D1626429

Environmental History of
East Africa

Environmental History of East Africa

A Study of the Quaternary

A. C. Hamilton

Department of Environmental Science
New University of Ulster
Co. Londonderry
Northern Ireland

1982

ACADEMIC PRESS

A Subsidiary of Harcourt Brace Jovanovich Publishers
LONDON   NEW YORK
PARIS   SAN DIEGO   SAN FRANCISCO   SÃO PAOLO
SYDNEY   TOKYO   TORONTO

ACADEMIC PRESS INC. (LONDON) LTD
24–28 Oval Road,
London NW1

U.S. Edition published by
ACADEMIC PRESS INC.
111 Fifth Avenue,
New York, New York 10003

British Library Cataloguing in Publication Data

Hamilton, A.C.
    Environmental history of East Africa.
    1. Glacial epoch—Africa, East
    I. Title
    551.7'92'09676   QE697

    ISBN 0-12-321880-2
    LCCN 81-68016

Printed in Great Britain at
The Pitman Press, Bath

Preface

This book is an attempt to provide an account of the environmental history of East Africa. By East Africa is meant the countries of Kenya, Tanzania and Uganda, but much information is included which is relevant to tropical Africa as a whole. The inter-disciplinary approach adopted is invaluable for the interpretation of the various strands of evidence and also helps to demonstrate the level of our ignorance and to highlight areas for future research.

East Africa is well known for its rich record of human evolution, with fossils dating from recent times back more than two and a half million years—a date which marks the beginning of the Quaternary Period. What sort of environment did early man occupy? What was the climate, what was the vegetation, what was the nature and frequency of environmental changes? This book attempts to provide answers to these and similar questions, drawing on a wide range of subject areas concerned with the reconstruction of the past. Several major fields, such as the glacial evidence, the evidence for changes in lake levels and the pollen record, are reviewed and these accounts are supplemented by the results of original research recently carried out by the author. The ways in which climatic fluctuations in East Africa relate to those in other parts of the world are discussed, as are the effects of these fluctuations on the distribution and evolution of plants and animals.

Modern East Africa is faced with severe environmental problems. To those concerned with the alleviation of these problems, a knowledge of environmental history provides a useful temporal perspective. Accordingly, recent trends in the environment are discussed, and there is an account of possible future developments.

Oct 1981   A. C. Hamilton

Acknowledgements

My interest in tropical biology was awakened by Professor E. J. H. Corner at Cambridge. Thanks to the thoughtfulness of Professor Sir Harry Godwin, I was able to travel to Uganda in 1966 to work on the history of the East African environment under the supervision of Dr Michael Morrison. Many people aided my studies in Uganda and of these I would like to single out George Reno, Professor Brian Langlands, Tony Stuart-Smith and Keith Thompson. The latter two acted as the supervisors of my thesis following the untimely early death of Michael Morrison. My work in Uganda was supported financially by the British Ministry of Overseas Development, the Nuffield Foundation and NORAD, to all of which organizations I am indebted. Professor E. M. van Zinderen Bakker assisted me greatly with publication of part of my doctoral thesis and ever since has remained a source of encouragement. After moving to Northern Ireland in 1972, I was fortunate to receive in 1975 a grant from the Natural Environment Research Council to continue work in East Africa. I am grateful to the Council, the Forest Department of Kenya, Kenya National Parks Department, the National Museums of Kenya, the Botany Department of Nairobi University, the British Institute in Eastern Africa, CNRS (Butare, Rwanda), Dr Andrew Agnew, Professor Simeon Imbamba, Christine Kabuye, Richard Leakey, Professor Palmer Newbould and many others for various types of assistance during the course of the project. Alan Perrott has been of great assistance both in the field and in the laboratory; he is responsible for counting the pollen diagram from Lake Kimilili on Mt Elgon. The Royal Society kindly made finance available for a brief visit to Arusha in 1978. Apollo and Rachel Musoke generously assisted with accommodation for my family and myself in Nairobi in 1979. Here in Coleraine I would like to express my gratitude to John Shaw for drawing the pollen diagrams as well as a few of the other figures, to Bob Simmons for printing the photographs and Dr David Riley for many helpful discussions on ecological and other matters and for major assistance with the text. My wife Naomi and John Beech kindly read the manuscript.

I am grateful to the following for permission to reproduce copyright material: Academic Press and Dr N. J. Shackleton for a figure in *Quaternary Res.* **3**; A. A. Balkema and Prof. E. M. van Zinderen Bakker for illustrations from *Palaeoecol. Afr.* **3, 9** and **11** (1967, 1976, 1979); Blackwell Scientific Publications Ltd for illustrations from the *J. Ecol.* (**56** and **62**); Elsevier Scientific Publishing Co. for a figure in *Palaeogeog. Palaeoclimatol. Palaeoecol.* **21**; Faber and Faber for illustrations of artifacts from "The Archaeology of Early Man" by J. M. Coles and E. S. Higgs (1969); The Geological Society of America for figures from their bulletin (**75**); The International Glaciological Society and Prof. P. H. Temple for a figure from the *J. Glaciol* **4**; Liverpool University for Fig. 4 (Annual rainfall, 30% probability) in the article by J. M. Kenworthy in "Geographers and the Tropics: Liverpool Essays", ed. R. W. Steel and R. M. Prothero (1964); Longman Group Ltd for two figures from "East Africa", ed. W. T. W. Morgan; MacMillan Journals for a figure from *Nature* **239**; the editor, *Revu Algologique*, for parts of a figure in **13** (1978); Thames and Hudson Ltd for three figures from "The Prehistory of Africa" by J. D. Clark (1970); Mme van Campo for two figures from *Pollen et Spores* (in press); the editor, *Vegetatio*, for figures from various volumes.

Contents

List of Tables

List of Figures

To Naomi, Susan, Patrick and Dave

Chapter 1

The Study of the East African Quaternary

The Quaternary is the most recent period of geological time and extends back from the present about 2·5 million years. In temperate parts of the world, the Quaternary has been marked by a series of ice ages, full glacials being characterized by the spread of very extensive sheets of ice over the northern part of North America, north-west Europe and elsewhere, and interglacials showing a return to ice-limits and climatic conditions more or less similar to those which prevail today. Within once glaciated regions the importance of ice age events in forming the modern landscape is often obvious. Glacially-eroded areas frequently show such features as U-shaped valleys, ice-excavated rock basins and shallow soils; areas of glacial deposition are characterized by sheets of till and spreads of outwash sand and gravel. Major Quaternary environmental changes were by no means restricted to glaciated regions. Thus, to the south of the old ice limits in the northern hemisphere there are very extensive deposits of wind-blown dust, in which the presence of fossil soils is a testament to former periods of stability. Again, ecosytems such as temperate forest are known to have been subjected to repeated and massive oscillations in distribution as a response to glacial/interglacial climatic changes.

Until comparatively recent times the tropics have escaped the detailed investigations of Quaternary environmental history such as those to which more northerly latitudes have been subjected ever since the last century. A commonly held view was that the tropics have been more stable than temperate zones during the Quaternary and stability has been invoked, for example, to help explain the species-richness of tropical forest. Systematic studies into the environmental history of East Africa began in the 1920s and 1930s with work on former high lake stands and on the past glaciations of the

Fig. 1   Countries of Africa.

high mountains. Enthusiasm was greatly kindled by the discovery of a rich and very long archaeological record and later by the finding of fossil hominids of great age. These early studies resulted in the development of a theory of Quaternary climatic change, which was believed to be applicable to the tropics generally and which came to be widely accepted. This "Pluvial Theory" proposed that glaciations were associated with cool moist climates in the tropics and interglacials with climates similar to those of today.

Since about 1960 there has been a revolution in our understanding of the Quaternary history of East Africa. The biggest single advance has undoubtedly been the widespread application of absolute dating techniques, especially the radiocarbon and potassium–argon methods, and this has permitted the development of a much more firmly based chronology than had existed hitherto. An early casualty of absolute dating was the Pluvial Theory and it is now known that those high lake stands formerly attributed to the last glaciation are actually of postglacial age.

The reconstruction of the course of human evolution and of man's changing relationship with his environment remains one of the driving forces behind studies of the East African past. This is a long-term project but there are much more immediate reasons for interest in environmental history. During the last 15 years large areas of the drier parts of East Africa have suffered rapid ecosystem degradation with often tragic human consequences. The problem of desertification is widespread in the continent as a whole and involves both climatic fluctuations and intractable socio-economic problems. It is hoped that research into environmental history will be of some use in understanding the causes of the problem and thus make a contribution to its alleviation.

Approaches to the Past

It is today realized that the Earth is in a state of constant flux and continual adjustment, and that the modern environment cannot be fully understood without reference to the past. During the Quaternary, environmental instability has been induced by both numerous major climatic changes and the unprecedented impact of man as his culture has developed and his population has grown. This book is not primarily concerned with the explanation of these particular phenomena, but rather with the detection of their effects on terrestrial ecosystems.

An investigation of a modern environment is incomplete without considering the ways in which past processes have moulded its characteristics, and a study of past environments is dependent on studies of modern processes and the ways in which these processes alter the components of the environment. The study of the past throws much light on the modern condition, and vice versa, and the principle "the present is the key to the past" can be balanced, with as much validity, by that of "the past is the key to the present" (cf. George, 1976).

A vast store of information could be tapped to help in the reconstruction of the Quaternary environmental history of East Africa. Needless to say, only a small part of this potential has yet been exploited; findings in some of the more important subject areas are discussed in later chapters. Each discipline has its own strengths and weaknesses, but all are complimentary and the evidence from one approach frequently helps to clarify and modify ideas in another. Thus, strengths of the evidence relating to past ice ages in East Africa are that the signs of ancient glaciation are often obvious and that the climatic controls over glacier formation are believed to be relatively simple. A weakness, however, is that the dating of ancient glaciations is rather imprecise. In contrast, the horizons in a sediment which has accumulated during the Upper Quaternary can sometimes be dated fairly exactly, but the controls which have determined some of the sediment characteristics, for example their pollen contents, are believed to have often been complex and are difficult to determine.

Dating plays a vital role in the study of past East African environments. Three aspects of dating can be distinguished: correlation, relative dating and absolute dating. Correlation refers to the determination of the temporal equivalence of past environmental events in different places, relative dating refers to the assignment of events to a temporal order, and absolute dating refers to the placing of events on an absolute scale of years. Absolute dating techniques, such as radiocarbon (^{14}C) or potassium–argon (K–A) dating, are based on the assumption that radioactive isotopes of elements decay at constant rates over time. Radiocarbon is constantly formed in the upper atmosphere through interaction of nitrogen with protons entering in the solar flux. The ^{14}C is oxidized and enters general atmospheric circulation and is incorporated into organisms. Radiocarbon is taken to have a half-life of 5568 years and measurement of the radiocarbon to stable carbon isotope ratios in fossil material allows an estimate of age. Radiocarbon dating is used on carbonaceous materials with ages of less than about 50 000 years and K–A dating on volcanic rocks older than about 0·25 million years. The methods and their limitations are described in Bowen (1978). A date in this book which is post-fixed by B.P. (before present— actually before 1950 A.D.) normally refers to ^{14}C years, which, it should be noted, do not always correspond exactly to sidereal years (Bowen, 1978). If, however, the date is older than about 50 000 years, then B.P. is used purely for convenience.

Scope of the Book

The contents of this book follow my own interests and, although I have attempted to provide a broad coverage, the work is not intended to be comprehensive. Vegetational history receives special attention and this is partly because it is my main research interest and partly because vegetation is a particularly key component of the environment. I apologize for the lack of information on fossil faunas; penetration into the large literature on this subject has proved too daunting.

The second chapter is an introduction to the East African environment and this is followed by accounts of knowledge about the past resulting from studies in a number of major research fields. These are succeeded by chapters on climatic change and on some of the implications of the findings, and then by a section on the position of man in Quaternary East Africa. In spite of the hazards of prophecy, I have concluded with some speculations on the future of the environment.

The area covered is mainly East Africa, by which is meant the countries of Uganda, Kenya and Tanzania (Fig. 2). From many points of view, the limits of the area so defined is highly artificial and I have had no hesitation in widening the perspective to scales more appropriate to particular problems. As used here, eastern Africa is not a precisely defined entity, but normally includes the area from Ethiopia to northern Mozambique and Malawi.

Finally, some comments about the use of geological terms are necessary. According to some more recent recommendations (e.g. West, 1977), the geological period known as the Pleistocene is regarded as equivalent to the Quaternary Era, both of which extend up to the present. The older use of the term Pleistocene is, however, more restrictive, the Quaternary being divided into two periods, the Pleistocene and the Holocene (or the Recent). The Pleistocene covers the bulk of the Quaternary, and the Holocene only that part following on from the last glaciation, or, according to some recommendations, after 10 000 B.P. One justification for changing the definition of Pleistocene is that the Holocene is too short to be worthy of the same rank as other geological periods, all of which lasted for well over one million years. There is something to be said for this, but the traditional definitions of Pleistocene and Holocene are retained here, mainly to facilitate reference to the literature.

Also by long-established tradition, the Pleistocene is divided into three categories, Lower, Middle and Upper. These were originally

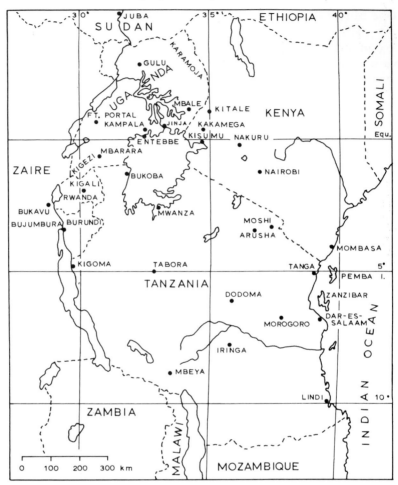

Fig. 2　East Africa: countries and towns.

defined on the basis of their stone-tool and mammalian assemblages and are rather vague categories. In an attempt at greater precision, Isaac (1975) has suggested that a convenient marker for separating the Lower from the Middle Pleistocene is the Brunhes-Matuyama reversal in the world's magnetic field, an event detectable world-wide and dated at approximately 700 000 B.P. The upper boundary of the Middle Pleistocene is taken as the upper boundary of the Acheulian culture, perhaps *c.* 100–50 000 B.P. These usages are employed here, but it must be noted that the categories, Lower, Middle and Upper Quaternary, are deliberately used without precise definition.

This book concentrates on the Upper Quaternary, a period for which there is a particular abundance of evidence, and for which environmental reconstruction is most certain. The lower boundary of the Pleistocene, and hence also of the Quaternary, is defined by reference to a geological section in Italy where it is taken as lying below the horizon which shows the first evidence of cooling. There are considerable difficulties in dating this boundary and in correlating it with strata elsewhere in the world. It is also noteworthy that the first signs of cooling occur much earlier in deep-sea cores than they do in the Italian section.

Chapter 2

Introduction to the East African Environment

Geomorphology

From the Precambrian (> 600 million years) until the onset of rifting during the Miocene, the bulk of Africa was little affected by major earth movements such as those which elsewhere pushed up the Alps and the Himalayas. This stability resulted in a generally subdued topography which in the case of East Africa was largely etched into Precambrian crystalline rocks. The surface of the continent is believed to have been moulded by differential uplift and subsidence into a gentle basin-and-swell pattern of large depressions separated by ridges (Fig. 3; Gill, 1974). This structure is still apparent today in those parts of tropical Africa, such as the Chad and Congo basins, which have been little affected by subsequent deformation.

The middle Tertiary (roughly 25 million years ago) witnessed the beginnings of a general elevation of extensive areas of central and eastern Africa (Gautier, 1967; Morgan, 1973). Remnants of the sub-Miocene erosion surface show that uplift has often been of the order of c. 700 m, though, in the case of Ruwenzori (5109 m), an upthrust block of Precambrian rocks contained within the Western Rift Valley, the sub-Miocene surface has been elevated by at least 3000 m. Uplift has been accompanied by a number of other disruptive activities such as rifting, faulting and volcanism, all of which have continued intermittently to the present day.

Rifting probably marks the initial stages of fragmentation of the African continent and, although the rates of separation across the rift

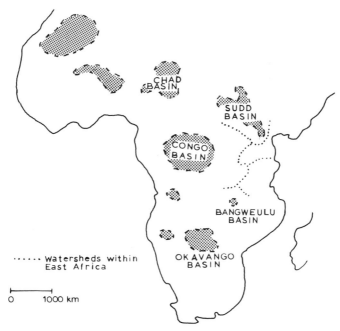

Fig. 3 Pre rift Africa showing some of the major sedimentary basins and, for East Africa, watersheds. Modified from Howell and Bourlière (1963) and Burke and Wilson (1972).

valleys are at present very slow by the standards of mature mid-oceanic ridges (Baker and Wohlenberg, 1971), at some distant time in the future it is envisaged that the present rift valleys may be sufficiently broad and deep to carry new oceans. The rift system extends from Lake Malawi, through the Western and Eastern (Gregory) Rifts of East Africa (Fig. 4), into Ethiopia and on, further north, as far as the Red Sea and the Jordan valley of western Asia. Tectonic activity associated with rifting has included the upwarping of domes along the rifts, the uplift of land along rift margins and, of course, the depression and down-faulting of the rift valleys themselves. One consequence of all this activity has been the disruption of drainage patterns in East Africa. It is thought that the pre-rift watershed lay approximately at the longitude of the Kenya/Uganda border, separating rivers running westwards to the Atlantic and eastwards into the Indian Ocean. Uplift of shoulders along the Western Rift caused the reversal of previously west-running rivers, such as the Kagera and Katonga, and the creation of the Lake Victoria and Kyoga basins. The drainage waters from the north-western part of East Africa

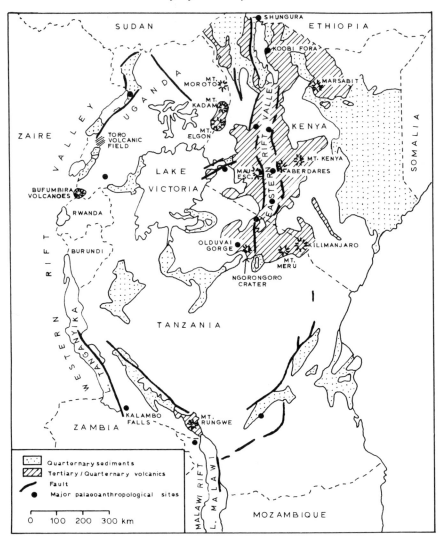

Fig. 4   Map of East Africa showing Quaternary sediments, Tertiary/Quaternary volcanics and major palaeoanthropological sites. Adapted from Morgan (1973) and Isaac (1976).

became diverted to the north and were eventually incorporated into the Nile system.

Since their formation the rift valleys have tended to act as traps for sediments and great thicknesses of fluvial, lacustrine and volcanic rocks have accumulated in some basins. Conditions have sometimes proved very favourable for the incorporation of animal fossils within these sediments and it is from exposures of rift sediments that the majority of the East African hominid finds has been recovered.

Volcanism has been a prominent feature of late Tertiary and Quaternary East Africa and several volcanoes remain active today (Baker and Wohlenberg, 1971). The oldest volcanoes, which tend to lie away from the main rift valleys, are of Miocene age and include Mts Moroto, Napak, Kadam and Elgon (4320 m), near the Kenya/Uganda border. More recent volcanic activity has been a more prominent feature of the Eastern and Ethiopian Rifts than of the Western and Nyasa Rifts and much of highland Kenya and Ethiopia is composed to volcanic rock. Three of the best known volcanic mountains are Kilimanjaro (5895 m), Mt Kenya (5199 m) and the Aberdares (3999 m). Along the Western Rift, the main volcanic centres are the Virunga volcanic field, with several large volcanoes including Mt Muhavura (4127 m), and the Toro-Ankole field with an abundance of small craters. Volcanism along the Western Rift has caused damming of some valleys and the creation of Kivu and other lakes.

Climate

Subtropical high pressure areas situated about 20–30° north and south of the equator are important controls of the climate of tropical Africa (Fig. 5; Boucher, 1975). These subtropical high pressure cells tend to move north during the northern summer and south during the southern summer, and the outflow of air from their centres is reduced during summer months as a consequence of thermal heating. The north-east trade-winds, which flow out from the north African and Arabian high pressure cells, are very dry and often laden with dust.

In the case of East Africa, the air of the north-east trades originates in Arabia and north-east Africa and benefits, at most, from only a short sea-fetch. The south-east trades, coming off the Indian Ocean, constitute the dominant air-stream over East Africa in July, but, although deep and moist, their passage does not result over most of the region in a July rainfall peak, probably because the air-stream is divergent. As well as the trades, the western part of East Africa is also under the influence of westerlies coming across the Congo basin. This air-stream, originating in the south Atlantic, is moist.

Rainfall data from East Africa indicate that most rain occurs during the passage of the inter-tropical convergence zone (ITCZ) (Boucher,

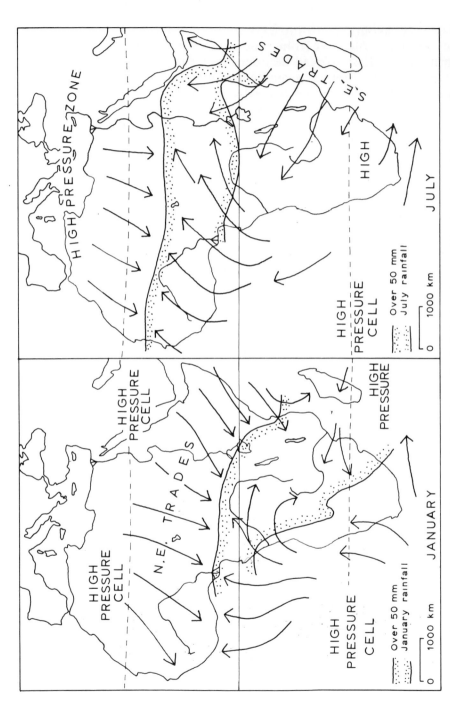

Fig. 5 Africa, showing features of the general circulation and rain belts in January and July. Adapted from Boucher (1975) and Grove (1967).

1975). The ITCZ is the ill-defined low pressure zone where the north-east and south-east trades converge and is characterized by convectional rainfall. The ITCZ migrates north and south with the sun and there is a tendency for there to be two well-marked wet seasons near the equator, but only one further to the north or to the south. The annual rainfall cycle follows the following course (Boucher, 1975). April is usually a wet month over East Africa, with the ITCZ lying between 3°S and 3°N. By June the rainfall belt has shifted north and rainfall diminishes towards September, the driest month of the year over most of the region. In November the rains start to move southwards and by December all Tanzania is under the influence of the ITCZ. A dry zone migrates southwards from North Uganda in December to include much of the rest of Uganda and nearly all of Kenya during the months of January and February.

Mean annual rainfall for East Africa is shown on Fig. 6. There are variations related to latitude, distance from the coast and topography, but the causes of the complex pattern are incompletely understood (Kenworthy, 1966). The association of many rainfall maxima with highland areas is apparent from comparison of maps, but it is noted that within any particular highland area there are invariably great variations in precipitation related to aspect and altitude. On Mt Kenya, for instance, where highest rainfall probably occurs at an altitude of 2500–3000 m, much less rain is received in the north than the south-west, the latter facing the local direction of the south-east trades. Lake Victoria and to a lesser extent other large lakes modify regional climatic patterns. The heavy rain on the western and northern margins of Lake Victoria is associated mainly with the presence of the large water body and, in the case of Lake Malawi, the funnelling of air northwards along the lake and then against the obstruction of Mt Rungwe creates a pocket of very high precipitation (Morgan, 1973).

Potential evapotranspiration is defined as the quantity of water which would be evaporated from a vegetated surface if water input is maintained at such a rate as to always meet plant needs. The difference between potential and actual evapotranspiration determines water deficit or surplus. It is estimated that only *c.* 3% of the land-surface of East Africa regularly receives annual rainfall in excess of potential evapotranspiration (Morgan, 1973). Extensive areas are subject to severe water deficit and have little potential value for agriculture (Table 1). Kenya, with its vast semi-arid north-east territory, is particularly unfortunate in this respect.

In montane areas precipitation tends to increase up to at least an

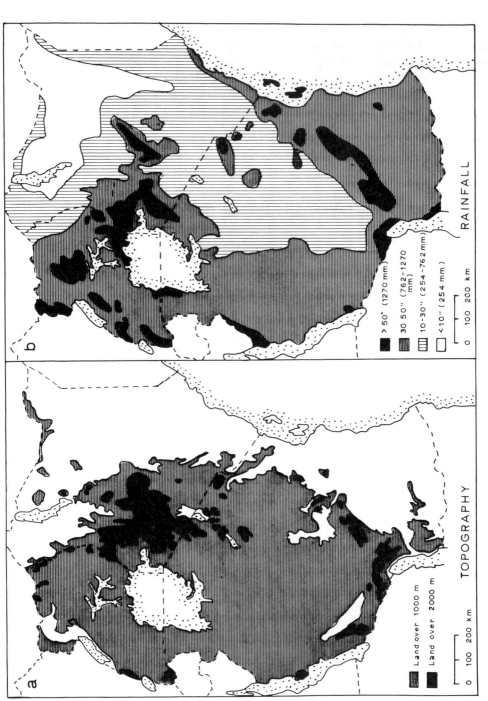

TOPOGRAPHY

Land over 1000 m

Land over 2000 m

0   100   200 km

RAINFALL

> 50" (1270 mm)

30 50" (762-1270 mm)

10-30" (254-762 mm)

<10" (254 mm)

0   100   200 km

Fig. 6 East Africa: topography and mean annual rainfall (the latter based on M. T. W. Morgan (1973) "East Africa" and reproduced with permission from Longman Group Ltd).

Table 1   Percentages of land area in East Africa receiving selected amounts of annual rainfall in 4 years out of 5. Also, basic limitations to land-use, as indicated by the East Africa Royal Commission of 1955 (data from Morgan, 1973).

Annual rainfall	Kenya	Tan-zania	Uganda	East Africa	Suitable agricultural use
Less than 508 mm (20 in)	72	16	12	35	Ranching only
508–762 mm (20–30 in)	13	33	10	20	Subsistence cultivation, ranching, sorghum millet
762–1270 mm (30–50 in)	12	47	72	41	Profitable maize growing
> 1270 mm (50 in)	3	4	6	4	

altitude of *c.* 2500 m. In addition, since temperature is one of the key determinants of potential evapotranspiration, there is a steady decline of potential evapotranspiration with altitude. Consequently, montane areas in East Africa play a vital role in maintaining perennial flow in rivers.

Vegetation

Vegetation is often regarded as one of the best indicators of general environment. This idea has been expressed by Perring (1959) in terms of the formula $v = f(cl, p, r, o, t)$, i.e. vegetational characteristics (v) are a function of regional climate (cl), soil parent material (p), topography (r), organisms (including available flora) (o) and time (t). There are numerous ways of classifying vegetation, usually involving a varible mixture of floristic and physiognomic characteristics. Physiognomy refers to the general appearance of vegetation and physiognomic attributes include height, structure, plant density and leaf size. The most generally useful classifications, that is those with the widest range of applications, are those in which the vegetational categories can be related to environmental factors.

Classifications of vegetation based on floristic composition can be very valuable on a local scale since within a confined area the distributions of species are believed to be largely determined by variations in environmental factors. As the scale of interest increases, however, the distributions of species become increasingly determined not only by the modern environment, but also by environmental history, and the value of classifications of vegetation based on floristic composition consequently declines. Except where there has been a change in the environment in the very recent past, vegetational physiognomy is generally regarded as being very responsive to immediate environmental conditions, and physiognomic attributes become of overwhelming importance in large-scale classifications of vegetation. One of the reasons for this is believed to be that, where some species are absent from an area for historical reasons, other species of similar physiognomy tend to increase in abundance to occupy the vacant ecological space, and it is also thought that the process of natural selection has tended to produce species of similar appearance for similar niches in different parts of the world.

For Africa as a whole, the following six main vegetation types may be recognized (Fig. 7).:

(1) Lowland tropical forest, characterized by dense woody vegetation with several tree strata and lacking narrow-leaved grasses in the herbaceous stratum. This type occurs within the well-watered tropics at comparatively low altitudes (below *c.* 1500–2000 m). Soils are typically deep and reddish in colour; nutrients and organic matter tend to be concentrated within a thin upper horizon.

(2) Montane tropical forest, of generally similar appearance to lowland tropical forest, but sometimes of lesser stature and with fewer tree strata, and occurring at higher altitudes. Soils are similar to those of (1), but become richer in organic matter with altitude.

(3) Moist savanna, characteristically with a single stratum of densely-spaced trees with relatively large leaves or leaflets and an herbaceous stratum of tall, narrow-leaved grasses. This type is found in areas which receive somewhat less effective precipitation than the forest zones. Soils tend to be deep, yellow or red in colour and sandier than the forest soils.

(4) Dry savanna, occurring in even drier areas than the above and usually differing in having smaller and more widely-spaced trees or shrubs, and a lower grass stratum. Soils tend to be less acidic and richer in exchangeable bases than those of the above categories.

(5) Semi-desert and desert, with little vegetation cover and restricted to the driest regions. Soils tend to be calcareous.

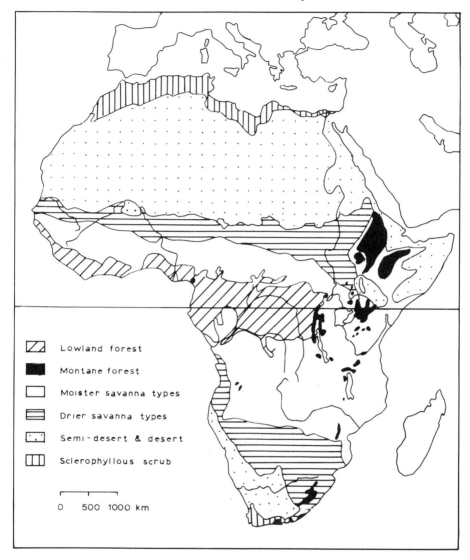

Fig. 7 Mainland Africa: vegetation types. From various sources.

(6) Sclerophyllous scrub, in areas of Mediterranean climate at the northern and southern extremities of the continent.

On a smaller scale the heterogeneity of these broad vegetational divisions becomes apparent and it becomes possible to map additional vegetation categories (Fig. 8). For East Africa, the latter include, for

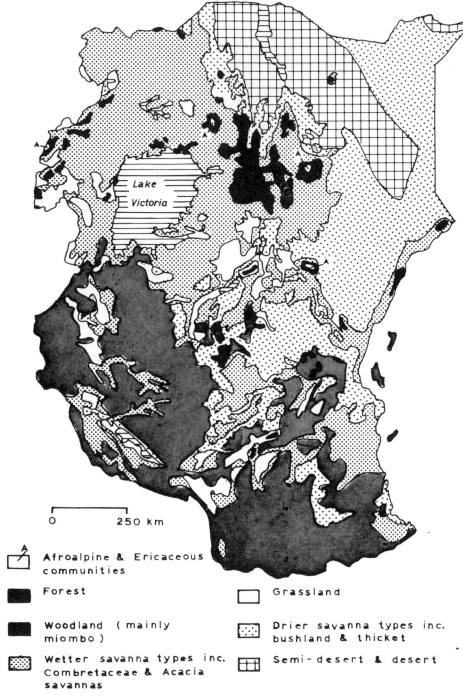

Fig. 8   East Africa: vegetation types. Adapted from Lind and Morrison (1974) "East African Vegetation" (Longman Group Ltd).

instance, the Ericaceous and Afroalpine Belts, present at very high altitudes on the taller mountains. With reduction in scale it becomes apparent that other environmental factors, in addition to climate, are important as determinants of the distributions of vegetation types. Thus, the fragmentary occurrence of lowland forest in Uganda is undoubtedly largely a consequence of human disturbance, climatic data suggesting that, in the absence of human activities, lowland forest would occupy two, possibly connected, zones, one extending around the northern shore of Lake Victoria and the other being situated along the eastern shoulder of the Western Rift (Fig. 9).

There are many instances in which the role of man as a determinant of the distribution and characteristics of vegetation types is poorly understood. Much debate, for example, has surrounded the relationship between man and miombo, a moist savanna type dominated by fairly tall (20 m) and densely-spaced leguminous trees, belonging to such genera as *Brachystegia, Isoberlinia* and *Julbernardia*. Miombo is very extensive in Tanzania, as well as elsewhere in south tropical Africa (i.e. Zambia, North Angola, Katanga), being found in areas with an annual rainfall of 750–1000 mm and a rather long dry season. Some ecologists believe that much of the area now covered by miombo would support dry forest types in the absence of human disturbance.

Man

The density of human population in East Africa (Fig. 11) is related to a number of environmental factors including rainfall, the existence of permanent water supplies and the distribution of tsetse fly infected areas (Kingdon, 1971; Morgan, 1973). Rainfall acts mainly through the association of higher biological productivity with better watered areas (Leith, 1975), and tsetse fly through its role as carrier of sleeping-sickness, a serious disease of man and animals. No less than 60% of Tanzania is infested with tsetse fly and this includes extensive areas which receive reasonable rainfall and which might be expected to be otherwise quite usefully productive.

Two contrasting agricultural systems are found in East Africa, one associated with the pastoral way of life (Fig. 10) and the other with an emphasis on cultivation. Ethnic differences often serve to maintain a clear distinction between these systems. Geographically, the divide between the systems is usually related to rainfall distribution; in drier areas, cultivation becomes an uncertain proposition and is confined

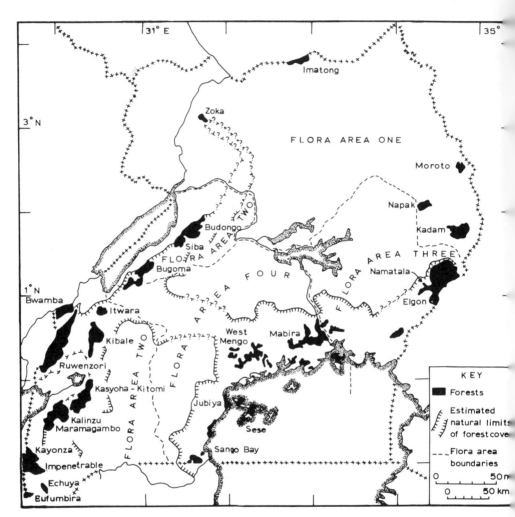

Fig. 9   Uganda: forests and extent of natural forest cover. From Hamilton (1974a).
Reproduced from Vegetatio with permission.

Fig. 10   Pastoralists at their homestead at 3000 m on the southern slopes of Mt Elgon. All the land in the photograph was probably at one time covered with forest.

to locally favourable micro-environments. It should be noted that cattle density is often higher in areas of high rather than low rainfall (Fig. 11), but in the former cattle do not play such important roles in either the biological or social environments and domestic stock is but one component of a relatively diverse agricultural economy.

Fire, the hoe and the panga are the chief tools employed in food production in most of East Africa. Fallowing forms part of the majority of traditional cultivation systems, and secondary vegetation is allowed to develop on land which has been cropped to assist in the build-up of soil fertility. Crops are grown for subsistence (e.g. sorghum, millet, maize, bananas, cassava, sweet-potatoes), export (e.g. coffee, cotton, tea, sisal) and sometimes for sale in local markets. Burning of savanna is a universal activity in East Africa and is a long-established practice which is carried out for a variety of reasons. Burning destroys dry standing vegetation and thus clears the ground for cultivation; nutrients released from the ash cause a temporary rise in soil fertility. Burning is also used to encourage the growth of fresh grass shoots during the dry seasons and as an aid in hunting.

Wood products form essential ingredients in East African econo-

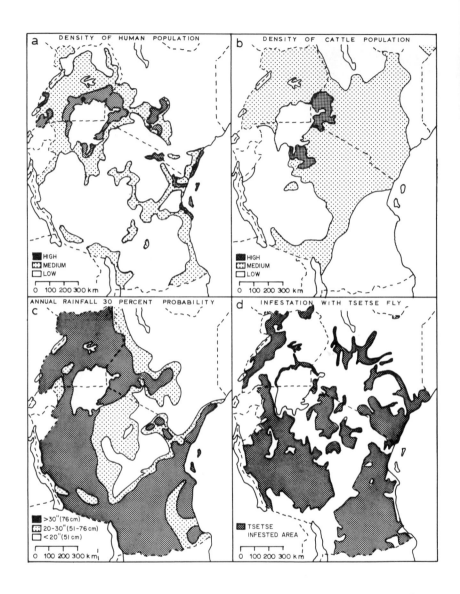

Fig. 11 East Africa: (a) density of human population, (b) density of cattle
population, (c) annual rainfall 30% probability and (d) infestation with tsetse fly.
The area with 30% probability of over 76 cm (30 in) mean annual rainfall is for the
most part suitable for cultivation; the remainder of East Africa is suitable only for
pastoralism. Figs (a) and (b) adapted from Morgan (1973); (c) from Kenworthy
(1964) and reproduced with permission from Liverpool University; (d) from W. T.
W. Morgan (1973) "East Africa", and reproduced with permission from Longman
Group Ltd.

mies. The biggest single use of wood is for fuel, the wood being used either in the raw state or as charcoal. Woody plants also provide poles and timber for construction. In many parts of East Africa, the gathering of wood for fuel is a major activity. It is worth noting the observation of Werger (1977) that, in the case of most rangeland (savanna) vegetation in Africa, the physiognomic appearance at a particular site is often dependant upon the time interval since fire last passed through the vegetation, or on the need for fuel by man in that area.

Chapter 3

East African Ice-ages

Historical Introduction

The first documented sighting of an ice-covered mountain in tropical
Africa was of Kilimanjaro by J. Rebmann in 1848 and this was
followed by a report of ice on Mt Kenya in the following year. The
third of the East African mountains with glaciers, the Ruwenzori
Range, proved more elusive to explorers, although several had
passed below its mist-shrouded slopes, and it was not until 1887 that
Henry Stanley caught a glimpse of the ice on its peaks (Johnston,
1902).

In 1893 Mt Kenya was visited by J. W. Gregory who recognized
old moraines and other evidence of past glaciation. For the first time
it became apparent that Equatorial Africa, like many other parts of
the world, had experienced major ice expansion during the Quaternary. Traces of old glaciations are now known, not only from Mt
Kenya, but also from Kilimanjaro and Ruwenzori, as well as from the
unglaciated mountains, Elgon and the Aberdares (Fig. 12). There is
an unconfirmed report of past glaciation on Mt Muhavura, one of the
Bufumbira Volcanoes and, from a long distance, I have clearly seen
moraines on Mt Meru, although these have not been described in the
literature. Elsewhere in Africa, there were glaciations on some of the
Ethiopian mts (Hastenrath, 1977; Messerli et al., 1980; Potter, 1976)
and it is also possible that there were once glaciers on two peaks in the
Hoggar Mts, Sahara (Messerli et al., 1980). The High Atlas Mts in
Morocco were glaciated, but no traces of Quaternary glaciations have
been reported from Mt Cameroon or from southern Africa. Fossil

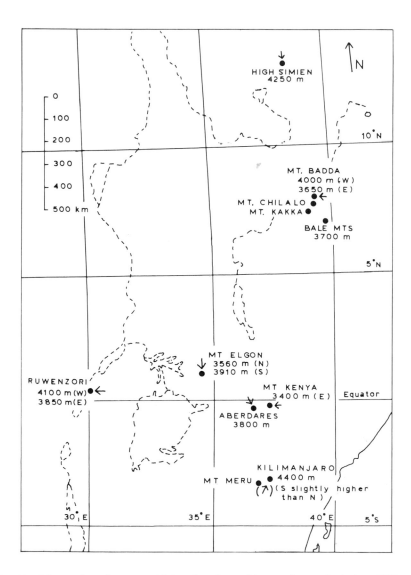

Fig. 12   Mountains of eastern Africa showing evidence of past glaciation. Kilimanjaro, Mt Kenya and Ruwenzori still carry ice. The altitudes are for firnlines during the last major glacial stage and arrows indicate those aspects of mountains on which firnlines were lowermost. The list of glaciated mountains is largely based on Baker (1967), Downie (1964), Hastenrath (1977), Nilsson (1931) and Osmaston (1965). The Mt Meru glaciation is my own observation. There is some controversy over the extent of ice in Ethiopia (Hastenrath, 1977; Messerli et al., 1980). Firnline data follow Messerli et al. (1980) for High Simien, Mt Badda (with assistance of data supplied to me by F. A. Street), Bale Mts and Mt Kenya, Osmaston (1975) for Ruwenzori and Kilimanjaro, and Hamilton and Perrott (1979) for Mt Elgon. The Aberdares estimate is based on work by R. A. Perrott and myself.

periglacial phenomena are widely found on the mountains of eastern Africa and on the Hoggar and Tibetsi Mts (Messerli *et al.*, 1980), and can also be seen on the Drakensburgs.

The first extensive study of past glaciations in East Africa and Ethiopia was undertaken by E. Nilsson, who visited East Africa for the first time in 1927–1928 as a member of the Swedish Geological Expedition to East Africa. On this first visit he concentrated on Mt Elgon, but also travelled to Mt Kenya, Ruwenzori and Kilimanjaro. Nilsson laid the foundations for subsequent studies, but his interpretation of the climatic history of East Africa (see Chapter 4), once widely accepted, is now known to be untenable. The 1950s witnessed a peak in the number of workers visiting the mountains to investigate present and past glacial features and we may note especially expeditions from Sheffield University (England) to Kilimanjaro (Downie, 1964; Downie *et al.*, 1956; Humphries, 1959, 1972), the various studies on Mt Kenya under the leadership of I. S. Loupekine (Charnley, 1959), and the six parties mounted at regular intervals between 1957 and 1961 to Ruwenzori, mostly by F. P. Hendersen (Whittow *et al.*, 1963). The detailed mapping of glacial features on Ruwenzori by Osmaston (1965, 1975) is noteworthy, as also are both his studies and those of Messerli *et al.* (1980) on the interpretation of past glaciations in terms of climatic change.

Modern Glaciers

The three East African mountains which at present bear glaciers are Kilimanjaro (5895 m), Mt Kenya (5199 m) and the Ruwenzori Range (5109 m). Kilimanjaro, Africa's highest mountain, stands on the southern side of the Kenya/Tanzania border some 350 km south of the Equator and *c.* 250 km from the Indian Ocean. This volcanic massif is *c.* 209 km in circumference at the base and rises from arid plains at *c.* 1220 m to culminate in three great peaks, Shira, Kibo and Mawenzi (Fig. 14). Of these, Kibo (5895 m) in the centre is the highest and the only peak to retain glaciers. Mawenzi (5150 m) to the east has semi-permanent snow patches, while to the west the Shira Ridge, rising to 4010 m, is presently unglaciated.

Kibo is a cone of 24 km circumference rising up from the level (*c.* 4270 m) of a saddle stretching across to Mawenzi. The summit region has subsided to form a spectacular caldera 2·4 km in diameter with an inner wall 180 m deep on the south side. Within the caldera there is an inner cone, rising to 5790 m and itself enclosing a crater 823 m in diameter. Within this second crater there is yet another cone, again with a central crater. The caldera wall is breached on the south-west side by the Great West Notch and the Kibo Barranco.

Inside the caldera wall there are isolated and rapidly disappearing masses of stagnant ice (Downie *et al.*, 1956). The major glaciers occur outside the caldera on the southern and western flanks commencing just below the crest of the caldera wall. The longest is the Penck Glacier reaching down to below 4875 m. The glaciers of the northern slopes originate within the caldera, but are more limited in extent, the lowest ice being at 5640 m. There is general agreement that the ice on Kilimanjaro is dead and will probably entirely disappear within a few decades (Downie *et al.*, 1965; Spink, 1949).

Mt Kenya is a heavily denuded volcano with the shape of a convex dome *c.* 90 km in diameter. A group of peaks rise near the centre of the cone, the two highest being Batian (5199 m) and Nelion (5188 m). Valleys proceed radially from the central peaks. Today, there are 12 small glaciers, seven of valley-type and the remainder hanging. Total plan area of the ice is *c.* 1·2 km².

The Ruwenzori is a 120 × 50 km range lying just north of the Equator and with its long axis bearing NNE–SSW. In contrast to all other large mountains in East Africa (which are volcanic), Ruwenzori consists mainly of Precambrian rocks, such as gneisses, migmatites, metamorphic shales and amphibolites; it is an upthrust block situated within the Western Rift Valley. Judging by terraces and ledges in the valleys, uplift has been intermittent (Whittow *et al.*, 1963). There are six ice-capped peaks, namely Stanley (5109 m), Speke (4891 m), Baker (4873 m), Emin (4802 m), Gessi (4769 m) and Luigi di Savoia (4665 m). (The latter may have lost its glaciers since the 1950s.) The number of glaciers is given as 37 by Whittow *et al.* (1963) and 42 by Osmaston (1975), but, whatever the true figure, there is no doubt that the extent of ice has decreased greatly during the last 50 years.

The Controls of Past and Present Glaciation and Their Determination

The most easily determined parameter of the extent of the past or present glaciations of East Africa is the altitudinal limit of the ice. This altitude is much influenced by both topographic and climatic variables and the relative effects of the two sets of factors can be difficult to disentangle. A better indication of the influence of climate is, however, given by the altitude of the snowline or firnline (Flint, 1959; Osmaston, 1975). Firn (or névé) is snow which persists from one year to the next and the firnline can be defined as the line which bounds the lower ends of firnbanks. It is noted that some of the methods which have been proposed for determining firnlines in East Africa apply strictly speaking to equilibrium lines, that is the limits between areas of net accumulation and net ablation. This is, however, unimportant since in tropical Africa the altitudes of firnlines and equilibrium lines on any particular glacier will always have been virtually identical.

Firnlines for modern glaciers can be estimated by direct observation of glacier surfaces and examination of their strata by the digging of pits. Estimated firnlines are successively lower on Kilimanjaro, Mt Kenya and Ruwenzori and there is general agreement that this is related to a gradient of increasing precipitation, acting both directly by increasing snow and ice fall and indirectly by reducing ablation under cloudier skies. On all three mountains the surfaces which define the firnlines are tilted down in the direction of presumed greatest precipitation, that is towards the south-west on both Kilimanjaro (Spink, 1949) and Mt Kenya (Charnley, 1959; Coe, 1967) and towards the east on Ruwenzori (Osmaston, 1975). The firnline dips on Kilimanjaro and Mt Kenya are related to the local direction of the moist south-east monsoon. Ruwenzori is situated in a more complex climatic region, receiving substantial precipitation from both westerlies moving across the Congo basin and from the East African monsoons. At lower altitudes, precipitation is greater on the western slopes (Robyns, 1948), but the eastern slopes receive more precipitation at high altitudes, perhaps because of an eddy effect (Osmaston, 1965).

Observations on modern glacier budgets have been made on the Penck Glacier, Kilimanjaro (Downie, 1964), the Lewis Glacier, Mt Kenya (Platt, 1966), and the Elena Glacier, Ruwenzori (Bergström, 1955; Whittow, 1960). In the case of Ruwenzori, the calculations of budgets is aided by the presence of prominent bands of dirt in the ice, the dirt consisting of dust and ash originating from erosion and savanna-burning in the lowlands. Deposition of the dirt is at a peak during the January–February dry season when a northerly air-stream carries dust south from the drier north and when burning is most pronounced. Sometimes another band is deposited in June–August. On Kilimanjaro, the summit of which lies below the firnline (Downie, 1964), the presence of melting ice and pools of melt-water during the day reflects a rate of ablation which, it is estimated, will cause the disappearance of the ice by 2000 A.D. Ice retreat has been preceding at a much faster rate on the drier north-east than on the south-west. The ice on Kilimanjaro is much less contaminated by dirt bands than that of Ruwenzori. Since at present Kilimanjaro lies in a more arid zone than Ruwenzori, this rarity of dirt appears inconsistent with the modern environment and this suggests that the Kilimanjaro ice was deposited during a cleaner era. On both mountains there are moraines dating, it is believed, to the Little Ice Age, *c.* 1500–1800 A.D. Ice must have been accumulating on Kilimanjaro at this time, which suggests that onset of high dust deposition rates occurred sometime during the last 200 years. It is considered that reduction of the albedo of the ice surface on Kilimanjaro must have helped to accelerate ice retreat. On Ruwenzori, where precipitation is higher, the dirt has become incorporated in the ice.

Osmaston (1965, 1975) has discussed the ways in which glacial landforms can be used in the study of climatic change. First, the various erosional and depositional traces of past glaciations visible on a mountain are mapped and then an attempt is made to assign the moraines and other features to stages on the basis of appearance, altitude and stratigraphy. In practice there is usually little difficulty in placing the great majority of the more recent moraines on a mountain in particular stages and it is held by Osmaston (1975) that all the moraines of each stage are likely to be roughly, though perhaps not exactly, contemporaneous. Firnlines or firn-surfaces are estimated for each stage using one or more of the various methods mentioned by Osmaston (1975). It is then possible to estimate temperature conditions for each of the firnlines, assuming present day temperature lapse rates and precipitation levels. The possible influence of variations in precipitation may become apparent if comparisons are made between different places, or with the aid of data on past temperature fluctuations available from other types of evidence. It is desirable to establish the dates of the glacial stages, either by absolute age determinations of material overlying or underlying glacial deposits or by determination of the degree of weathering of moraines, the state of the vegetation contained within various glacial limits, and other means. The response time of East African glaciers to climatic events is uncertain, but is unlikely to be great. Smaller glaciers are said to show lags in response of 3–40 years (Embleton and King, 1968) and there is evidence that the response of modern Ruwenzori glaciers is very fast (Morton, 1968).

Past Glaciations of Kilimanjaro

Kilimanjaro has a peculiar advantage over the other glaciated East African mountains for determining the succession of glaciations during the Quaternary (Downie, 1964). It is the only glaciated mountain in East Africa on which volcanism has continued until recent times and which displays the interbedding of glacial deposits and volcanic rocks (Fig. 13). This has permitted the recognition of a

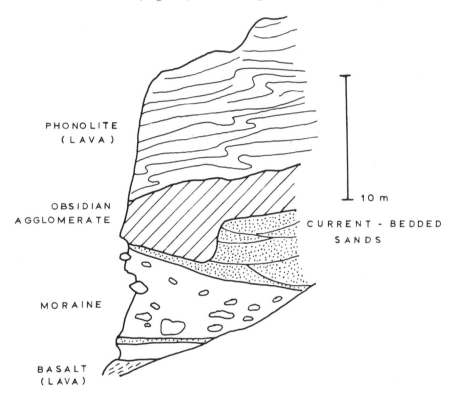

Fig. 13   Section at 4000 m in the Bastionsbach, south-west of Kibo summit, showing a moraine of the Second Glaciation with capping volcanic deposits. After Downie (1964). Reproduced with permission of The Geological Society of America.

greater number of glacial episodes than on the other East African mountains. There is considerable evidence that the ice cover of Kibo was greatly reduced or absent during long periods of the Quaternary and that much volcanic activity took place at these times.

Four major glaciations of Kilimanjaro have been recognized (Table

Table 2   Possible correlations between glacial stages in East Africa

Kilimanjaro	Mt Kenya	Ruwenzori	Mt Elgon	Date
Recent Glaciation	Recent Stage	Lac Gris Stage	(absent)	Little Ice Age (*c.* 1500–1800 A.D.).
Little Glaciation	(undescribed)	Omurabaho Stage	Cirque Stage?	Shortly before 11 500 B.P.?
Main Glaciation	Main Stage	Mahoma Stage	Main Stage	Perhaps *c.* 18 000 B.P.
+ 3 earlier major stages	+ one earlier major stage	+ 2 earlier major stages	(not known)	?

2). Most of the obvious glacial features belong to the last of these (the Main Glaciation) (Fig. 14). At its maximum extent, the ice of the Main Glaciation covered 390 km², when both Kibo and Mawenzi were ice-capped, but Shira carried only small patches of ice. On the ice-capped peaks the ice sheet was broken below *c.* 4420 m by rock ridges, and below 3500–4270 m the glaciers separated into ice tongues which terminated at 2740–4180 m. The radial pattern of these glaciers was disrupted on the Saddle, where the head-on collision of glaciers from Kibo and Mawenzi resulted in a deflection of ice-flow down the north and south flanks.

The Main Glaciation has left large moraines on the south and west sides of Kibo, while on the north and east the moraines are smaller, less definite in pattern and in places difficult to locate (Downie, 1964). The glaciated valleys on the southern slopes tend to be both longer and deeper than on the north. This evidence suggests that the direction of the main rain-bearing winds was from the south west, as is the case today, but a note of caution is necessitated by the remark of Nilsson (1931) that there is not much difference in the altitudes of moraines on the different slopes. The latter view has indeed been substantiated by the work of Osmaston (1975), who has demonstrated that firnlines were at about the same altitude on the south-west and north-west slopes of Kibo during the Main Glaciation (Table 3). There was probably much less contrast between the climates of the northern and southern slopes than is the case now, probably because the differences in the humidity of the north-east and south-west trades was less pronounced. Osmaston has calculated the difference in firnline elevation between the Main and the Recent

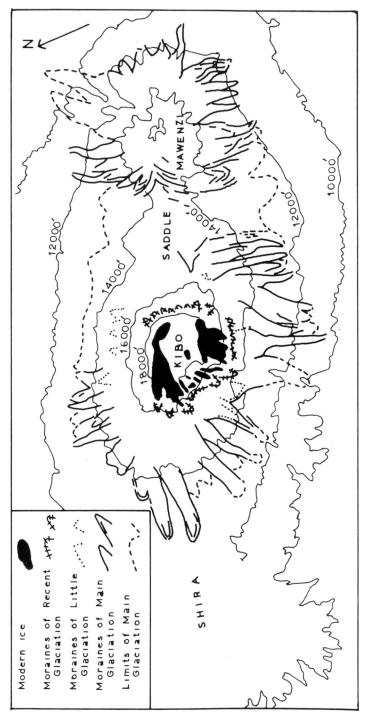

Fig. 14 Moraines of Kilimanjaro. After Downie (1964) and reproduced with permission of The Geological Society of America.

Table 3   Regional firnline altitudes of the Main and Recent Glaciations, Kilimanjaro

	$K = 1^a$		$K = 2^a$	
	Altitude of firnline (m)	Altitudinal difference between stages (m)	Altitude of firnline (m)	Altitudinal difference between stages (m)
S.W. Kibo				
Main Glaciation	4484		4328	
		762		771
Recent Glaciation	5246		5099	
N.W. Kibo				
Main Glaciation	4447		4337	
		902		909
Recent Glaciation	5349		5246	

Note: these figures are adjusted for ice thickness.
[a] These two separate calculations of firnlines are based on Kurowski's Method, in the first case assuming a linear mass balance/altitude relationship ($K = 1$) and in the second case a mass balance/altitude relationship consisting of two linear segments, that below the firnline having twice the gradient of that above ($K = 2$). After Osmaston (1975), to which reference should be made for details of the technique.

Stages at *c.* 777–762 m on the south-west slopes and 903–910 m on the north-west slopes (Table 3), and he infers that, if precipitation and other non-temperature variables were as today, temperatures during the Main Glaciation were depressed by 6°C.

Two relatively minor glacial stages succeed the Main Glaciation. The older of these is the Little Glaciation, marked by moraines situated altitudinally *c.* 300 m above those of the Main Glaciation. The moraines are smaller and less continuous than those of the Main Glaciation, suggesting shorter duration, and there is evidence from one valley on Kibo that a warmer period intervened between the Main and Little Glacial Stages. The Little Glaciation was thus a phase of ice advance, rather than being a standstill episode during general glacial retreat.

The Recent Glacial Stage is represented by a set of very fresh and usually multiple moraines forming an almost complete girdle around Kibo. Each tongue of the present ice has a corresponding moraine, the altitudinal interval between modern ice and the Recent Stage moraines varying between 60 and 360 m, and being greater on the north-east than the south-west. Comparison of the present ice front with that when records began in 1888 shows that the ice has retreated rapidly and extrapolating from observed rates it can be inferred that deposition of the Recent Stage moraines ceased *c.* 200 years ago. It was only at some time between 1898 and 1904 that it became possible to walk into the caldera through a pass.

Past Glaciations of Mt Kenya

Following earlier work by Nilsson (1931) and others, Baker (1967) mapped the glacial features of Mt Kenya, recognizing two major glaciations and one more recent minor glacial stage. He confirmed an earlier suggestion of Gregory that the mountain had once been completed covered by a dome of ice through which only the crags and peaks projected. The oldest glaciation recognized by Baker is marked by poorly preserved moraines situated just below the moraines attributed to the second stage. There is an unconfirmed report of morainic boulders at an altitude as low as 2850 m in the Buguret valley in the WNW (Jeannel, 1950, quoted in Hedberg, 1951).

The second glaciation has left the most prominent traces and is marked by conspicuous moraines at altitudes of *c.* 3500 m in the valleys which radiate out from the centre of the mountain. According to a cursory examination of aerial photographs by R. A. Perrott and myself, the moraines on the east-facing slopes are usually the largest and the lowest in altitude. Glacial features on a subsidiary peak, Ithanguni, show that the firnline on the east must have been below 3894 m and probably lay at *c.* 3400 m. At maximum glaciation the ice area was *c.* 430 km^2. The difference in temperature between this stage and the present is estimated to have been *c.* 5°C, other factors being constant (Osmaston, 1975).

The most recent glacial stage is marked by large, often multiple moraines, situated at altitudes of 4270–4420 m and 500–800 m in front of the present glaciers (Charnley, 1959). A plant community with mature giant groundsels and lobelias ends abruptly in front of these moraines, suggesting that ice retreat has been fairly recent. There is historical evidence that in the 1890s the glaciers lay close to the inner side of these moraines (Charnley, 1959) and Coe (1967) suggests that the glacial stage dates to the Little Ice Age. Glacial retreat has resulted in a decline in the number of glaciers, figures given by Spink (1949) being 15 in 1899, 14 in 1926 and 10 by 1943/1945.

Past Glaciations of Ruwenzori

Osmaston (1965, 1975), following earlier work by Heinzelin (1951, 1953), Whittow *et al.* (1963) and others, has identified several glacial stages (Table 4). The main depositional features are the large converg-

Table 4   Glaciations of Ruwenzori: firnline altitudes

	Firnline difference from modern (m)
Complete deglaciation	+ 300
Modern conditions	0
1906 firnline	− 75
Lac Gris Stage	− 105
Omurabaho Stage	− 180
Mahoma Stage	− 630
Rwimi Basin Stage	− 720
Katabarua Stage	− 630

Data from Osmaston (1965, 1975).

ing lateral moraines of the Mahoma Glaciation. These moraines extend down to 2100 m, which is no less than 2400 m below the present lower limit of the ice. The moraines are up to 5 km long and 150 m high and it is possible that they have accumulated over several glaciations (Livingstone, 1962). A ^{14}C determination for basal organic sediments in Lake Mahoma, which occupies a kettlehole at 2960 m on the moraines, gives a minimum age for deglaciation of 14 700 ± 290 B.P. (Livingstone, 1962).

Below the Mahoma moraines the valleys are U-shaped for some distance and in some there are irregular mounds, apparently remains of terminal moraines. Osmaston gives an order of magnitude estimate of 100 000 years for this Rwimi Basin glaciation. A still older glaciation is indicated by the presence of old moraines on the flat interfluves between the U-shaped valleys of Rwimi Basin age. These Katabarua moraines are protected from river erosion and are morphologically well preserved. Their great age is shown by the deep onion-skin weathering of their boulders and the major inversion of topography which occurred between the Rwimi and Katabarua Glaciations.

Above the Mahoma Lake moraines it is possible to identify a consistent series of much smaller moraines, the Omurabaho moraines, at 3600–3900 m. These are not well dated, but Osmaston has pointed out that the volume of material in them is very much less than the volume of rock in the screes formed more recently. He concluded that they must be close in age to the Mahoma Lake moraines and suggested an age of 15–10 000 B.P. Finally, small, fresh moraines (the Lac Gris moraines) at *c.* 4200 m and only a relatively short distance below the modern glaciers are believed to have an age of 100–700 years.

Osmaston has made a detailed study of the shape and altitudinal distribution of each of the former glaciers and also estimates of firnline altitudes (Table 4). The firnlines of all past glaciations lie approximately parallel to one another and to the modern firnline, being tilted down towards the east. From this it is assumed that wind circulation patterns were similar at glacial maxima to the present. Assuming temperature depression alone to have been responsible for firnline movement, Osmaston estimated a lowering by 3–4°C during the Mahoma Glaciation and depression would have been of a similar order during the earlier Rwimi Basin and Katabarua Glaciations.

The extent of the ice has been observed at intervals beginning with the Duke of Abruzzi's expedition in 1906. All glaciers examined retreated rapidly up to 1961, with an apparent acceleration in melting since the 1940s (Fig. 15). Six glaciers disappeared completely between 1906 and 1959 and several others split into smaller units. In marked contrast to their former behaviour, the Speke, Elena and Savoia glaciers (the three Ruwenzori glaciers which have received the most attention) showed a well-marked advance in 1961/1962. This was followed between 1962 and 1966 by further retreat, though apparently at a slower rate than before. Between 1966 and 1968 there were modest advances of the Elena and Savoia Glaciers, and virtually no change in the Speke Glacier. Morton (1968) suggests that climatic change is responsible for these alterations, noting that 1961/1962 and to a lesser extent 1967 were years of high precipitation. The lag period between increased precipitation and glacial advance is thus thought to be very short. The Moore Glacier, all of which lies below the present firnline, retreated rapidly between 1958 and 1968.

Past Glaciations of Mt Elgon

Mt Elgon (4320 m) is a quiescent Miocene volcano and one of the highest, presently unglaciated mountains in tropical Africa to have carried ice during the Quaternary. The mountain rises gently from a surrounding plateau and covers a very large area extending *c.* 80 km

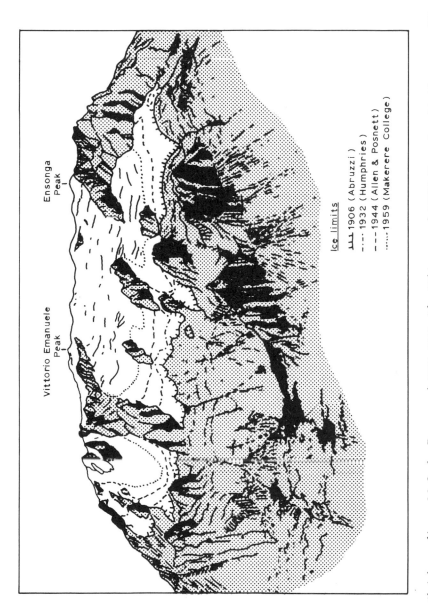

Fig. 15 Shrinkage of ice on Mt Speke, Ruwenzori, 1906–1959. After Whittow *et al.* (1963). Reproduced (with some modifications) from the Journal of Glaciology by permission of the International Glaciological Society.

from north to south and *c.* 50 km from east to west. It is surmounted by a large caldera, *c.* 8 km in diameter and surrounded by a ring of peaks. The general altitude of the caldera floor is 3660–3960 m and that of the peaks 3960–4270 m. The caldera has been breached in the ENE by the River Suam which flows out through an impressive rocky gorge. Drainage on the outer slopes is by a large number of radial streams. The volcanic sediments are mainly ashes and agglomerates, the more resistant strata in places forming prominent cliffs.

A map of the glaciations of Mt Elgon based on a very extensive ground survey was prepared by Nilsson (1931). Nilsson lacked aerial photographs, as well as the excellent 1:50 000 maps which later became available, and a new map was published in 1979 showing moraines and other glacial features which are visible on aerial photographs (Hamilton and Perrott, 1979; Fig. 16). The extent of glaciation can conveniently be shown in radial profile (Fig. 17).

The most conspicuous depositional glacial feature of Mt Elgon is a series of termino-lateral moraines, found both in external valleys and within the caldera. In many valleys this series is represented by two or three associated moraines which are taken to represent minor ice adjustments within the same glacial stage. The altitude of the external moraines varies with aspect, being lowest in the north (*c.* 3350–3430 m) and highest in the south (*c.* 3660–3730 m). [14]C determinations for basal organic sediments in Lake Kimilili (4150 m), at the head of a valley on the southern slopes, shows that deglaciation at this site occurred shortly before 11 000 B.P. (Hamilton and Perrott, 1978); the date of retreat from the main morainic series could have been considerably earlier. No moraines assignable to older glaciations have been detected. At altitudes above those of the main moraines, minor moraines occur in some valleys, but these are neither sufficiently numerous nor well correlated from valley to valley to be assignable to a glacial stage. There seems little justification for the detailed scheme of three glacial stages advanced by Nilsson (1931). Within the caldera there are several prominent moraines in the southern sector, but morainic development is very poor in the north.

Nilsson (1931) noted that a remarkable feature of the present topography is a shelf inside the caldera, especially prominent in the south, south-west and east, but also present in the north, and in places more than 1 km broad. This shelf can be very clearly seen on modern maps and on aerial photographs, being marked on the latter by a concentric pattern of light coloured, poorly-vegetated rock outcrops, alternating with darker bands of *Alchemilla* scrub. In the

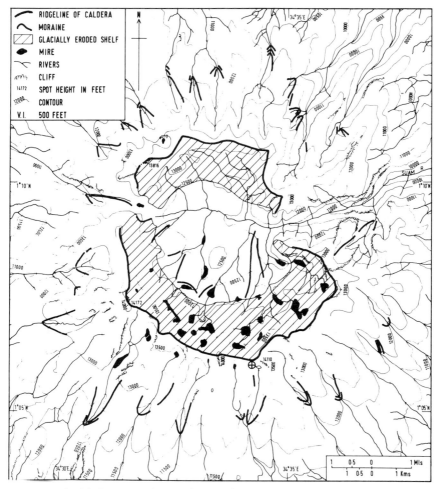

Fig. 16   Glacial features of Mt Elgon. The mires occupy glacially eroded rock basins. The circled cross indicates the site of Lake Kimilili. From Hamilton and Perrott (1979). Reproduced from Palaeoecology of Africa with permission from A. A. Balkema and E. M. van Zinderen Bakker.

southern part of the caldera, the edge of this shelf is associated with moraines and it is clearly a product of glacial erosion. As can be seen on Fig. 16, nearly all mires inside the caldera lie on the southern side. These mires mark the sites of ice-scooped basins, and erosion must have been more active in the southern part of the caldera than in the north.

In addition, there are other geomorphological contrasts between

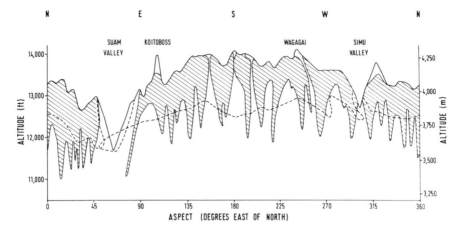

Fig. 17   Extent of ice on Mt Elgon at maximum glaciation. Notice the higher altitude of the glaciers on the south as compared to the north. From Hamilton and Perrott (1979). Reproduced from Palaeoecology of Africa with permission of A. A. Balkema and E. M. van Zinderen Bakker.

the northern and southern parts of the mountain. The northern rim of the caldera is generally rounded and it appears that glaciation here took the form of an ice-cap, with ice tongues extending down external valleys. The southern rim of the caldera is generally higher and more rugged, with frequent cliffs and pinnacles. Within the southern part of the caldera, glaciation caused fairly uniform semi-circular cut-back into the caldera rim. The various glaciers in the south failed to coalesce into a single ice-cap and many summits and ridge-crests escaped glaciation. A number of external valleys on the south are headed by prominent rock-dammed cirques. In contrast, on the north there is only one rather poorly developed cirque: this is noteworthy in having a prominent cliff to its north so that in consequence it faces roughly south-west (i.e. a similar direction to the other cirques), rather than north, as might be expected from its position on the mountain. It is thought that the head-wall backed glaciers on the south had access to a much greater supply of sediment than the ice-capped glaciers on the north. The greater scouring-ability of the southern glaciers, as evidenced by the larger moraines and the distribution of rock hollows, presumably owes much to this factor.

Reconstruction of the firn-surface, using the morainic method described by Osmaston (1975), shows that it must have been tilted up from north to south, standing at c. 3560 m on the north and c. 3914 m on the south, a difference of 264 m (Hamilton and Perrott, 1979). Since the highest peaks on the northern and southern slopes are 4211 and 4320 m respectively, the minimum depression of the firnline during glaciation is calculated to have been 561 m on the north and 406 m on the south. This corresponds to a temperature reduction by at least 3·5°C, assuming no change in precipitation.

It is quite likely that differences in altitude of the north and south rims of the caldera are the result of differential erosion during a succession of Quaternary glaciations. Assuming the rim of the caldera in preglacial times to have been approximately equi-altitudinal in relation to aspect and there to have been a number of glaciations with rain-bearing winds coming predominantly from the north on each occasion, then during early glaciations erosion of the rim is likely to have been more intensive on the north than on the south. It is envisaged that lowering of the northern rim eventually allowed an ice-cap to form on this side. Ever since the development of this ice-cap, the northern glaciers have continued to be the lower in altitude, but the southern glaciers, with their readier access to rocks, have been the more erosive.

Other Glaciations in Eastern Africa

The Aberdares consists of two peaks, Satima (3999 m) to the north and Kinangop (3906 m) to the south, separated by an extensive undulating plateau at *c.* 3000–3300 m. Whether Kinangop was glaciated is uncertain. Satima shows clear signs of past glaciation; at least two valleys facing north-west carry moraines and show U-shaped cross-sections. The main moisture-carrying winds were presumably northerly or north-westerly.

In Ethiopia past glaciations show a progressive decrease in the altitude of the firnline and a progressive increase in the extent of glaciation from north to south (Messerli *et al.*, 1980). The northern Simien mountains have 17 glaciated valleys orientated towards the west, north or north-east; the firnline is estimated to have been at *c.* 4250 m. Glaciation on the Bale Mts (including Mt Batu) was far more extensive, with a firnline at *c.* 3700 m. The influence of aspect has not been determined. The intermediately-situated Arussi Mts include three glaciated summits, Mts Badda, Chilalo and Kakka. The Mt Badda glaciers reached lower altitude on the east as compared with the west, that is 3260–3500 m as against 3700–3740 m (Street, personal communication). If we follow Messerli *et al.* (1980) in placing the firnline on the western slopes of Mt Badda at *c.* 4000 m, then that on the eastern slopes could have been at *c.* 3650 m. A ^{14}C determination of 11 500 B.P. for basal peat in a bog at 4040 m on Mt Badda gives a minimum date for the deglaciation of that mountain.

Comparison Between the Mountains

There is general agreement that two glacial stages can be correlated over wide areas (Downie, 1964; Osmaston, 1965) (Table 2). One of these is the stage which marked the last major ice advance (the Main Glaciation of Kilimanjaro, the Mahoma Glaciation of Ruwenzori, etc.), and the other is that which is marked by moraines close to modern ice limits (the Recent Glaciation of Kilimanjaro, the Lac Gris stage of Ruwenzori). It is also possible that the Little Glaciation of Kilimanjaro and the Omurabaho stage of Ruwenzori belong to a stage which is of intermediate age and to which the cirques at the heads of external valleys on the southern slopes of Mt Elgon also belong. The only doubt concerning the contemporaneity of the main glacial stage has been raised by Messerli *et al.* (1980) who agree that glaciation on the Bale Mts belongs to the main glacial stage of East Africa, but suggest that the glaciations of the Arussi Mts and the Simien Mts may have been more recent.

The ^{14}C date for basal Lake Mahoma sediments indicates that the maximum of the main glacial stage occurred before 14 700 B.P., but the exact period of maximum glaciation and its relationship to changes in precipitation and temperature remain open questions. Gasse *et al.* (1980) have suggested that maximum glaciation in Ethiopia may date to the period *c.* 27 000–21 000 B.P. when there could have been a particularly favourable combination of cold temperatures and relatively high precipitation. Alternatively, maximum glaciation could have occurred or have persisted into the succeeding climatic phase, after *c.* 21 000 B.P., when the climate is believed to have been colder and drier. More absolute dates are needed. It is noted that, on a world scale, maximum glaciation was at *c.* 18 000 B.P.

The altitudes of the firnlines and the direction of firn-surface tilt at maximum glaciation are of great interest (Fig. 12). According to Osmaston's estimates, firnline depress on was greater on Kilimanjaro than on Ruwenzori, Mt Kenya being intermediate. The actual temperature fall on these three mountains was probably similar (estimated at 6·7–8·3°C by Livingstone, 1980). It is believed from other evidence that there was an absolute reduction in precipitation on all three mountains. It therefore follows that the reduction in precipitation was relatively small on Kilimanjaro.

The apparent reversal in the direction of the main rain-bearing winds at maximum glaciation on several of the mountains is striking. It is thought that the north-east trades existed during the last glaciation. It is suggested that the presence of a stronger and perhaps more southerly Saharo–Arabian high pressure zone forced the north-east trades to adopt a more southerly route giving them a longer sea-passage over the Indian Ocean.

^{14}C determinations from Mt Elgon and Mt Badda are taken to show that the ice had disappeared completely from these mountains by 11 500/11 000 B.P. The possible high altitude cirque-based glacial stage on Mt Elgon would probably have occurred shortly before this date. The distribution of cirques assigned to this stage suggests that the main rain-bearing winds were from the south-west, as they are today. This would imply that by this time the south-easterly trades had become the moister wind stream. It should be possible to test this idea by studies of the Little Glaciation on Kilimanjaro and the equivalent stage reported by Downie (1964) to be present on Mt Kenya.

It is agreed by all that there was a minor glacial readvance on Kilimanjaro, Mt Kenya and Ruwenzori during the Little Ice Age which dates to *c.* 1500–1800 A.D. and which was marked by ice expansion in many parts of the world. That this event was recorded by the East African ice, and indeed the general correlation of the last major glacial maximum in eastern Africa with that found world-wide, demonstrates the inter-dependency of climates in different parts of the world.

On a world scale, the number of major glaciations during the Quaternary considerably exceeds four, which is the maximum number of major glacial stages recognized on any one East African mountain. It is therefore likely that East Africa has witnessed glacial episodes of which no evidence survives.

The retreat since the Little Ice Age is believed to be due partly to world-wide climatic trends, and partly to the effects of increased influx of dust onto the ice surface. There has been no marked trend towards drier climate overall since the turn of the century in East Africa (indeed the early decades of the century were drier than the rather wet 1950s and 1960s) and therefore it is likely that the recent retreat of the ice on the East African mountains is largely a symptom of ecosystem degradation at lower altitudes at the hands of man.

Chapter 4

Past Lakes, Rivers and Deserts

Historical Introduction

It has been known for some time that many African lakes once stood at substantially higher levels than they do today. These high lake stands have generally been held to provide some of the most convincing evidence that tropical Africa witnessed major alterations in climate during the Quaternary and their existence, backed up by other supposed indications of past climatic events, resulted in the emergence in the 1930s of a generally held theory (the "Pluvial Theory") of Quaternary climatic change (Leakey, 1931, 1965; Nilsson, 1931, 1940; Wayland, 1934, 1952). According to the Pluvial Theory, wet and dry climatic periods have alternated during the Quaternary, the wet periods being correlated with glaciations in temperate parts of the world (and on the mountains of eastern Africa) and the dry periods being correlated with interglacials. The determining factor was held to be temperature change and it was envisaged that during glaciations lower temperatures were experienced at all latitudes resulting in the tropics in decreased potential evapotranspiration and hence higher effective precipitation. Changes in rainfall *per se* seem to have been regarded by adherents of the Pluvial Theory as being relatively unimportant. At the time when the Pluvial Theory was widely accepted, it was commonly believed that there had been four major European glaciations and from this it was often supposed that there had been four major pluvials in Africa (e.g. Cole, 1964). Although uncertainties as to the dating of some of the high East African lake stands or other phenomena attributed to climatic vicissitudes remained, the Pluvial Theory appeared to many workers to be sufficiently well established by the mid-1950s to constitute the basis for a formal climo-stratigraphic scheme to be used by Quaternary palaeo-environmentalists working in tropical Africa (Clark and Cole, 1957).

Since the late 1950s, the Pluvial Theory has come under increasing criticism (Bishop, 1963, 1967, 1969; Bishop and Posnansky, 1960; Cooke, 1958; Flint, 1959; Isaac, 1966; McCall *et al.*, 1967). In particular, it became widely doubted whether the Pluvial Theory was meteorologically soundly based. The demise of the Pluvial Theory was due above all to the introduction of ^{14}C dating, a method not available to earlier workers, and today it is unequivocally established that the most recent of the high lake stands (those once attributed to the Gamblian Pluvial) actually occurred during postglacial times and not at the time of the last glaciation as was formerly believed. There has been little progress in dating high lake stands too old to be dated by ^{14}C dating (> *c.* 40 000 B.P.) and workers have understandably been cautious in correlating these either with one another or with climatic events in temperate parts of the world. Additionally, it becomes more difficult to disentangle the possible roles of tectonic activity and other non-climatic variables in controlling water-levels with older high lake stands.

Lakes

(a) *Some characteristics of modern lakes*

It can be seen from Fig. 18 that most lakes in eastern Africa are associated with the rift valleys. The catchments of the lakes of the Western and Nyasa Rifts receive relatively high precipitation and all of the larger lakes are presently externally drained. In contrast, the climate of the Eastern and Ethiopian Rifts is relatively arid and all lakes here lack outlets. With the exception of Lake Turkana, these lakes tend to be rather small and saline. Lake Victoria occupies a shallow basin, believed to have been impounded by the same earth movements which led to the formation of the rifts.

Some characteristics of selected eastern African lakes are shown on Table 5. Biologically, the lakes fall into three categories, each characterized by a certain range in electrical conductivity (Beadle, 1974). First, there are those lakes with a conductivity of less than *c.*

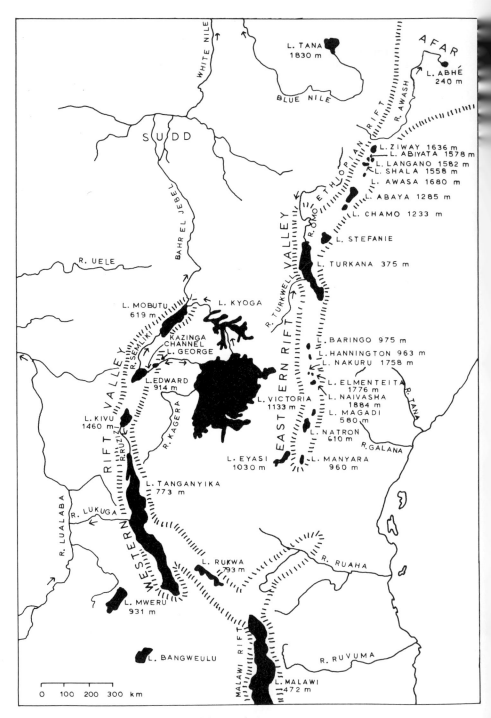

Fig. 18   Eastern Africa: major lakes and rivers.

Table 5 Some characteristics of modern lakes

Lake	Altitude (m)	Area (km²)	Max. depth (m)	Conductivity (K_{20})	Salinity (g l^{-1}‰)	pH (spot or range)
Malawi Rift						
Malawi	472	—	770	210	0·192	8·2–8·9
Western Rift Valley						
Tanganyika	773	34 000	1470	610	0·530	8·0–9·0
Kivu	1460	2055	485	1240	1·115	9·1–9·5
Edward	914	2325	112	925	0·789	8·8–9·1
George	914	270	3	200	0·139	8·5–9·8
Mobutu	619	6800	56	735	0·597	8·9–9·5
Eastern and Ethiopian Rift Valleys						
Elmenteita	1776	15	1·9	22 500	4	—
Nakuru	1758	40	2·8	162 500	45	—
Naivasha	1884	180	18	250	—	—
Turkana	375	7500	73	3300	2·482	9·5–9·7
Shalla	1558	329	266	—	—	9·7
Others						
Victoria	1133	69 500	79	96	0·093	7·1–8·5
Chad	280	15 000	12	180	0·165	8·0–8·5

Data from Beadle (1974), Butzer et al. (1972), Hecky and Degens (1973) and Lind and Morrison (1974). Conductivity (K_{20}) is the reciprocal of the electrical resistance (ohms^{-1}) of 1 cm of water at 20°C. Salinity is expressed as weight (g) per volume of water (1) and is given in parts per thousand. With the exception of very saline lakes, electrical conductivity is a measure of the total concentration of major ions. Differences between altitudes given here and those given elsewhere in the book are due to differences in the literature sources. A dash indicates that I have been unable to obtain information.

40 ohm^{-1} cm^{-1}. In these there is some evidence that ionic deficiencies, at least in calcium, influence their biotic composition. None of the lakes dealt with at some length in this chapter fall into this category. Second, there are lakes with conductivities between *c.* 40 and 6000 ohm^{-1} cm^{-1}. This category includes the great majority of normal "freshwater" lakes. Beadle maintains that there is no evidence that differences in the composition of the water in respect of the major chemical constituents have any effect on the distribution of organisms within lakes of this category. This opinion is, however, questioned by Hecky and Degens (1973) who suggest that diatom differences between Lakes Edward and Mobutu may be due to the relative richness in silica and poverty in phosphate of the former. The third of Beadle's categories includes the hypersaline lakes with conductivities exceeding *c.* 6000 ohm^{-1} cm^{-1}. Very few species can tolerate the hypersalinity of these lakes.

The recycling of nutrients from deeper waters into the photic zone is very important for maintaining a high biological production in a lake. Lakes such as Chad and George, which are shallow enough to be frequently stirred to the bottom by surface wave action, are often very productive, though even these can become deoxygenated at depth during calm periods. Most lakes of moderate depth, including Mobutu, Victoria and probably Turkana, are stratified for part of the year but are thoroughly mixed by seasonal winds. Pulses of increased algal productivity result from the stirring. Finally, deep lakes can be permanently stratified, the lower water being always free of oxygen. Anoxic conditions are present in Lakes Kivu (below 70 m), Malawi (200–250 m) and Tanganyika (100–200 m). Lake Edward has a deep trench containing more or less permanently anoxic water, but for the most part it is only seasonally stratified. Production in permanently stratified lakes is reduced by nutrient deficiency. There is some evidence of nutrient recycling within Lakes Malawi and Tanganyika making them somewhat more productive than would otherwise be the case, but Lake Kivu, a very unproductive lake, is particularly firmly stratified and there is probably a complete lack of circulation within the anoxic region. There are remarkably large increases in temperature and salinity below 70 m in Lake Kivu caused by deep seepage of warm saline water from volcanic sources, and the presence at depth of large quantities of dissolved gases. According to Hecky and Degens, the latter are of mixed volcanic (CO_2) and predominantly biological (H_2S, CH_4) origin.

Diatom frustules are by far the most abundant microfossils in Rift Valley lake sediments (Hecky and Degens, 1973). The diatom flora is principally determined by the chemistry of the surface water and by the range of habitats present, and can thus respond to lake level changes and to changes in the state of stratification. The study of the ecology of diatom taxa can therefore be important for the reconstruction of limnological history (Richardson, 1964).

(b) *Methods of detecting lake level changes*

The reconstruction of limnological history can be based on several types of evidence, including the modern distributions of aquatic organisms, the topography of the lake sediment surface, the characteristics of lake sediments and raised beaches, and other evidence of high lake stands.

Lake sediments contain a wealth of information relating to the development of lakes and their catchments and may be collected for study either by means of under-water coring devices or more simply from exposures above present water-levels. Many attributes of the sediments, including lithology, mineralogy, fossil contents and magnetic properties, can be investigated and a common problem facing the researcher is to select from the many sediment properties those which provide the greatest insight into the past. Some sort of model of the factors which determine sediment characteristics is essential; a good example is provided by the work of Gasse (1975), who infers changes in the lacustrine environment from diatom assemblages using studies of the ecology of modern diatoms as the basis for interpretation.

(c) *The controls over lake levels*

Several factors can influence lake levels. Non-climatic variables include changes in drainage patterns, heights of outflows, tectonic events and vegetational changes in catchments. The main climatic determinants are precipitation and evaporation, both in the catchment and on the lake itself. In reconstructing climatic history from lake level history, it has to be appreciated that lake level fluctuations may not be in phase with climatic events. Soil moisture, which in short-term hydrological investigations can represent an important lagged storage, can probably be neglected on the longer time-scales dealt with here, but the size and the topography of the catchment are important influences over the response time of a lake. Consideration must also be given to the relative importance of overland and groundwater flow; lakes which are primarily fed by groundwater can show greater lags in their responses to climatic events (Gasse and Street, 1978).

(d) *History of Western and Malawi Rift lakes*

(i) *Lake Mobutu (Albert).* The Lake Mobutu basin contains a great thickness of sediments deposited during the Quaternary and perhaps also at earlier times. Boreholes and seismic records indicate the presence of over 2·4 km of sediment at the south end of the basin (Beadle, 1974), but detailed palaeo-environmental investigations of the great bulk of these sediments have not been undertaken.

Two series of sediments have been exposed around the present lake by earth movements (Beadle, 1974; Bishop, 1969). The older of these, the Kaiso beds, is believed to date to the Lower or Middle Quaternary and consists of over 600 m of sediment. All but one of the 25 species of molluscs described from these beds are now absent fom Lake Mobutu. A similar "Kaiso fauna" is known from sediments exposed in the Lake Edward basin and three of the species are found in the early Pleistocene Gaza beds in the Lake Turkana basin. The fauna includes several genera which are now confined to Lake Tanganyika suggesting greater environmental stability here than in the more northern lake basins. The younger series of sediments in the Mobutu basin is believed to be of Upper Quaternary age. The mollusc fauna is modern, giving an upper time limit to the catastrophe which overtook the Kaiso fauna. Beadle (1974) suggests that the disappearance of the Kaiso fauna could have been due to severe desiccation.

Sediment cores have been collected by Harvey (1976) and Hecky and Degens (1973). According to Harvey the lake overflowed at 28 000–25 000 B.P., lacked an outlet at 25 000–18 000 B.P., was freshwater at 18 000–14 000 B.P., and lacked an outlet again up to 12 500 B.P., when the modern overflow period commenced. Chemical analyses of sediment cores collected by Hecky and Degens show higher values of carbonate and organic carbon after *c.* 5000 B.P. and productivity is estimated to have increased by a factor of two. This was probably due to increased nutrient input which, according to Hecky and Degens, could have been channelled into the lake by the Semliki River from the fresh volcanic sediments of the Toro-Ankole volcanic field. A ^{14}C determination for volcanism in the Fort Portal area gives a date of 4070 ± 120 B.P. (Osmaston, 1967).

(ii) *Lake Edward.* Three series of Quaternary sediments are exposed in the lake basin (Beadle, 1974; Bishop, 1969). Lower Quaternary sediments are similar to the Kaiso beds of Lake Mobutu and contain, in addition to the molluscs, fossils of crocodile and of two fish genera, all lacking from the present-day fauna of the basin. The Middle Quaternary Semliki series is afossiliferous and coarser-grained than the Lower Quaternary sediments, suggesting a period of active uplift (Beadle, 1974) or perhaps of drier climate. Upper Quaternary sediments dating from 10 000–8000 B.P. are exposed at Ishango and contain human remains, stone tools and harpoons. Two fishes recorded from these beds, *Lates niloticus* (Nile perch) and *Barbus bynni*, are now absent from the lake but persist in Lake Mobutu. It is possible that their extinctions were caused by volcanism; volcanic ash overlies the sediments containing the artifacts at Ishango.

Five lake sediment cores were collected from Lake Edward in 1972 (Hecky and Degens, 1973). The two from deeper water (102 m, 120 m) were laminated (the light bands being diatom-rich) and the three from shallow water (< 80 m) were unlaminated, suggesting an approximate limit to seasonal mixing at 80–102 m. Chemical examination of one core revealed ash layers and lead peaks at 5600 B.P. and again at < 1200 B.P., dates more or less corresponding to periods of hydrothermal activity at Lake Kivu.

(iii) *Lake Kivu.* Lake Kivu is believed to have been formed by imposition of the Virunga volcanic field on northward-flowing drainage originating in the Lake Tanganyika basin. Today the lake drains southwards by way of the Ruzizi River into Lake Tanganyika. Sediment cores were collected in 1971 and 1972 by expeditions from the Woods Hole Oceanographic Institution. These cores range in length up to 8 m and are from various parts of the lake and from beneath various depths of water. The following account is based largely on the results of examination of these cores (Hecky and Degens, 1973). Dating is by ^{14}C determinations on the sediments, with correlations and extrapolations based on the determinations.

Seismic profiles show that there are more than 500 m of sediment beneath the deep (to 485 m) northern part of Lake Kivu, suggesting that the lake is rather old. Where water depth is less than *c*. 300 m, there is only a thin veneer of sediment and the lake probably stood 300 m below its present level during relatively recent times. This has been confirmed by sediment cores, which showed the presence of beach deposits at −310 m and which provided a date range of > 13 700–12 500 B.P. for the low phase.

At 12 500 B.P. the water level began to rise and, with the exception of a major low stand between 11 000 and 10 000 B.P., continued to do so until overflow at 9 500 B.P. Evidence for this rise in water level is demonstrated, *inter alia*, by a core collected beneath 86 m of water and based by a soil horizon which became submerged at 12 130 B.P. and by a core from the Bukavu basin, which is separated from the main lake by a 30 m deep sill and which is shown by the core to have become connected to the main lake at 10 000 B.P. A 100 m terrace in the Kivu basin is believed to mark the height of the water surface at overflow.

There is evidence of volcanic activity at 12 000 B.P. and again at 5500–5000 B.P. and 1200 B.P. The latter two events are marked in the sediments by increased quantities of TiO_2 and Al_2O_3 from volcanic ash and were closely followed by hydrothermal spring activity, injecting warm, metal-rich and CO_2-charged groundwater into the lake. This is shown in the sediments by big increases in lead and by the absence of $CaCO_3$, the latter being attributed to dissolution of $CaCO_3$ particles falling into the CO_2-rich, and thus acidic, deep water. Calcium carbonate deposition was renewed between 4000 and 1200 B.P., a period when the lake level dropped and the lake once again became closed. Dolomite was precipitated in the Bukavu basin which may have been only intermittently connected to the main lake. High lake levels, with overflow, were resumed at 1200 B.P. and have persisted to the present day.

The close association of volcanism and increased hydrothermal spring activity at 5500–5000 and 1200 B.P. suggests that there may be a causal relationship between them (Hecky and Degens, 1973). As the water of the springs is meteoric, climatic processes may be involved and it is postulated that the climatically determined availability of water for deep percolation through the porous lavas and ash present in the catchment might regulate the volcanic activity. The water, by mixing with hot magma, would be transformed to steam and the consequent volume changes would fracture or dislodge confining overburden and allow the release of volcanic ejecta and lava. It is thus possible that the African sequence of pluvials and interpluvials may have been associated with periods of activity and quiescence in volcanic and rifting processes.

Two main diatom zones can be recognized in the sediments. In the older, which lasted from 13 700 to 5000 B.P., the most common species is *Stephanodiscus astraea* which together with *Nitzschia fonticola* and *N. spiculum* account for over 95% of the diatom flora. Rather minor changes in the relative abundance of these three species during the zone are attributed to changes in water level and in the stability of stratification in the lake. The second zone, dated 5000–0 B.P., is very different from the first. Its distinctive character is believed to be due to changes in lake chemistry consequent on increased hydrothermal spring activity. Two different diatom assemblages are present in this zone, one dominated by rod shaped species of *Nitzschia* such as *N. palea* and *N. accomodata* and the other by needle-shaped species of *Nitzschia*, such as *N. bacata, N. mediocris* and *N. spiculum*. The most abundant microfossil with the first assemblage is actually not a diatom, but the chrysophyte *Paraphysomonas vestita*.

(iv) *Lake Tanganyika.* After Lake Baikal, Lake Tanganyika at 1470 m is the deepest lake in the world. The fauna is rich and of a relict nature, indicating the long persistence of the lake and the absence of any periods of hypersalinity. Structurally there are two deep basins, one in the north and the other in the south, separated from one another by a relatively shallow sill. Outflow today is westwards into the River Zaire system by way of the Lukuga River.

Former lake level depression on several occasions is suggested by seismic investigations (Capart, 1949, cited in Hecky and Degens, 1973). Multiple echoes recorded beneath water depths of 150–850 m are believed to be caused by alternating light and dense sediments. Where the lake is less than 150 m deep, multiple echoes are lacking and the trace indicates a hard bottom (sandy silt according to Beadle, 1974). At depths of over 850 m, the echo sounder recorded only a single diffuse trace, attributed to a single layer of very soft sediment. Within the 150–850 m zone, as many as eight traces occur above 550 m, but only two at greater depths. The denser material is believed to have been deposited during periods of low water level and the lighter material during periods of high water table. Further evidence for low lake levels is provided by the indentation of many river courses into the floor of the lake at depths of up to 550 m. It has been suggested that the hard bands in the sediment are horizons of volcanic ash, but this explanation does not account for their distribution in relation to depth.

Cores have been collected from various parts of the lake (Hecky and Degens, 1973). The basal part of a 2 m core from under 550 m in the central shallower zone was rich in montmorillonite and lacked pyrite, contrasting with the kaolinite-dominated and pyrite-containing upper part of the same core and of the entire lengths of cores obtained from deeper parts of the lake. It is thought that the lower part of the sill core was deposited under oxidizing conditions, suggesting a much lower lake level than now. The base of this core is ^{14}C-dated to > 28 200 B.P. A 10·74 m core collected by Livingstone (1965, 1975) from beneath 440 m of water at the southern end of the lake lacked a soil horizon. Only a single ^{14}C date of 11 690 B.P. at 5·75 m is available, giving a date of 22 000 B.P. for the base of the core by linear extrapolation. According to Hecky and Degens (1973), such extrapolation may not be valid and they suggest that the base of the core may be much younger.

Hecky and Degens (1973) have calculated the effects on the level of Lake Tanganyika if temperature lowering and precipitation changes at *c*. 13 700–12 000 B.P. had been similar to those estimated for nearby Lake Kivu. If rainfall was two-thirds of modern values and if temperatures were depressed by 3°C, the lake is calculated to have been lowered by over 600 m, a sufficient reduction to split the lake into two separate basins.

The loss of drainage from Lake Kivu between *c*. 4000 and 1000 B.P. would have been sufficient by itself to have lowered the level of Lake Tanganyika by 75 m, i.e. well below the modern outlet (Hecky and Degens, 1973). This estimate assumes no climatic change, but, since it is probable that the lowering of the Lake Kivu was climatically induced and since climatic trends would have followed a similar pattern over both the Kivu and Lake Tanganyika catchments, then even lower levels of Lake Tanganyika are probable. Capart (1949) suggested that the very thin sediment cover at depths of > 150 m could be a consequence of this low stand. The earliest historical record of the Lukuga outlet from Lake Tanganyika shows that in 1854 it was completely blocked. Overflow occurred in 1878 and flow has been continuous ever since. Considering the long response time of the lake, it is possible that 1878 A.D. marks the first overflow of Lake Tanganyika since *c*. 4000 B.P.

(v) *Lake Rukwa.* Two ^{14}C dates for a high lake stand are 9740 ± 130 and 8060 ± 120 B.P. (Butzer *et al.*, 1972).

(vi) *Lake Malawi.* There have been few palaeo-environmental investigations of this long-established lake (Beadle, 1974). An undated raised shoreline occurs at + 100 m above the present lake level (Beadle, 1974). The lake today overflows by the River Shire into the Zambezi, but this overflow is tenuous and, although present from before 1865 to 1915 A.D. and since 1936, it was absent during the intervening years (Hecky and Degens, 1973). The sediments are similar to those of Lake Tanganyika, but have not been examined in detail. Several peaks in lead in the sediments suggest hydrothermal activity in the basin.

(c) *History of Eastern and Ethiopian Rift lakes*

The Eastern and Ethiopian Rifts are today mostly situated in a drier climatic zone than the Western and Nyasa Rifts. There have been considerable climatically-induced fluctuations in lake levels in the area of the Eastern and Ethiopian Rifts during the Quaternary, but according to Isaac (1975) the general contrast in aridity between the two rift valley areas is long-standing. Lake Turkana has always been in a fairly arid area and, although there have been fluctuations in the size of the saline lake and in the intensity of aeolian sediment transport at Olduvai, these have never been of sufficient amplitude to remove the basin from a semi-arid hydrological regime.

(i) *Lakes Nakuru, Elmenteita and Naivasha.* These three lakes (Fig. 19) lie just south of the Equator, at a point where the floor of the Eastern Rift Valley reaches its greatest elevation. Lake Naivasha is the largest and freshest, while Lakes Elmenteita and Nakuru are smaller, shallower and highly saline. The basins of these lakes have probably received greater attention from palaeo-environmentalists than any other areas of comparable size in eastern Africa. The following account largely follows Butzer *et al.* (1972). (See also Richardson, 1966; Richardson and Richardson, 1972; Washbourn, 1967; Washbourn-Kamau, 1970, 1975.)

The modern potential outlet of the Nakuru-Elmenteita basin stands at 1949 m, which is 191 m above the modern level of Lake Nakuru (1758 m). Two raised shorelines can be traced in the basin. The older of these, the Gamble's Cave shoreline, is represented by prominent shoreline notches and littoral deposits along the outer slopes of Menengai Crater, on the Karterit volcanic cone and at Gamble's Cave. Lake level stood at + *c.* 180 m and the enlarged lake is believed to have seeped into Menengai Crater, perhaps over an outlet since blocked by volcanic deposits. ^{14}C dates for littoral deposits indicate that the shoreline dates to 10 000–8000 B.P. The younger of the two raised shorelines, the Misonge shoreline, is 49 m above the present Lake Nakuru level. It is represented by a shoreline notch cut into soft pyroclastic deposits which are believed to have been derived from the last major eruption of Menengai.

In the Naivasha basin a possible beach ridge and the presence in

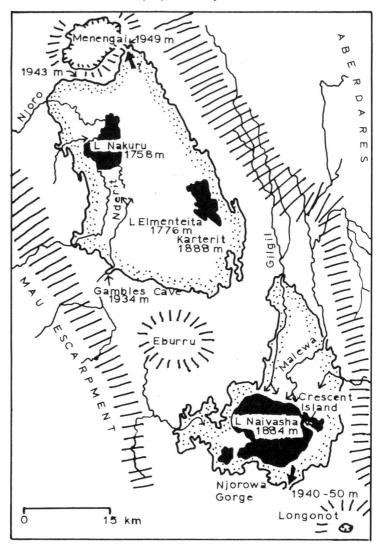

Fig. 19   The Nakuru and Naivasha basins showing the modern and expanded early Holocene lake margins (the latter indicated by heavy lines). Spillways shown by arrows. Adapted from Butzer *et al.* (1972) and Beadle ("The Inland Waters of Tropical Africa", 1974, Longman Group Ltd).

many places of beach gravels indicate that the lake once stood at 2000 ± 10 m, compared to its 1972 level of 1890 m (Washbourn-Kamau, 1975). There is no conclusive proof of raised shorelines at lower altitude. The lake overflowed down the Njorowa Gorge, the floor of which then stood at a higher level than its present-day altitude of 1940–1950 m. According to modern opinion, the lake did not connect with the Nakuru-Elmenteita basin during the high phase.

Three sedimentary lacustrine units, A (the oldest), B and C, separated by conspicuous disconformities, are present in the area south of Lake Nakuru. The strata of unit A indicate alternating contraction and expansion of the lake, the lake reaching a level approaching that of its modern potential outlet on at least three occasions. A ^{14}C sample from fluvial beds in the upper part of unit A has given a date of 19 000 B.P. A widespread unconformity occurs between units A and B; during this period the lake was low and drainage lines were deeply incised into the floor of the basin. Unit B, which is widespread and lithologically varied, is correlated with the Gamble's Cave shoreline. Unit C is probably correlated with the Misonge shoreline.

Lake sediment cores have been collected by Richardson from all lakes, including a 50 m core from Lake Nakuru, a 23 m core from Lake Elmenteita (basal ^{14}C date, 29 320 B.P.) and a 27 m core from Lake Naivasha (basal ^{14}C date, 9200 B.P.). Cores from Lake Naivasha indicate lake overflow at 9000–5600 B.P.

There is widespread evidence of tectonic deformation in the Nakuru-Elmenteita and Naivasha basins and this has certainly influenced both sedimentological and hydrological history. It is thought, however, that rapid oscillations of lake levels with amplitudes of 60–190 m are likely to have been largely climatically determined. Butzer *et al.* (1972) have attempted to model the hydrological systems at the time when the lakes were standing at the levels of their outlets and, with reasonable assumptions concerning temperatures and runoff, have concluded that precipitation could have been at least 65% greater than at present in the case of the Nakuru-Elmenteita basin and 50% in the case of the Naivasha basin.

Lake Nakuru has been dry at least once during the 70–80 years for which records exist. The levels of all lakes rose slightly after the high rainfall of the early 1960s.

(ii) *Lake Magadi.* Magadi (604 m) is an ephemeral lake lying at the lowermost point of the southern part of the Eastern Rift. Silts and clays (the High Magadi Beds) form a discontinuous shelf 12 m above the modern lake level and were deposited at a time when the water level was seasonally higher and somwhat more stable than it is today (Butzer *et al.*, 1972). Fish fossils in this deposit have yielded a ^{14}C date of 9120 ± 170 B.P. A core from the lake sediments shows chert at 61–48 m, silty tuffaceous siltstones at 41–35 m and trona at 34–0 m. It is thought that the siltstones formed at a time of higher lake level than the other strata.

(iii) *Lake Turkana (Rudolf)*. Lake Turkana is the largest lake lacking an outlet in eastern Africa. The biggest inflow is the Omo River with a catchment which includes part of the Ethiopian Plateau. The Suam/Turkwell River originating on Mt Elgon also drains into the lake.

Pliocene and Quaternary sedimentary and volcanic formations dating back *c.* 6 million years outcrop extensively around the lake (Coppens *et al.*, 1976). Although the characteristics of these formations do indicate some climatic changes, it is only for the tectonically undeformed uppermost formation, the Kibish, that unequivocal palaeoclimatic conclusions can be drawn (Butzer, 1976). However, the topography, the disposition and altitude of the various earlier sedimentary formations, as well as the types of aquatic fossil animals contained within them, all point to repeated hydrological links with the Nile System. Each formation culminates at an altitude of 450–460 m, that is at the level of the Turkana-Nile threshold (Butzer, 1976).

The Kibish Formation consists of littoral, deltaic and fluvial beds dating from the mid-Pleistocene to the mid-Holocene (Butzer, 1976; Butzer *et al.*, 1972). An early lake level *c.* 60 m higher than the modern level has been dated by the Th/U method at 130 000 and a later high stand at + 60–70 m occurred shortly before 35 000 B.P. Deltaic and littoral sediments are absent for the period 35 000–9500 B.P. and the lake is thought to have been low. Aridity is also suggested by carbonate horizons and by desert varnish on lag pebbles. The youngest Kibish units (Members IVa and IVb) are well exposed, preserve considerable surface morphology and have received a number of ^{14}C determinations. The maximum level during Member IVa times was attained by 9500 B.P. and the lake level fluctuated between + 60 and + 80 m until a little after 7500 B.P., when the lake shrunk to its present size. Member IVb records a transgression which began shortly before 6600 B.P., reaching a level of + 65–70 m by *c.* 6200 B.P. This level was maintained until after 4400 B.P. and was followed by a brief transgression to + 70 m a little before 3000 B.P. The lake has been relatively low since 3000 B.P., with rapid fluctuations over a range of over 40 m. In common with all other East African lakes, there was a rise in level in 1962–1966.

Connection with the Nile system is believed to have been achieved during at least parts of the 9500–7500 and 6200–3250 B.P. high stands.

(iv) *Lakes of the Ethiopian Rift and Afar Region.* Following earlier studies by Grove *et al.* (1975) and others, Gasse and Street (1978) and Gasse *et al.* (1980) have published detailed comparisons of Upper Quaternary lake level fluctuations in the Ziway-Shala Basin of the Main Ethiopian Rift with those in the Afar depression in north-east Ethiopia/Djibouti. Following a high-lake stand in the early part of the Upper Quaternary, Lake Abhé dried out during a period believed to date to 70 000–60 000 B.P. A second high stand between well before 40 000 and *c.* 30 000 B.P. witnessed a deep, alkaline lake rich in organic matter and containing tropical diatoms. Following a brief recession at *c.* 30 000 B.P., there was a third lacustrine phase lasting from *c.* 30 000 to 21 000 B.P., or perhaps slightly later. The diatom flora consisted of a combination of tropical and temperate forms and there are indications of a high content of suspended sediment in the lake water. The period *c.* 17 000–10 000 B.P. was hyperarid and was marked by drying up of the lake and dune development. During the Holocene three or possibly four high stands occurred in the Abhé basin. The first two, dated 9400–8400 and 7000–4000 B.P. respectively, were of large amplitude and were interrupted by a very rapid and pronounced recession. A small recession occurred shortly after 6000 B.P. Soon after a big fall at 4000 B.P. the lake level reached its present level and there have since been only minor fluctuations, including a transgression at *c.* 2700–1000 B.P. and possibly another about a century ago. The level of Abhé has been determined principally by inflow of the River Awash from the highlands and it is interesting to note that lakes in the Afar region, differing from Abhé in being mainly fed by groundwater, lacked the *c.* 8400–7000 recession. This is presumed to be due to the greater response time of the groundwater reservoir. It is thought that only arid intervals of long duration, such as that which followed 4000 B.P., are registered in such lakes.

Two pre-Holocene high lake stands are recorded in the Ziway-Shala basin. The second of these terminated at *c.* 22 000 B.P. and, as at Abhé, this was followed by a very dry phase and then by high levels during the early Holocene. Prior to 10 000 B.P., the exact form of the lake level curve is uncertain, but there is evidence for an initial lake rise, beginning perhaps around 12 000 B.P., followed by a brief recession. The main transgression took place at *c.* 10 000 B.P., with two major high stands dated at *c.* 9400–8000 and *c.* 6500–4000 B.P. interrupted by a brief recession. The lake level then fell rapidly, with a minor high at *c.* 3000–2000 B.P. and a very slight positive oscillation during the last few centuries.

The Pleistocene high lake stands, both at Afar and in the main Ethiopian Rift, are marked by relatively low detrital influx into the basins and it is considered that rates of physical erosion in the catchments were low. The terminal Pleistocene arid phase was in contrast marked by an upsurge in detrital influx with, for example, very extensive gravel fans containing huge boulders developed throughout the Central Afar. Deep water Lower Holocene sediments are more calcareous than the corresponding sediments of upper Pleistocene age and Gasse and Street (1978) speculate that this may have been due to a leaching of soils which, in the area as a whole, became carbonate enriched as a result of input of carbonate-rich desert dust from Arabia and India during the terminal arid phase, a time when trade-wind circulation was intensified.

(f) *History of Lake Victoria*

The Lake Victoria basin is believed to have originated by uplift of land along the eastern shoulder of the Western Rift Valley and the reversal of previously west-flowing rivers, such as the Kagera. The present drainage of the lake is northwards by the Nile into Lake Kyoga and on into Lake Mobutu.

A series of strandlines have been detected around the lake (Temple, 1964, 1966, 1967). The older of these range in 'height up to 66 m above the present lake surface and are tilted up towards the west, showing that tectonic events have been at least partly responsible for their formation. Temple (1964) has accurately surveyed the raised beaches on the northern shoreline of the lake and has shown that these are untilted and stand at heights of 3·0, 13·7 and 18·3 m (10, 45 and 60 ft) above the modern lake. Temple discusses possible dates and causes. Changes in inflow into the lake due to drainage evolution, downcutting of the lake outlet and climatic change could all have contributed. [14]C dates of 3700 B.P. and 3240 B.P. have been obtained for the lowest, which is also the youngest, level. It is concluded from these dates that Lake Nabugabo on the northern shore of Lake Victoria was cut off from the main lake within the last 4000 years.

Sediment cores have been collected by Kendall (1969) from the northern part of the lake. The longest, from Pilkington Bay near Jinja, represents *c.* 15 000 years and is ^{14}C-dated in 28 places, allowing considerable precision in the estimation of the accumulation rates of sediment constituents. Mineralogical, pollen and diatom analyses have been undertaken. Near the base of the section there is an erosional unconformity ^{14}C-dated at 14 730 B.P. and the lake was clearly much lower than now. Below this unconformity the sediment contains much inorganic matter and microfossil preservation is poor. Further coring by Livingstone (1980) has established that the level of the lake was actually depressed by at least 75 m and the lake must have been virtually non-existent. Above the unconformity the sediment is uniformly lake mud but shows some chemical differentiation. Before 12 000 B.P., the sediment was rich in exchangeable bases, calcite was deposited and the lake was clearly closed. Overflow of the lake occurred at 12 000 B.P. and, except for a brief period of closure at *c.* 10 000 B.P. the lake has remained open ever since. Historical changes in lake level are described in Beadle (1974).

(g) *Upper Quaternary lake level fluctuations elsewhere in tropical Africa*

Lake Chad is a large lake in semi-arid to arid West Africa, deriving its waters principally from the Chari-Logone Rivers draining savanna country to the south. The results of investigations of studies of lake level fluctuations are given in Grove and Pullan (1963), Rognon and Williams (1977), Servant and Servant-Vildary (1980). There are slight differences between some of these accounts, but a general summary is as follows. The lake was very high between *c.* 40 000 and 20 000 B.P., with a periodically dry phase at *c.* 30 000 B.P. A long period of desiccation with associated aeolian activity then ensued and this terminated shortly before 12 000 B.P., when the lake began to fill. Expansion was interrupted a little before 10 200 B.P., but was then continued, the lake reaching its maximum level at *c.* 10 000 B.P. when there was overflow into the Benue and thus the Niger Rivers. At its greatest extent this lake "Mega-Chad" had an area of 400 000–300 000 km², about five times the size of modern Lake Victoria. A minor recession at *c.* 7000 B.P. was followed by a major recession at 4000–3500 B.P., after which the lake rose to a last, but minor, high stand at 3500–2500 B.P. During the present century the lake has fluctuated in area between 10 000–25 000 km², with a low at 1913–1950 and then higher levels up to a maximum at 1964–1972.

In Mauritania, lakes which are now dry or shallow, were very high between *c.* 40 000 and 20 000 B.P. (Charnard, reported in Rognon and Williams, 1977). There were rapid falls between *c.* 20 000 and 17 000 B.P., dramatic rises after *c.* 11 000 B.P. and increasingly low levels after 7000 B.P. The latter were interrupted by minor high stands at *c.* 6000–4000 B.P. and again during the Little Ice Age.

Lake Bosumtwi in Ghana is contained within 1·3 million year old meteor-impact crater in the forest zone (Talbot and Delibrias, 1977, 1980). There is a clearly defined bench at + *c.* 110 m above the modern lake, this height being determined by the level of the potential outlet of the crater. Twenty-eight ^{14}C dates are available for dating evidence of lake level changes. Prior to 13 000 B.P. and probably for a fairly long period lake levels were low. There was a rise just after 13 000 B.P., followed by a brief recession at *c.* 10 500 B.P. The highest lake levels were achieved in the early Holocene between 10 000 and 4500/4000 B.P. with a brief recession at *c.* 8000 B.P. Generally lower lake levels have prevailed since 4000 B.P., with somewhat higher levels at *c.* 3000–1000 B.P. An early Holocene fossil leaf flora is described from sediments in the catchment (Hall *et al.*, 1978).

In the Arabian Desert there is evidence of moister conditions than now between 30 000 and 21 000 B.P. and again between *c.* 9000 and 6000 B.P. (McClure, 1976). Dune building phases precede and antedate the later moist period.

(h)　*Rivers*

During the Quaternary many of the rivers of tropical Africa have undergone great changes in flow and in their abilities to erode channels or deposit sediments. The best investigated river system is probably that of the Nile, which today drains extensive areas of East Africa. The history of Nile sedimentation is complex and is discussed at length by Adamson and Williams (1980), Butzer (1980) and Williams and Adamson (1980). Extensive evaporites, which have yielded ^{14}C dates of > 40 000–25 600 B.P., are present along the White Nile and, taken in conjunction with the dates of Lakes Mobutu and Victoria overflow of 12 500–12 000 B.P., it is possible that there was no major contribution of water into the Nile system from the East African lakes between > 40 000 and 12 500/12 000 B.P. Sedimentary evidence along the White Nile shows that the river was higher than at present at 12 500–11 400 B.P. and on a number of occasions thereafter.

The Gezira plain near Khartoum has been a site of sediment deposition for the Blue Nile and other rivers emerging from upland Ethiopia. ^{14}C dates for Gezira sediments show that from *c.* 18 000–12 000 B.P. the Blue Nile was a highly seasonal braided river transporting gravels and sands during flood, while between *c.* 12 000 and 5000 B.P. it was a sinuous river flowing slowly through permanent swamps in which it deposited silty clays (Rognon, 1980). Williams and Adamson (1980) have discussed the controls over erosion and sedimentation along the Blue Nile and have concluded, *inter alia*, that vegetation cover was much reduced on the Ethiopian highlands during the pre-12 000 B.P. stage. Vegetation cover in the highlands must have been sufficiently dense after 12 000 B.P. to prevent much removal of large-sized particles. The presence of abundant fossils of the terrestrial mollusc *Limicolaria flammata* in Blue Nile sediments dating to 8000–4500 B.P. indicates that isohyets must have been 200–300 km further north than they are today (Williams and Adamson, 1980).

The history of river systems further west in tropical Africa is dealt with very briefly here. A number of large and essentially relict river systems are present in the Sahara. Stratigraphic examination of the sediments in some of the large rivers which used to flow southwards from the central Sahara into the Niger has revealed a clearly defined band of silts and clays interbedded among predominantly coarse-grained sands. ^{14}C dates show that the humid period of deposition of the fine-grained sediments was *c.* 12 000–10 000 B.P. (Talbot, 1980). During the arid phase which preceded this wet period, it is believed that the Upper Niger became lost in the expanded desert, with an inland delta to the west of Timbuktu. The course of the River Senegal is believed also to have been blocked by dunes.

(i) *Deserts*

It can be seen from Fig. 20 that fixed dunes are very common in Africa. The most spectacular development is a belt stretching from the Atlantic coast as far east as the Nile, with a southern margin more or less parallel to the modern limit of active dunes and displaced 600–400 km to the south (Mainquet *et al.*, 1980). ^{14}C determinations for upper and lower horizons date this dune-building phase to 20 000–12 000 B.P. (Talbot, 1980). In addition to this most prominent stage, the modern Sahel Zone also contains an older series of (massive) dunes of unknown age, but predating 40 000 B.P., and also some younger dunes. Some of the latter have been dated at somewhere between 8000 and 6000 B.P. and others to post-4000 B.P. (Talbot, 1980).

Dunes in the Sahara today are active only where the rainfall is less than 25–50 mm (Talbot, 1980). Since the main fixed dune stage

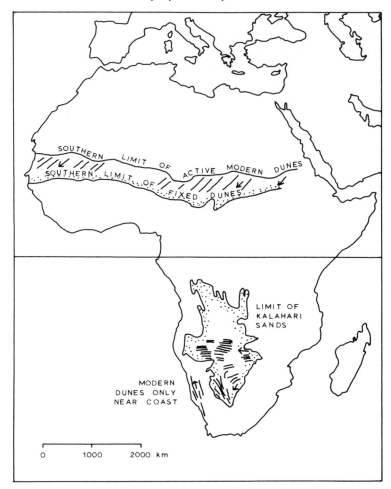

Fig. 20   Features of modern and fixed dunes in Africa. Dune limits for the southern Sahara after Mainguet *et al.* (1980). The limit of the Kalahari Sands is after Lancaster (1979a). The heavy lines indicate the alignment of fixed dunes, and arrows show postulated wind directions (after Lancaster, 1979a; Sarnthein, 1978).

extends across northern Africa at about the 800 mm isohyet (Mainguet *et al.*, 1980), rainfall was probably greatly diminished at 20 000–12 000 B.P. There is much evidence that monsoonal winds were more active at that time than now and this could have contributed to the aridity. Dune alignment shows that predominant wind directions during the main fixed dune stage were similar to the present (Mainguet and Callot, 1976; Talbot, 1980). It has been shown that the shapes of the fixed dunes in Upper Volta and W. Niger were modified by subsidiary winds blowing from the south and, assuming that these winds were blowing at the same time as main dune formation, it has been argued that the northern limit of the inter-tropical convergence zone must have been further north (Talbot, 1980). The inference is that atmospheric circulation over west tropical Africa must have been rather similar to the present, and that the dryness was a result of a general decrease in rainfall rather than any southerly displacement of the northward movement of the inter-tropical convergence zone.

Evidence of past changes in humidity in the form of both fixed dunes and of fossil drainage networks occurs widely in the Kalahari and neighbouring areas of south-west Africa, indicating that the climate was, at times, both much drier and much moister than now (Lancaster, 1979a). The Kalahari Sands are terrestrial beds of very extensive distribution, being found as far north as the River Zaire and as far east as Zimbabwe (Fig. 20). The sands are believed to be mainly of aeolian origin and there have probably been several phases of reworking since intitial deposition in the late Tertiary or early Quaternary. There is evidence of wet conditions in the northern Kalahari at 30 000–20 000 B.P. when the Makgadikgadi depression was occupied by a greatly expanded lake. This was then followed by an arid phase which probably began at *c.* 20 000 B.P. in the north, but possibly later in the southern Kalahari (Lancaster, 1979b). Although the dating of past events in the Kalahari region is still rather poor, it is thought that dune-building and subtropical aridity was more or less contemporaneous in both hemispheres during the Later Pleistocene (Lancaster, 1979a; Sarnthein, 1979; see also Heine, 1979). Dune alignment suggests that during this arid phase the South African anticyclone was larger and had a more northerly position than at present (Lancaster, 1979a). There is evidence that the lower Holocene was wetter than the upper Holocene in the Kalahari.

General Conclusions

It is clear that there have been some striking similarities in the patterns of Upper Quaternary lake level changes in different basins, not only within East Africa, but right across the African tropics (Fig. 21). To summarize:

(1) The period before a rather poorly dated upper boundary of *c.* 22 000/20 000 B.P. was marked by high lake levels in at least some

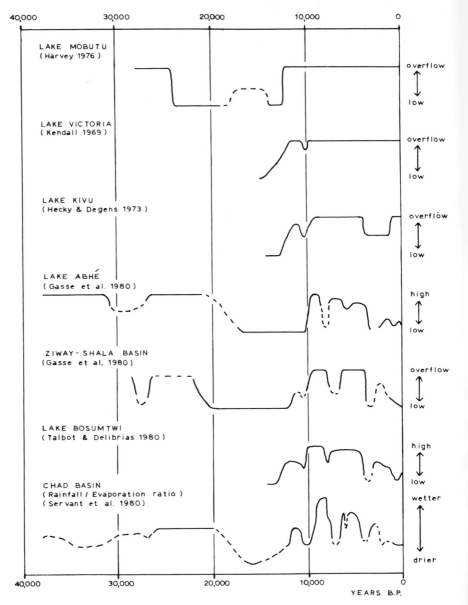

Fig. 21 Lake level changes in selected basins. Basins ordered from top to bottom roughly in order of increasing responsiveness to climatic events. Firm lines are fairly well established; dashed lines indicate greater uncertainty.

basins. The Nile system appears anomalous, both in terms of the early 26 000 B.P. decline from overflow level of Lake Mobutu, and also because of the evidence of evaporite deposition at > 40 000–25 600 B.P. along the White Nile. More work is needed to clear up this matter, but I am inclined to the view that the climate of much of tropical Africa was moister than now before 22 000/20 000 B.P. This period predates the last world glacial maximum.

(2) The period between *c.* 22 000/20 000 and *c.* 12 000/10 000 B.P. was marked by greater dryness than now in all basins. River flow was low in many areas and the White Nile was, at most, a seasonal stream. The southern boundary of mobile dunes in North Africa lay 600–400 km south of its present position and it seems certain that a great expansion of desert in south-west Africa also dates to this period.

(3) Higher lake levels have generally prevailed since 12 000/10 000 B.P., a date which in north-west Europe marks the transition to postglacial conditions. Despite the generally high levels, there have been variations within this period. In detail, there is evidence from several basins of a dry interlude at or just before 10 000 B.P. Conditions between 10 000 and 8000 B.P. seem to have been wetter than at any other time. Some basins show recessions at roughly 8000–6000 B.P. The most important general change was probably a switch to lower levels at around 4000 B.P., a time which also witnessed expansion of the Sahara and the demise of the "Saharan Neolithic". The last 4000 years have been marked by some fairly major lake level fluctuations, including high levels during the early and mid-1960s.

There are striking similarities between the times of lake level fluctuations in the various basins, and there is no doubt that climatic changes have been important determinants of lake fluctuations. Some of the differences in the timing of events in different places are probably due to variations in data quality and some may be related to differences in the responses of different basins. In general, considerable effort has been expended in the collection of dates to establish lake level curves, but inadequate knowledge of the hydrological systems means that the curves are not always easy to interpret in terms of climatic and ecosystem fluctuations.

Chapter 5

Pollen Diagrams: Guide to Interpretation

Pollen analysis is one of the principal tools used in the study of the Quaternary environment. The technique involves the extraction and examination of fossil pollen grains contained within hard rocks, sediments and soils. It is customary to include not only true pollen grains (the male spores of angiosperms and gymnosperms), but also the spores of ferns and some bryophytes (especially *Sphagnum*). The importance of the pollen record is partly due to two properties of pollen grain walls: they are very resistant to decay and they display a wide range of design, the latter often permitting identification of fossil grains to the genus level. Many plants, particularly those which are wind-pollinated, produce pollen grains in vast numbers and some of these come to rest in sites where conditions are favourable for their preservation. In East Africa, well-preserved pollen grains can usually be found in peat deposits, which are present in basins in wet areas above *c.* 1500 m, and in sediments beneath permanent lakes at all altitudes. Tuffs, high altitude alluvial clays and coprolites can also contain pollen and there may well be some other, as yet unknown, types of material which could be of use to the palynologist. It is usual to collect a sequence of samples for pollen analyses down a rock, sediment or soil column using either an open section or a sampling device (see West, 1977) according to the type and depth of the deposit. The pollen is extracted from each sample by physical and chemical methods (Bonnefille, 1972; Faegri and Iversen, 1964), mounted on slides and the pollen grains identified and counted. The results are expressed in terms of a pollen diagram showing changes in the relative or absolute abundances of different types of pollen up the column. In a relative diagram, abundances at each level are calculated as percentages of a pollen sum, which is the total number of grains of specified types present at that level. In an absolute pollen diagram abundances are expressed as numbers of grains in a given weight or volume of sediment, or, if the sediment accumulation rate is known, as the numbers of grains which have accumulated per unit time.

The advantages of studying fossil pollen for the reconstruction of past environments are several. First, fossil pollen provides a record of past vegetation and vegetation is usually regarded as a good indicator of the general environment of an area. Second, sites where pollen is preserved are fairly frequent. Third, pollen is often present in a sediment sequence, allowing the reconstruction of vegetation change over time. Fourth, pollen can be well dispersed and a proportion of the pollen in a sediment is usually derived from more or less distant vegetation, thus creating the possibility of reconstructing relatively long-distance, as well as local, past vegetation. Exactly how past vegetation and environment can be reconstructed from pollen diagrams is, however, a matter of debate and differences in the assumptions of authors have led to contrasting interpretations of the same diagrams (e.g. Coetzee, 1967; Livingstone, 1967).

Interpretation can be considered as having two components: reconstruction of vegetation from the pollen record, and reconstruction of the environment from the reconstructed vegetation. Studies of the contemporary relationships between species distributions, pollen rain and environmental factors clearly help to provide answers to these questions, and the contributions of these approaches are described later in this chapter. It would be a mistake to suppose that such studies alone provide a complete understanding of these matters. Pollen diagrams themselves are important sources of information concerning the dispersal characteristics of pollen grains and the ecology of species, supplementing and modifying views derived from other lines of evidence.

The identification of Quaternary fossil pollen grains is based on comparison of their morphological characteristics with those of the pollen of modern plants. No comprehensive key for the East African pollen flora is available, but there are a number of publications dealing with selected groups (Bonnefille, 1971a, 1971b; Bonnefille and Riollet, 1980; Hamilton, 1976b; Livingstone *et al.*, 1973) and papers relating to geographically neighbouring areas are useful (Maley, 1970; Straka, 1966 etc.). The level of identification achieved by palynologists is partly dependent on the distinctiveness of pollen types and can be the family (e.g. Gramineae), the genus (e.g.

Podocarpus) or the species (e.g. *Olea africana*). All identified pollen grains known from the Pliocene and later in eastern Africa are present in the contemporary tropical African flora (Bonnefille, 1976). In this context it is pertinent to mention that many of the seeds and fruits recorded from the rich Miocene flora of Rusinga Island, Lake Victoria, (Chesters, 1957) and dated to *c.* 22 million years (Bishop, 1967) are remarkably similar to those of modern species. Since form and function in plants are believed to be closely linked, this morphological constancy is evidence that the ecology of many African plant taxa has undergone little change over a long time. This is an assumption basic to the reconstruction of past environments from the pollen record, and is one that the palynologist only abandons when there is strong evidence to the contrary.

Two strategies have been adopted by palynologists interested in reconstructing the Pliocene/Quaternary environmental history of eastern Africa. The first approach, pioneered by Hedberg (1954) and Osmaston (1958) recognizes the relative abundance of Upper Quaternary pollen-bearing sediments (dating to, say, the last 30 000 years) and the fact that horizons in such sediments can often be accurately dated by ^{14}C determinations, and workers have attempted to reconstruct relatively recent vegetational and environmental history in some detail. Following the phraseology of Livingstone (1975, p. 274), this period includes a "specimen ice age" (centred on *c.* 18 000 B.P.) and a "specimen interglacial" (the postglacial; after *c.* 12 000/ 10 000 B.P.). Authors have displayed various degrees of confidence in extrapolating patterns of vegetation and climate determined for the Upper Quaternary back through time. The other approach has been the "direct" reconstruction of Lower Quaternary/Pliocene environments by studying the pollen contents of rocks dating to this early period. The rocks chosen have generally been those found at fossil hominid localities and have often proved disappointingly poor in pollen. Localities used for palynological investigations of Quaternary or Upper Pliocene environments in East Africa are shown on Fig. 22.

The Montane Environment of East Africa

(a) *Introduction*

Most Upper Quaternary pollen diagrams are from montane areas and montane vegetation has been selected for special attention here. The geographical region considered is that to which the majority of

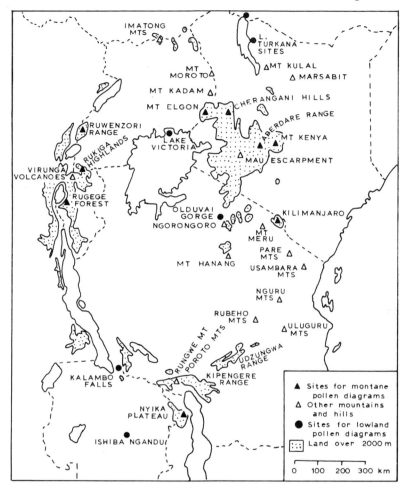

Fig. 22 East Africa: montane localities and sites for pollen diagrams.

diagrams relate, extending from the Western Rift in Uganda and Rwanda, across Kenya and as far east as Kilimanjaro in northern Tanzania. Within this area there are a substantial number of montane localities, each distinguished by its own environmental peculiarities and its degree of geographical isolation. The Western Rift montane localities include Ruwenzori (5109 m), the Bufumbira Volcanoes and the rift-shoulder mountains of south-west Uganda (the Rukiga Highlands), Rwanda and Burundi. The three Bufumbira Volcanoes,

Muhavura (4127 m), Mgahinga (3474 m) and Sabinio (3634 m), are more or less fresh volcanic cones standing on an east–west line along the Rwanda/Uganda border. They form part of the extensive Virunga volcanic field which is found also in Zaire. The rift-shoulder mountains are composed predominantly of Precambrian rocks (as Ruwenzori) and barely attain 2500 m altitude. They are heavily populated and extensively cultivated and only four fairly large forests remain, namely Rugege Forest in Rwanda and Bwindi (Impenetrable), Echuya and Mafuga Forests in Uganda. Of these forest remnants, Echuya is a bamboo forest of uncertain seral status and Mafuga is a young secondary forest.

The Western Rift montane localities are separated from those further east by extensive lowlands. The first mountains encountered on travelling eastwards are three isolated Tertiary volcanoes, Moroto (3083 m), Kadam (3070 m) and Napak (2539 m), arising from the Karamoja plain, and Mt Elgon (4320 m) which stands on the western extremity of the Kenyan highlands. Kenya has an extensive land area at *c.* 2000–2500 m and some of the higher summits are the Cherangani Hills (3370 m), the Mau Escarpment (3098 m), the Aberdares (3999 m) and Mt Kenya (5199 m). A number of mountains stand away from the main Kenyan montane block and these include Marsabit (1695 m) and Kulal (2412 m) to the north and Kilimanjaro (5895 m), Mt Meru (4566 m), the Ngorongoro Hills (3188 m) and Mt Hanang (3418 m) to the south.

Knowledge of the ecology of montane taxa is derived effectively from the detection of their patterns of distribution and the relating of these patterns to those shown by environmental factors. There has been little physiological work and perhaps no attempts at growing montane plants in controlled environments. There is much variation in the montane environment, particularly in respect of temperature, moisture availability and human disturbance and it can be particularly valuable to compare altitudinal variation in vegetation in different montane areas and between environmentally contrasting localities within the same area. In making such comparisons, particularly when distances are great, it must be remembered that historical factors help to determine the ranges and abundances of species, setting one limit to the amount of information which can be deduced about the ecology of species from distributional evidence alone. Thus, a species may be absent from an area, not because of an unsuitable environment, but rather because it has been unable to migrate to the area from elsewhere. Again, even if a species is present in an area, slow response to a past change in environment can result in the species being more or less abundant today than it would be at equilibrium. It also has to be borne in mind that the full ecological potential of a species is not necessarily revealed by its modern distribution.

The areas of montane vegetation form scattered enclaves and their biotic isolation has produced many differences between their floristic lists. When considering any particular environmental type, it is often possible to recognize vicarious communities (Hedberg, 1964) which differ floristically from mountain to mountain, but display similar physiognomy throughout. In the Afroalpine Belt the taxonomic equivalence of vicarious communities is often close, for example, various shrubby species of *Alchemilla* replace one another as dominants in *Alchemilla* scrub on different mountains. The concept of vicarious communities, however, need not be limited to communities so closely related taxonomically. Thus, the various isolated patches of forest which are included in the Moist Lower Montane Forest Zone can be regarded as vicarious equivalents, even though floristic diversity is great. As Chapman and White (1970) have also suggested, major vegetation categories are best recognized on the basis of physiognomic and environmental characteristics, as well as by floristic lists.

Species show varying degrees of morphological variation and, in the case of such widely distributed and morphologically variable species as *Prunus africana*, it is likely that there is much related ecotypic variation. An example of a species with the unusual feature of growing in different communities on different mountains is *Valeriana kilimandscharica*. This species is often abundant in *Alchemilla* scrub on Mt Elgon and the Aberdares, but this is not the case on Mt Kenya where it also occurs (Hedberg, 1964).

In the following account, I refer particularly to a study of the vegetation of Mt Elgon carried out by R. A. Perrott and myself in 1976 (Hamilton and Perrott, 1980, in press b) This survey was based on analysis of aerial photographs (Fig. 23), and the recording of sample plots along two altitudinal transects up the mountain, one on the relatively dry eastern slopes (the Koitoboss transect), and the other on the relatively moist southern slopes (the Kimilili transect). In so far as any mountain can be considered to be so, Mt Elgon is a typical East African mountain, in terms of both climate and vegetation. The regular oval shape of the mountain and the relatively subdued topography ensure that differences in vegetation related to aspect are obvious, at least within the Montane Forest Belt. It should be noted that, while the lower altitude forests on the Koitoboss transect clearly belong to the Dry Lower Montane Forest Zone and

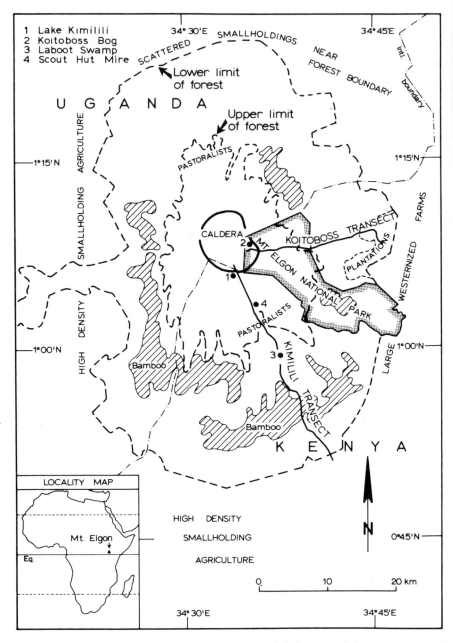

Fig. 23 Mt Elgon: general features. Based on aerial photograph interpretation and published in Hamilton and Perrott (in press, b). Sites 1 to 4 are localities for which pollen diagrams are available. Reproduced from "Pollen et Spores" with permission of Mme van Campo.

those on the Kimilili transect to the Moist Lower Montane Forest Zone, according to the classification used on Fig. 25, neither transect is situated on a climatically extreme aspect of the mountain.

(b) *The montane environment*

Two important climatic determinants of the distribution patterns shown by plants are temperature and moisture availability. With comparatively minor exceptions, the relationships between many temperature variables and altitude are similar throughout East Africa, at least up to 3000 m (Griffiths, 1962; Kenworthy, 1966). There is a shortage of long-term measurements from high altitude, making it difficult to determine accurately temperature variation with altitude. Hedberg (1964) considered that a fair approximation to mean annual temperature at high altitudes is provided by short-term measurements and, if such measurements are included, then the lapse rate for mean annual temperature can be calculated to be 1°C in 157 m (6·37°C in 1000 m) (Hamilton, 1972). This is similar to the 1°C in 161 m (6·20°C in 1000 m) rate estimated for East Africa by Griffiths (1962), though notably higher than the 1°C in 193 m (5·19°C in 1000 m) rate calculated for Malawi by Lancaster (1980). The lapse rate varies little throughout East Africa, but there is some variation in the constant of the altitude/temperature regression line (Griffiths, 1962). For present purposes the most significant such variation is depression of mean and mean maximum temperatures in wetter places, cloudiness decreasing the quantities of incoming radiation (Kenworthy, 1966). To take an example, Mt Kenya and the west Kenyan highlands have mean annual maximum temperatures a little over 1·7°C higher than those found at equivalent altitudes on the mountains of western Uganda (Griffiths, 1962); the mean annual minimum temperatures are the same in both areas, since, in both, clear conditions normally prevail at night.

In contrast to the relative constancy of the temperature/altitude relationship, the mountains of East Africa vary greatly in climatic moistness. This is indicated by climatic records, only a few of which are available for altitudes above 2200 m, by casual observations and by vegetation, including the degree of development of terrestrial and epiphytic lichens and bryophytes. There are wide divergencies, not only between different montane areas considered as individuals, but also between different aspects of the same mountain and between different altitudes on the same vertical transect. Judging by available evidence (much of it summarized in Coe, 1967; Hamilton, 1972; Hedberg, 1964) and taking each montane locality as a whole unit, the wettest montane area being considered here is Ruwenzori, closely followed by the mountains of south-west Uganda and Rwanda. Kilimanjaro, Mt Meru and the Karamoja Mts fall at the dry end of the spectrum and Mt Elgon, the Aberdares and Mt Kenya are climatically intermediate, Mt Elgon probably being somewhat drier than the other two.

Variation in precipitation with aspect is probably marked on all mountains, in most cases being at a maximum on that side of the mountain which faces the "south-east" monsoon. Due in part to local variations in the direction of this monsoon, it is not necessarily the south-east slopes of mountains which are the wettest; for example, the highest rainfall on Elgon is received on the south-west and west slopes. The mountains along the Western Rift are influenced, not only by the East African monsoons, but also by moist westerlies. Ruwenzori, for instance, has a higher rainfall on its western than its eastern slopes, at least at lower altitudes (Osmaston, 1965; Robyns, 1948). Rainfall records along extensive altitudinal transects are available for Ruwenzori (Osmaston, 1965) and for Mt Kenya and Kilimanjaro (Hedberg, 1964), and isolated high altitude rain gauges have been operated on Elgon and Mt Sabinio (East African Meteorological Dept. 1967 a, b). Despite the limitations of the measurements (Hedberg, 1964), the results do show that rainfall at high altitudes follows the same seasonal trends as at lower altitudes and also that there is much variation from place to place in the rainfall/altitude relationship. Thus, rainfall in the Afroalpine Belt of Kilimanjaro is very low and erratic (Hedberg, 1964), while on Ruwenzori rainfall can be just as high above the Montane Forest Belt as within it (Osmaston, 1965).

There are usually clear differences in vegetation with position on slope. It is thought that this catenary variation is largely related to differences in soil-water availability (cf. Johannesen *et al.*, 1967; Radwinski and Ollier, 1959), though other factors such as soil nutrient status undoubtedly also play a part. Vegetation catenas are particularly pronounced on rugged Ruwenzori and on the mountains of south-west Uganda and Rwanda (Hamilton, 1969; Lind and Morrison, 1974).

The importance of man as a determinant of montane vegetation varies widely from place to place and is dependant on both the type and level of disturbance. In contrast to Ethiopia, where crops are grown at over 3000 m, cultivation is virtually restricted to the lower part of the Montane Forest Belt in East Africa, often occurring up to an artificially maintained forest boundary at *c.* 2150 m. The only mountain to support a permanent high altitude population today is Mt Elgon, with scattered settlements of pastoralists at 3000–3300 m on the northern and south-eastern slopes. These people, together with the cattle smugglers who utilize trails running over the mountain, have increased the extent of grassland through burning. Fires, presumably usually started by man, are also common on some of the other mountains, such as Mt Kenya, Kilimanjaro and the Aberdares. It is possible that these three mountains once supported high altitude populations, perhaps at times of drought, or, as has been shown to be the case for Elgon (Weatherby, 1962), of warfare.

The role of soil properties as determinants of vegetation has been little studied, but a case-study of the influence of soil maturity on vegetation in a climatically moist region is worthy of note (Fig. 24). The three Bufumbira Volcanoes are composed of porous lavas; erosional differences indicate that Mt Muhavura is the youngest and Mt Sabinio the oldest, Mgahinga being of intermediate age. The absolute dates of volcanism are unknown, though it is probable that Muhavura, at least, has erupted during the Upper Quaternary. With the exception of altitudes above 3660 m, where fairly normal Afro-alpine communities are reported to be present (Hedberg, 1964), much of Muhavura from 2000 m upwards is covered by grassland and scrub, suggesting that successional development is slow on porous soils. Sabinio has the most normal vegetation zonation, *Senecio*, *Philippia*, *Hagenia-Rapanea* and bamboo communities all being present, though the vegetation deviates from the typical in that the bamboo stems are thin and wiry, rather than stout and tall. On Mgahinga, woodland, containing drought-tolerant trees, extends up to 2750 m, which is well above the woodland limit on Sabinio (2450 m), bamboo is confined to high altitudes (2750–3000 m) and *Hypericum revolutum* forest replaces both the *Hagenia-Rapanea* and *Philippia* communities.

(c) *Montane vegetation types*

The classification usually used for the broad divisions shown by montane vegetation in East Africa is that of Hedberg (1951). Three vegetation belts, termed Montane Forest, Ericaceous and Afroalpine (or Alpine) Belts, are recognized (Fig. 25). The Montane Forest Belt is distinguished by an abundance of broad-leaved hardwood trees and contains some conifers, the Ericaceous Belt has many small-leaved

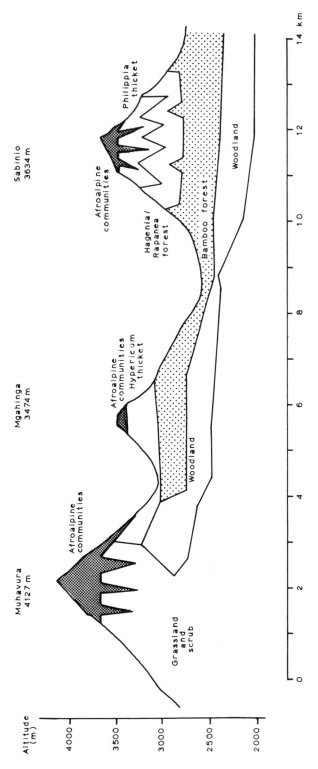

Fig. 24 Vegetation zonation on the Bufumbira Volcanoes (northern aspect). From a diagram by B. Kingston, drawn in 1967.

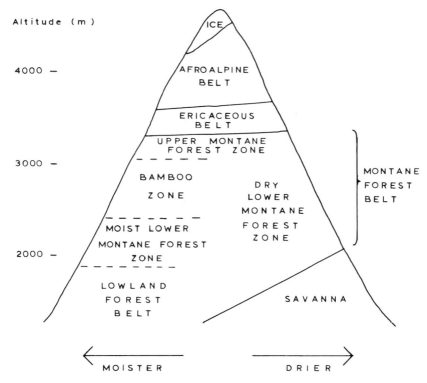

Fig. 25   Belts and zones of vegetation on the mountains of East Africa. Modified from an original idea of Hedberg (1951).

trees and shrubs, especially members of the Ericaceae, and the Afroalpine Belt, which varies greatly in appearance from mountain to mountain and includes various scrub, giant groundsel and grassland communities, is defined as "the zone situated above the Ericaceous Belt, i.e. above the upper limit of more or less continuous Ericaceous (tree- or shrub-) vegetation" (Hedberg, 1951, p. 167). While this classification is valuable for general descriptive purposes, it is emphasized that there are instances when the boundaries between the belts cannot be drawn with any degree of precision. Thus, on Mt Elgon, burning by man has resulted in extensive replacement of microphyllous thicket by grassland, obscuring the former location of the boundary between the Ericaceous and Afroalpine Belts while, on Ruwenzori, Ericaceous trees are abundant in what would normally be regarded as the upper part of the Montane Forest Belt. If a comprehensive classification scheme is required for all montane communities, then vegetation types, such as lower altitude grassland, woodland and cultivated land communities, can be assigned to particular vegetation belts according to altitude.

Various systems have been proposed for the classification of the montane forest vegetation of East Africa (e.g. Chapman and White, 1970; Hedberg, 1951). For reasons given in detail elsewhere (Hamilton and Perrott, 1980, in press, b), the scheme adopted here is that proposed for Ugandan vegetation by Langdale-Brown *et al.* (1964) which is believed to be applicable to East Africa as a whole. This classification stresses the relative floristic similarity of higher altitude montane forests situated in different places, and the divergence which occurs at lower altitudes, where geographical variations in precipitation become more pronounced. The practice of Langdale-Brown *et al.* (1964) of providing their zones with titles incorporating the names of particular plants I regard as unfortunate. Many of the plants so used can be found, sometimes abundantly, outside the vegetation types for which their names have been borrowed. It also sometimes happens, probably principally for historical reasons, that a taxon can be absent from its nominal zone.

I suggest that montane forest be divided into upper and lower altitude categories, with the adjectives moist and dry being used where appropriate. Bamboo (*Arundinaria alpina*) forest is such an obvious and distinctive vegetation type, being found mainly in wetter areas, that it is convenient to treat it as a distinct zone. Normally, four zones would be recognized on a mountain such as Mt Elgon, which shows substantial climatic and vegetation contrasts at lower altitudes: Upper Montane Forest, Bamboo, Moist Lower Montane Forest and Dry Lower Montane Forest. These are equivalent, repsectively, to the following zones of Langdale-Brown *et al.* (1964): *Hagenia-Rapanea* Moist Montane Forest, *Arundinaria* Montane Bamboo Forest, *Prunus* (*Pygeum*) Moist Montane Forest and *Juniperus-Podocarpus* Dry Montane Forest. Of the two montane forest categories described by Chapman and White (1970), Submontane seasonal rain forest seems to be equivalent to Moist Lower Montane Forest and Montane forest *sensu stricto* to the remaining zones.

Alchemilla scrub is the most widespread vegetation type above 3800 m on Mt Elgon (Fig. 26); it is common locally down to *c.* 3600 m. On Elgon, *Alchemilla* scrub is dominated by *Alchemilla elgonensis* and *A. johnstonii*, growing 30–60 cm tall over *Valeriana kilimandscharica* and a bryophyte and grass mat. Scattered giant groundsels (*Senecio johnstonii*) up to 5 m tall are generally present

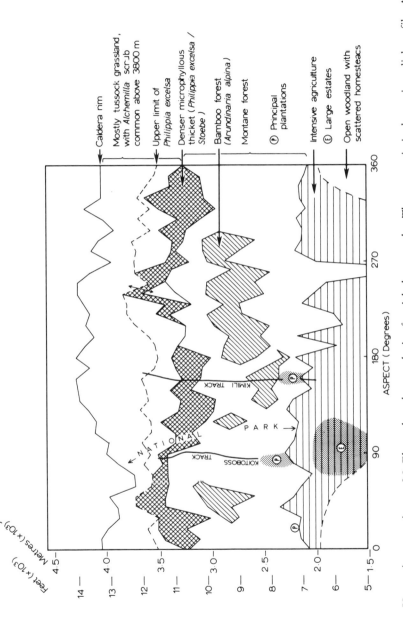

Fig. 26 Vegetation zonation on Mt Elgon, based on analysis of aerial photographs. The mountain is shown in radial profile. After Hamilton and Perrott (in press, b). The distribution of remnant forest patches and of intensive agriculture suggests that before forest destruction by man the forest boundary on the drier slopes probably lay at c. 2000 m and below 1370 m on the wettest slopes. It is possible that the Elgon forests were contiguous with the lowland forests around Lake Victoria. Reproduced from *Vegetatio* with permission.

above the *Alchemilla*, forming an open woodland, and other taller species, all locally abundant, are *Euryops elgonensis, Helichrysum amblyphyllum, Lobelia telekii* and *Peucadenum kerstenii*.

The actual species or varieties of *Alchemilla* forming the dominants in *Alchemilla* scrub vary to some extent from mountain to mountain. Hedberg (1964) has pointed out that *Alchemilla* scrub is widespread on the relatively moist mountains, Elgon, Kenya and Muhavura. On the driest of the tall mountains, it is scarce, being virtually absent from Meru and restricted to boggy places on Kilimanjaro. *Alchemilla* scrub can be seen locally on the plateau area of the Aberdares (altitude *c.* 3000 m), but it is uncommon in the Afroalpine Belt, perhaps, as indicated by Hedberg (1964), because of replacement by tussock grassland through recurrent burning. On Ruwenzori locally extensive patches of *Alchemilla* scrub are found on some moraines (Osmaston, 1965) and on flushed ground on the margins of *Carex* bogs, but the total area covered is not great. In contrast to Mts Elgon, Kenya and Muhavura, the understory of *Senecio* forest on Ruwenzori does not consist of *Alchemilla* scrub, but rather is composed of a luxuriant carpet of bryophytes containing occasional angiosperms, mainly grasses.

Giant groundsels (*Senecio*, subgenus *Dendrosenecio*) are a characteristic floristic component of Afroalpine vegetation (Fig. 27) and, as with the Alchemillas, a number of taxa are present. General requirements seem to be comparatively deep soil and a good supply of more or less mobile soil water (Hedberg, 1964). They are generally most prominent in the vegetation of the wetter mountains, being relatively uncommon and restricted to edaphically moist places on Kilimanjaro and being absent from Mt Meru (Hedberg, 1964). Extensive areas of closed-canopy giant groundsel forest are found only on climatically moist Ruwenzori and Bufumbira Volcanoes, being taller (8 m) on Ruwenzori than on the porous soils of the Bufumbira Volcanoes (2 m). On Mts Elgon and Kenya giant groundsels grow to 5–6 m and occur most abundantly over *Alchemilla* scrub, forming very open woodland rather than forest. On both mountains, giant groundsels can occasionally be seen in high altitude grassland, but patterns of regeneration suggest that such individuals are often relicts of once more extensive spreads of *Alchemilla* scrub.

Giant groundsels are not restricted to the Afroalpine Belt, being frequently common in the Ericaceous Belt, especially in valleys, and also in the understory of Moist Upper Montane Forest, as on Ruwenzori and on the western slopes of Mt Elgon. The contrast on Mt Elgon between the abundance of giant groundsels (to 8 m tall) at

Fig. 27   Giant groundsels (*Senecio johnstonii*) at about 4000 m on Mt Elgon. Most of the land is covered by tussock grassland. The shrubs include *Alchemilla elgonensis* (bottom left) and *Helichrysum* (with white flowers).

c. 3200 m in Upper Montane Forest on the western slopes with their absence or rarity at a similar altitude in forests on the drier eastern slopes is striking and is an example of the tendency shown by many taxa to extend their altitudinal ranges to lower altitudes in moister places.

A variety of vegetation types is found on thin soils at high altitudes. On Mt Elgon, where rocky ground is widespread only within the formerly glaciated region and in a peripheral zone extending down to *c.* 3400 m, the vegetation varies from a low cover of lichens, bryophytes and *Crassula* to *Helichrysum* scrub 1 m tall. *Helichrysum* scrub is recorded from a similar situation on many of the other mountains (Hedberg, 1964), achieving its maximum luxuriance on rocky Ruwenzori, where it reaches a height of 2 m, grows very densely, and is perhaps the most widespread of all Afroalpine vegetation types. On Kilimanjaro, *Helichrysum* scrub is very abundant in the lower part of the Afroalpine Belt (below 4300 m), but it is not restricted to areas of thin soil and its wide occurrence is probably related to climatic aridity (Hedberg, 1964).

The extent of grassland varies greatly between montane localities, being at a maximum on the drier and less steeply sloping mountains and on those which are most frequently burnt (Hedberg, 1964). Judging by the vegetation of Muhavura, grassland can also act as an early stage in the colonization of lava. In the case of Mt Elgon, grassland is the most widespread non-forest vegetation type (Fig. 28), with a main distribution between (3000−) 3350 and 3800 m, but it is also extensively present at higher and lower altitudes (Fig. 26). Lower

Fig. 28   Ericaceous Belt vegetation on Mt Elgon, photographed at about 4000 m on the western slopes. Notice the extent of grassland and the dense development of *Philippia excelsa* in the Simu Valley in the background.

altitude (below *c.* 3200 m) grassland on the wetter slopes of Elgon is often dominated by turf-forming species, especially *Pennisetum clandestinum*: similar grass swards, nearly always obviously maintained by the grazing of mainly domestic animals, are widely present throughout the altitudinal range of the Montane Forest Belt in moister parts of East Africa. Elsewhere on Elgon, that is at all altitudes on drier aspects and above *c.* 3200 m on moister aspects, grassland is dominated by tussock-forming species such as *Andropogon amethystinus*, *Festuca* spp., *Pentaschistis borussica*, *Sporobolus africanus* and *Themeda triandra*.

In general, variation in vegetation related to aspect on Elgon is less pronounced in the Ericaceous and Afroalpine Belts than it is in the Montane Forest Belt; this is also the case on Mt Kenya (Hedberg, 1968). Any such variation, which may occur in high altitude grassland on Elgon, is in any case overshadowed by major differences associated with the frequency of burning (Fig. 29). In little-burnt grassland, living tussocks are relatively large and are interspersed with dead tussocks, the density of which is often as great as that of the living tussocks. Small plants are common between the tussocks and the general topography of the soil/tussock surface is rounded. In over-burnt grassland, on the other hand, much bare soil is exposed, 50% of the ground being a typical figure, and sheet erosion by surface wash can readily be observed during storms. The grass tussocks are situated on soil pedestals, and the soil surface consists of slightly sloping flat areas separated from one another by miniature cliffs. Dead tussocks are entirely absent and small angiosperms are not only less frequent between the tussocks than in little-burnt grassland, but many of those which are present are annuals, rather than perennials. A prominent superficial organic soil horizon, similar in appearance to that found under *Alchemilla* scrub or Ericaceae thicket, is present in little-burnt grassland, but absent from over-burnt grassland.

There is almost no high altitude grassland on Ruwenzori, Mgahinga or Sabinio, all wetter mountains than Elgon. At the other end of the climatic spectrum, tussock grassland is the most extensive vegetation type above 4300 m on Kilimanjaro and in the Afroalpine Belt on Mt Meru: on both mountains, the grassland is very open and the vegetation is perhaps best referred to as Alpine desert (Hedberg, 1964). Widespread burning, probably nearly always initiated by man, undoubtedly encourages the spread of grassland at the expence of such fire-sensitive communities as *Alchemilla* scrub and Ericaceous thicket, and former burning has been invoked as the reason for the

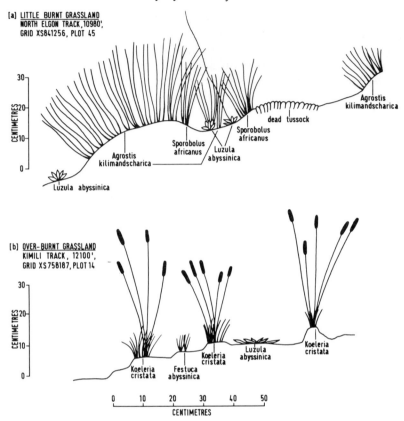

Fig. 29   Grassland profiles on Mt Elgon. The upper example is from the National Park, from which pastoralists are excluded and where there is little burning, and the lower example is from a frequently burnt area on the Kimilili Track. Observations suggest that these profiles are structurally typical of little and frequently burnt high altitude grassland on Elgon. Note: according to Hedberg (1957), *"Koeleria cristata"* of the above figure is correctly *K. gracilis.*

extensive presence of tussock grassland at high altitudes on the Aberdares (Hedberg, 1964) and Mt Kenya (Hedberg, 1968). There is a gap in the Montane Forest Belt on the northern side of Mt Kenya (Hedberg, 1968) and perhaps also on the same aspect of the Aberdares (Hedberg, 1951). Possibly the climates on these slopes are too dry to support forest, but comparing these mountains with others, I think that this is unlikely, and hold past forest destruction by man to be the likely cause.

Microphyllous thicket dominated by giant heathers of the genus

Philippia, or more rarely *Erica*, is a common vegetation type in the Ericaceous Belt. As with the giant groundsels, giant heathers are tallest and generally most abundant on wetter mountains and on those with a lower frequency of fires; they become stunted and tend to be replaced by grassland on drier mountains and on those with much burning. A comparison between Ruwenzori and Mt Elgon is instructive. On Ruwenzori, which is wet and little burnt, tree heathers are exceptionally abundant and there are at least three common species, *Philippia trimera*, *P. johnstonii* and *Erica bequaertii*. *Philippia trimera* thicket, to 15 m tall, is the most widespread vegetation type between 3300 and 3600 m, occurring in most topographic situations; *Philippia johnstonii* thicket, containing *inter alia* *Rapanea rhododendroides* and, at lower altitudes, *Podocarpus milanjianus*, is found between 2700 and 3300 m, particularly on ridges; *Erica bequaertii* thicket grows in swampy valleys between *c.* 2750 and 3200 m. All these Ruwenzori giant heather forests have a great development of lichens and bryophytes; *Sphagnum* is common and can be seen even under ridge-top *Philippia johnstonii* thicket. On Elgon, Ericaceous thicket is lower in stature (often *c.* 5 m), generally less extensive and, unlike Ruwenzori, there is a clear-cut boundary between Ericaceous thicket and montane forest. Although *Erica arborea* is locally abundant at *c.* 3750 m, only one species, *Philippia excelsa*, is dominant over extensive areas, particularly between *c.* 3000 and 3650 m (Fig. 26). Occasional trees, especially *Hagenia* and *Rapanea,* are found with the *Philippia* and there is often a shrub stratum, frequently with *Anthospermum usambarensis, Clutea robusta, Erlangea fusca, Hypericum revolutum* and *Stoebe kilimandscharica*, and a grass-rich herb stratum. Bryophytes and lichens are common, but not nearly as conspicuous as on Ruwenzori; *Sphagnum* does not occur.

The distribution of *Philippia johnstonii* thicket on north and south-facing slopes on a sharp east–west running ridge at 3300–3600 m on Mt Sabinio, Bufumbira Volcanoes, is of great interest (Hamilton, 1972). The ridge itself and the drier northern slopes are covered by *Philippia johnstonii* thicket with occasional *Senecio* trees, while the moister southern slopes are clothed in dense *Senecio* forest, entirely lacking *Philippia*. This is an excellent example of the common tendency for the lowering of the upper altitudinal limits of taxa in wetter areas.

Various microphyllous trees and shrubs, in addition to members of the Ericaceae, can be abundant in the Ericaceous Belt. One such species is *Stoebe kilimandscharica* (Compositae), prominent on some of the drier mountains from Mt Elgon eastwards and also known from the Virunga Volcanoes (Robyns, 1947; Weimarck, 1941). It is absent from western Uganda and probably also from Rwanda. On Mt Elgon *Stoebe* has a total recorded range of 2750–3750 m; it is common in the understory of *Philippia* thicket and grows occasionally in open places in upper montane forest, but its most conspicuous role is as a shrub of grassland in which it sometimes forms thickets. *Stoebe* is more fire-resistent than *Philippia* which it tends to replace with increasing human disturbance. An insight into the relationship between *Stoebe* thicket, *Philippia* thicket and montane forest on Elgon is provided by vegetation patterns which are present over the altitudinal range 3000–3300 m on the Koitoboss transect and are believed to have developed following a great reduction in human pressure when the national park was created in 1968. On this transect, though not at equivalent altitudes on the Kimilili transect, where regular burning and grazing have persisted, forest boundaries frequently show a narrow outer zone particularly rich in *Hagenia*, and two narrow thicket zones, the inner of *Philippia* and the outer of *Stoebe*. Both the *Philippia* and *Stoebe* zones contain abundant tree seedlings. These observations suggest that montane forest is often the natural vegetation type of Elgon between 3000 and 3300 m, that both *Stoebe* and *Philippia* are able to extend their ranges downwards with forest destruction by man and that *Stoebe* is an earlier colonizer of abandoned grassland than *Philippia*.

Two other small-leaved trees which can be abundant in the Ericaceous Belt are *Cliffortia nitidula* (Rosaceae) and *Hypericum revolutum* (Guttiferae). *Hypericum revolutum* is widely distributed, but *Cliffortia* seems to be more local, being unrecorded from western Uganda and probably rare in Rwanda and Burundi. Both are present, but infrequent on Mt Elgon. Judging by the literature and my own observations, the two species fill a rather similar niche; they are predominantly early colonizers of the Upper Montane Forest Zone and the lower Ericaceous Belt in moist localities. Scattered patches of one or the other species are common at *c.* 3000 m on the plateau of the Aberdares. This plateau has exceptional vegetation diversity, carrying, additionally, areas of tussock grassland, bamboo forest, *Hagenia* forest and assorted other vegetation types, and it is likely that the complicated pattern present is a product of both climatic effects, such as temperature inversion, and the activities of man and animals (Hedberg, 1951).

Montane forest forms a girdle around Mt Elgon. The upper forest boundary lies between 3000 and 3450 m, being depressed in places inhabited by pastoralists, and the lower forest boundary generally follows a cut-line at *c.* 2150 m, but descends to 1350 m in one place on the west (Fig. 25). Altitudes of very approximately 3300 and 2150 m are commonly encountered upper and lower limits of montane forest on the East African mountains. Intergradation of montane forest with Ericaceous Belt vegetation, as on Ruwenzori, can make determination of the upper altitudinal limit difficult and there can be much variation related to topography and sometimes to human influence. It is uncertain whether there is a tendency for the upper forest boundary to be altitudinally depressed in climatically wetter places. Concerning the lower limit, the altitude of *c.* 2150 m was frequently selected by colonial administrators as the lower limit of the forest reserves which were declared on virtually all mountains, primarily to conserve water supplies and prevent soil erosion. Forest destruction below this line is today virtually complete. In the case of drier localities, the natural lower limit of forest development is probably also often *c.* 2150 m or perhaps slightly lower.

A bamboo zone at *c.* 2450–3050 m is a common feature of moist montane forest in East Africa. Thus, bamboo is very widespread at (2200−) 2450–3000 (−3300) m on Ruwenzori, at 2500–3200 m on west Mt Kenya (Hedberg, 1951) and at 2400–3000 m on east Aberdares (Hedberg, 1951), but is absent from drier localities which include the Karamoja mountains (Hamilton, 1972) and the northern slopes of both Mt Kenya and Mt Meru (Hedberg, 1951). It is of very limited extent on Kilimanjaro (Wimbush, 1947). The distribution of bamboo on Mt Elgon is informative (Fig. 26). On the wetter south-west and west, the lower and upper boundaries of bamboo forest rather closely follow the 2450 and 3050 m contours and, since there is little evidence of past or present human disturbance in the central and upper parts of the Montane Forest Belt on these aspects of the mountain, there is no reason to suppose that a bamboo zone is anything but a natural feature of the forest. Bamboo patches are absent from north Mt Elgon, but occur sporadically and sometimes outside the 2450–3050 m band on the east and south-east. On the south-east, in particular, there is considerable evidence of human disturbance in the Montane Forest Belt, with patches of grassland, scrub and secondary forest, as well as bamboo, dispersed through a general cover of more mature forest types, and it is suggested that bamboo is here acting as a colonizing phase in montane forest regeneration.

Bamboo is not generally abundant on the rift shoulder mountains of south-west Uganda, Rwanda and Burundi and this is perhaps not surprising since the land here rarely exceeds 2450 m. In Bwindi Forest, where the maximum altitude is actually only 2450 m, bamboo is restricted to a few sites above *c.* 2400 m (Hamilton, 1972), and a similar distribution seems to hold also in Rugege Forest. Bamboo is recorded from 1700–2300 m in Burundi, but it never forms extensive stands, and always seems to be present in a colonizing role (Lewalle, 1972). Echuya Forest is the exceptional site for bamboo among rift-shoulder forests, with an extensive dominance of bamboo over the unusually low altitudinal range of 2260–2450 m. Temperature inversion is undoubtedly a regular event in the virtually enclosed valley in which the forest lies, but since similar sites in Bwindi and Rugege Forests carry normal non-bamboo montane forest other factors are probably involved. In my opinion, the area may well have once been used as agricultural land and the bamboo represents a colonizing forest stage. Undoubtedly the upper metre of peat in Muchoya Swamp, a bog lying in the centre of the forest, contains important evidence relating to this problem, but no pollen diagram for this metre is yet available.

Bamboo apparently produces little pollen, which in any case is difficult to separate from that of many other members of the grass family. This is a serious limitation to the Quaternary palynologist and has resulted in an interest in the associates of bamboo. Isolated trees and patches of trees are regularly found scattered through bamboo stands and a large number of species has been recorded. Our work on Mt Elgon suggests that, in terms of presence or absence of species, the Bamboo Zone has no special features; passing from below the Bamboo Zone to above it, there is a gradual change in the floristic composition of all vegetation strata (Hamilton and Perrott, in press, b). Nevertheless, some species are particularly abundant in the Bamboo Zone. Common trees in the Bamboo Zone on Ruwenzori include *Dombeya goetzenii*, *Philippia johnstonii*, *Podocarpus milanjianus* and *Rapanea rhododendroides*, while *Hagenia* is much the most abundant tree on west Mt Elgon. The understory varies with the density of the bamboo stand; shrubby Acanthaceae are common under more open groves, and grasses, sedges and herbaceous Urticaceae are found in shady places. *Dombeya*, *Hagenia* and *Philippia* are all light-requirers and are probably capable of rapid growth; this may be a reason for their abundance in the Bamboo Zone. Normally, *Arundinaria alpina* flowers and dies over restricted areas at intervals variously estimated at either 15 (Dale, 1940) or 40 (Tweedie, 1965) years. Several of the shrubby species of Acanthaceae found in bamboo forest also display periodic mass-flowering (Tweedie, 1965).

It may well be that fast-growing trees have a better than average chance of becoming established in the occasional open gaps which result from death of bamboo or perhaps also shrubby Acanthaceae.

Available evidence suggests that the tree flora of the Upper Montane Forest Zone varies rather little from locality to locality within East Africa. *Rapanea rhododendroides* and *Hagenia abyssinica* are generally prominent and *Afrocrania volkensii, Dombeya goetzenii, Hypericum revolutum* and *Prunus africana* are often also present. In the case of Mt Elgon the tree stratum is *c.* 15–20 m tall on both wetter and drier sides of the mountain, but structural differences associated with aspect can be seen in the lower vegetation strata. On drier slopes, the understory is a grass-rich meadow-like sward, while on wetter slopes giant groundsels (to 9 m) and lobelias (to 6 m) are common under the tree canopy and the understory consists of a dense tangle, 2 m tall, of grasses, lush herbs and shrubs (Fig. 30). On Ruwenzori much of the land over the altitudinal range 3000–3300 m is dominated by Ericaceae and forest is of local occurrence. *Rapanea* is common (Ross, 1955) and *Afrocrania, Hagenia* and *Maytenus acuminata* are all present; there is much *Hypericum revolutum* in the understory and giant groundsels and lobelias are abundant.

It is thought that forests of climatically dry and moist localities become more and more similar in their floristics with increasing altitude. This claim is supported by numerical classifications of both the trees and the herbs/shrubs recorded from plots situated along the relatively dry Koitoboss transect and the relatively moist Kimilili transect on Mt Elgon (Fig. 31). In each case, the primary division in the classification separates lower from higher altitude plots, irrespective of transect. With further divisions in the classification up to at least the five cluster (vegetation type) level, higher altitude plots at similar altitudes on the two transects remain within the same categories. In contrast, plots at lower altitudes on the two transects fall into different clusters.

Moist lower montane forest has structural and floristic similarities to lowland forest (Chapman and White, 1970). On the Kimilili transect, trees over 30 m tall are common between 2100 m (base of transect) and 3000 m and two tree strata, as well as an Acanthaceae-rich shrub stratum, can often be distinguished at altitudes below 2600 m. On Mt Elgon, Moist Lower Montane Forest is richer in species than Dry Lower Montane Forest, particularly at lower altitudes, and contains, *inter alia, Aningeria adolfi-friederici, Entandrophragma excelsum, Olea welwitschii, Polyscias* spp. and *Prunus africana.* All of these are found in moist lower montane forests

Fig. 30   The Upper Montane Forest Zone at about 3200 m on the western slopes of Mt Elgon. This is a moist lush forest type with abundant epiphytic lichens and bryophytes and an understory containing giant groundsels and lobelias (visible in the photograph). Trees present include *Hagenia*, *Prunus* and *Rapanea*.

elsewhere in East Africa. Montane forests at suitable altitudes along the Western Rift are nearly all referable to the Moist Lower Montane Forest Zone. Some of these forests, particularly Rugege Forest and, to a lesser degree, Bwindi Forest are richer in species than moist lower montane forest on Mt Elgon, additional trees including *Cassipourea ruwensorensis, Chrysophyllum gorungosanum, Ficalhoa laurifolia, Myrianthus holstii, Newtonia buchananii, Ocotea usambarensis, Parinari excelsa, Symphonia globulifera* and *Tabernaemon-*

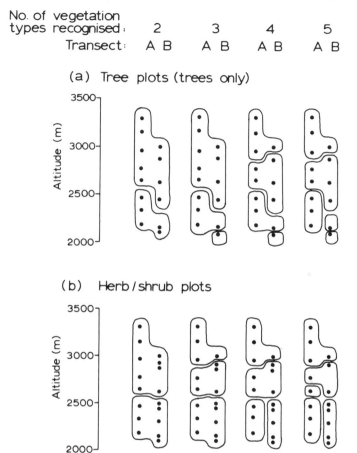

No. of vegetation
types recognised :   2   3   4   5
Transect: A B   A B   A B   A B

(a) Tree plots (trees only)

(b) Herb/shrub plots

Fig. 31 Classifications of forest tree and forest herb and shrub plots on Mt Elgon. The two transects are (A) the Koitoboss transect and (B) the Kimilili transect. The classifications are numerical and use Squared Euclidean Distance as the dissimilarity coefficient and incremental sums of squares for clustering. The classifications of both trees and herbs/shrubs are similar in that the initial divisions in the classifications separate plots according to altitude and that subsequently lower, but not higher altitude plots fall into different categories according to transect. From Hamilton and Perrott (in press, b) and reproduced from Vegetatio with permission.

tana holstii. Some of these are found on Mt Kenya. It is considered that the present environment of Mt Elgon could support many of these species and their absence is attributed to historical factors.

On Mt Elgon, an abundant species of Dry Lower Montane Forest (Fig. 32) is *Podocarpus gracilior*, individuals of which attain enor-

Fig. 32 Lower Montane Forest on Mt Elgon at about 2300 m. This photograph was taken in the National Park on the eastern slopes and the forest is of a relatively dry type. The trees visible include *Cassipourea malosana* (dark coloured).

mous dimensions; heights of over 40 m are common at 2450–2900 m on the Koitoboss transect. Other species of Dry Lower Montane Forest on Mt Elgon are *Celtis africana, Diospyros abyssinica, Juniperus procera, Olea africana, O. hochstetteri* and *Teclea nobilis*; forests of similar floristic composition are found on the Karamoja mountains (Langdale-Brown *et al*., 1964) and fairly widely in climatically suitable places in Kenya and Tanzania (Battiscombe, 1936; Lind and Morrison, 1974). During the survey of Mt Elgon, *Juniperus* was recorded both as a freely-regenerating tree at 2100–2500 m in the Dry Lower Montane Forest Zone and as a colonizer of burnt ground at *c*. 3000–3100 m. According to Logan (1946), *Juniperus* forests tend to grow in drier parts of montane Ethiopia than *Podocarpus gracilior* forest and this could also be the case in East Africa. The role of *Juniperus* as a colonizing species of burnt land is well attested (Lind and Morrison, 1974).

Montane woodland may usually be distinguished from montane forest by the openness and low stature of its tree statum and by having a field layer dominated by savanna-type grasses. In moister places montane woodland is clearly often a secondary vegetation type, following on from forest with human disturbance, but in climatically or edaphically dry localities its status can be difficult to judge. In the case of Mt Elgon, montane woodland is local within the altitudinal range of the Montane Forest Belt. Two types are present, a sclerophyllous type with much *Agauria salicifolia* at *c*. 3000–3300 m in areas heavily exploited by pastoralists and *Acacia hockii* woodland at *c*. 2000–2400 m, representing a colonizing stage on land once cleared of forest by man. Montane woodland, and related montane thicket and secondary forest communities, are known at *c*. 2000–2500 m on the Rukiga Highlands (Hamilton, 1969; Langdale-Brown *et al*., 1964; Snowden, 1953) on Ruwenzori and in Burundi (Lewalle, 1972) and must also occur in Rwanda. Among the common trees and shrubs in these woodlands are *Agauria, Dodonaea viscosa, Erythrina abyssinica, Hagenia abyssinica, Myrica salicifolia* and *Nuxia* spp. and some of these, as well as *Albizia gummifera, Macaranga kilimandscharica, Polyscias fulva* and *Prunus africana*, are also abundant in secondary forest. Woodland is common on the Virunga Volcanoes and on associated lava fields (Fig. 24). Common species on the Bufumbira Volcanoes include *Agauria, Hagenia* (above 2650 m), *Hypericum revolutum* and *Nuxia congesta* (below 2650 m). *Afrocrania-Agauria* woodland is present at 2300–2800 m on two of the Virunga Volcanoes in Zaire (Lebrun, 1942, quoted in Lind and Morrison, 1974), and *Myrica* is very common on lava fields in the

Albert National Park (Robyns, 1948). Derived woodland on the dry Karamoja mountains contains *Faurea saligna, Myrica salicifolia, Nuxia congesta* and *Protea gaguedi* (Hamilton, 1972; Langdale-Brown *et al.*, 1974; Wilson, 1962).

(d) *Some distributional trends shown by montane species*

The first question considered is whether floristically critical altitudes are present within montane vegetation. A floristically critical altitude is an altitude or narrow altitudinal band at which a disproportionate number of species attain one limit of their altitudinal range. It has been claimed that floristically critical altitudes are present within montane vegetation in Biafra (Boughey, 1954–1955) and Malaya (van Steenis, 1935), and evidence of their existence in East Africa would certainly influence the expected responses of montane species to climatic change and the ways in which pollen diagrams are interpreted.

In my opinion, the problem of critical altitudes is partly one of scale. If a very narrow vertical transect is considered, there is a good chance that local environmental features will cause large numbers of species to appear or disappear at particular altitudes. Such sudden local changes could be caused by changes in slope, changes in land-use, the local altitude of the forest/savanna boundary, the presence of particularly vigorous species excluding others over part of the transect, and so on. It is therefore possible that an apparently critical altitudinal change at one site might not be reproduced at others. There has been an unfortunate tendency for zonal schemes to be devised for more or less extensive parts of tropical Africa apparently on the basis of ascents by authors of one or two paths up mountains.

Assuming that an adequate scale is being considered, it is possible to argue on theoretical grounds that in undisturbed communities, species behave as groups in response to environmental gradients. But the most detailed evidence available in respect of altitude in East Africa does not support this hypothesis, indicating rather that species behave individualistically. Hedberg (1969a) presented information on the lower altitudinal limits of species which grow in the Afroalpine Belt which suggests that no particular altitudes can be singled out as critical for this group of plants. Studies of the altitudinal distributions of forest trees in Uganda also failed to reveal any floristically critical altitudes (Hamilton, 1975a) and the distributions of both trees and plants of the herb/shrub layer in the Montane Forest Belt of Mt

Elgon also suggest that there is a continuous gradient of floristic change with altitude (Hamilton and Perrott, in press, b).

On any particular and relatively narrow altitudinal transect, taxa generally occupy only part of the total altitudinal range which they display in East Africa as a whole. Of the two limits, the upper altitudinal limit of the range of a species appears to be usually the more constant from place to place (Hamilton, 1972). Thus, if present in an area, *Rapanea* is usually found up to c. 3400 m, *Afrocrania* to c. 3200 m, *Macaranga kilimandscharica* to c. 2600 m, *Cyathea manniana* to c. 2350 m and *Croton macrostachyus* to c. 2300 m, and these species are never found at much greater altitudes than these, but vary greatly between areas in their degrees of downward range extension. It is thought that part of the explanation is that temperature plays a more important role in limiting the upper than the lower altitudinal limits of species (cf. Grubb, 1977; Smith, 1977). The lack of floristically critical altitudes indicates that species vary widely in their tolerance to low temperatures.

The importance of temperature as a factor determining the upper limits of species ranges is supported by a number of observations. First, Hedberg (1959) has found no fewer than 18 species of vascular plants which reach their highest known altitude in the immediate vicinity of a hot spring at 3580 m on Mt Elgon. To this list should be added *Hagenia*, which I recorded in 1968 and which must have arrived since Hedberg's visit. Second, inversion of vegetation zones can sometimes be seen in valleys which are more or less enclosed and thus liable to strong temperature inversion. Third, given the overall similarity of the upper altitudinal limits of species in different localities, there is nevertheless a tendency for at least some taxa to occur at higher altitudes in drier places. It is thought that this is likely to be related to the higher mean maximum temperatures of such sites. The distribution of *Philippia* on Mt Sabinio, which has already been noted, is a case in point.

Many taxa descend to lower altitudes in moister places, for example descending further in areas which are climatically moister, or in edaphically moist river valleys. It is thought that decreased potential evapotranspiration and, to some extent, increased precipitation ensure that there is a general increase in the amount of water available for plants with increasing altitude (Langdale-Brown *et al.*, 1964). Some species of normal dryland situations at high altitudes carry the above tendency to an extreme by being found in wetlands at low altitudes. For example, *Podocarpus milanjianus*, a species of freely-draining soils in the Montane Forest Belt, is present on

Kamarinzovu Swamp (1950 m) and in seasonal swamp forest at 1200 m on the north-west side of Lake Victoria (Lind and Morrison, 1974). *Ilex mitis, Rapanea rhododendroides* and microphyllous Ericaceae are other taxa which share this distributional trend: all can be found growing on acidic peat at relatively low altitudes.

Two other cases of apparent changes in the habitats of species at different altitudes are mentioned here, but their possible causes are not discussed. First, some species which grow widely over the catenary sequence at higher altitudes tend to become restricted to ridge and upper slope sites at lower altitudes. Interestingly, *Podocarpus milanjianus, Rapanea rhododendroides* and microphyllous Ericaceae, mentioned in another context in the preceding paragraph, show this trend. Second, some species, which are members of more mature stages of vegetation at high altitudes tend to become restricted to more secondary types of vegetation at low. Thus, *Hagenia*, though always a light-demanding species, is widely present in Upper Montane Forest, but is restricted to forest edges and derived woodland in the lower part of the Montane Forest Belt. Again, *Prunus* can be common in Upper Montane Forest, as on Mt Elgon, but it is restricted to forest edges in the lowland forests which grow around the northern shore of Lake Victoria.

Finally, it is noted that human disturbance can result in changes of vegetation similar to those which are induced by a shift to drier climate. This is true of both vegetation structure and floristics and can create problems in the interpretation of pollen diagrams.

(e) *Mire vegetation of montane East Africa*

A substantial proportion of the pollen in many Quaternary sediments is believed to have been derived from plants growing on the surface of the accumulating sediment. Typically, sites of sedimentation in montane East Africa are wetlands, the vegetation of which is usually very different from that of surrounding dryland environments. There is a great range of wetland vegetation types, including lake, mire and marsh communities. Mire sediments are differentiated from marsh sediments by a higher organic content and are a more valuable source of pollen evidence. Marsh and lake vegetation is not considered here. An account of lacustrine vegetation is given in Lind and Morrison (1974) and further information on mire and swamp vegetation may be sought in Deuse (1966), Lind (1956), Snowden (1953) and Thompson (1973).

High altitude mires in East Africa are generally dominated by one of two tussock-forming species of Cyperaceae, *Carex runssoroensis* and *Pycreus nigricans*. *Carex runssoroensis* is the typical dominant above *c.* 3300 m and is absent only from the driest of the tall mountains, namely Kilimanjaro and Mt Meru (Hedberg, 1957). *Pycreus nigricans* replaces *Carex runssoroensis* at lower altitudes; I have seen it up to 3380 m on Mt Elgon and, although Thompson (1973) reports it as low as 1700 m in south-west Uganda, the lower limit of its range is more commonly *c.* 2200 m. More local high altitude mire dominants include *Carex monostachya* and some tussock grasses, the latter probably occupying flushed mesotrophic sites.

Carex and *Pycreus* tussocks vary greatly in size; for example, *Carex* tussocks grow to 1 m tall on Ruwenzori, but only to 20 cm on drier Mt Elgon. A number of associated species are found in *Carex* and *Pycreus* mires and these show a micro-distributional pattern which is determined mainly by the tussock/hollow pattern imposed by the *Carex* and *Pycreus* plants (Hamilton, 1969). Shrubby species of *Alchemilla* are among the commoner associates of *Carex* on both Ruwenzori and Mt Elgon, but they have not been reported from *Pycreus* mires. *Sphagnum* is prominent on the *Carex* mires of Ruwenzori and the Aberdares and on the *Pycreus* mire known as Muchoya Swamp in south-west Uganda, but it is absent from all but one mire on Mt Elgon, presumably partly because of the relatively dry climate. *Sphagnum* is not, incidentally, restricted to montane sites in East Africa; it can be found locally in suitably moist and oligotrophic places at *c.* 1200 m around the Lake Victoria shore (Lind and Morrison, 1974).

A variety of mire types are present at altitudes below the level of *Pycreus* mires. This account concentrates on those found above *c.* 1800 m along the Western Rift, which is the most relevant region from the point of view of Quaternary palynological studies. Thompson (1973) lists the following dominants of herbaceous mires: *Miscanthidium*, *Phragmites*, *Typha* and Cyperaceae such as *Cladium* and *Cyperus* (Fig. 33), including *Cyperus papyrus* (to 2100 m). To these may be added the *Xyris*-dominated type mentioned by Deuse (1966) and also types rich in *Sphagnum*. According to Deuse (1966), *Cladium*, *Phragmites* and *Typha* are present on mires and swamps of relatively high pH (see also Lind, 1956), *Cyperus* mires are found on mires of moderate pH and *Miscanthidium*, *Xyris* and *Sphagnum* are characteristic of the most acidic sites.

Various trees and shrubs can be found on mires and are sometimes sufficiently abundant to form closed-canopy forest or thicket. Scat-

Fig. 33   Katenga Swamp, Kigezi, S. W. Uganda, 1950 m. The photograph shows a marginal wet zone with clumps of *Cyperus*. The swamps in this part of the Rukiga Highlands contain a palynological record of forest clearance.

tered giant groundsels and giant lobelias are often present on *Carex* bogs and lobelias can also be seen on many *Pycreus* mires. Various species of *Erica* are known from acidic sites between *c.* 1950 and 3200 m, and other woody plants found on mires include *Myrica kandtiana, Rapanea rhododendroides* and *Syzygium cordatum* (Fig. 34). According to Deuse (1966), *Syzygium* forest is often the end-point of autogenic succession on Rwandese mires at *c.* 1700–2000 m; he gives the *Syzygium*-dominated forest on Kamiranzovu Swamp (1950 m) as an example of this final stage. It is, however, now known that this forest is growing on a surface which has been stagnant for thousands of years and Deuse's theories of successional development require revision.

Fig. 34 *Syzygium* swamp forest at about 1830 m in the Ishasha Valley near Kabale, S.W. Uganda. By analogy with Kamiranzovu Swamp (see Chapter 6), it is possible that this forest is growing on a peat surface which has stagnated since about 12 000 B.P.

Modern Pollen Deposition

Pollen grains contained within sediments can be derived from a variety of sources and one of the problems in pollen analysis is to interpret the pollen record at a particular site in terms of changes in the distribution and abundance of parent taxa in the surrounding area. Often, interpretation may be facilitated if it is possible to distinguish between pollen derived from the wetland (or local) vegetation of the sedimentary basin from that which has been produced by plants growing on well-drained soils (Fig. 35). Within the second category, it is desirable to separate pollen which has originated from adjacent vegetation from that of long-distance vegetation; adjacent vegetation includes plants growing sufficiently close to the sample site to be subject to approximately the same climatic conditions as prevail at the sample site itself, and long-distance vegetation includes plants growing further afield. The sharp

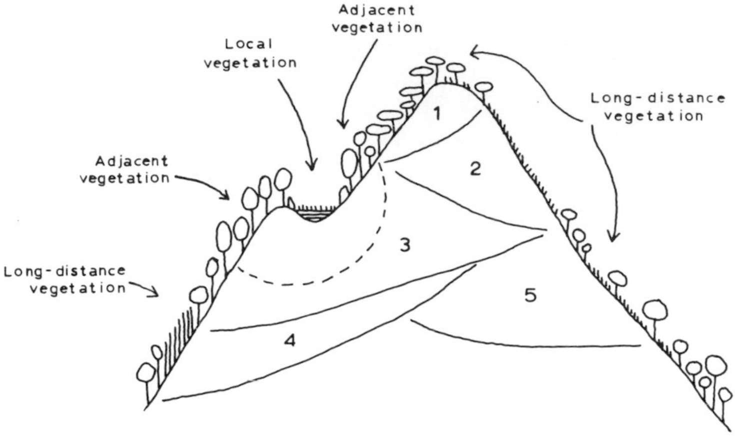

Fig. 35 Classification of vegetation in relation to the site of a montane pollen diagram. The diagram is for the sediments over which the local vegetation is growing. The limit of adjacent vegetation is indicated by the broken line. Arbitrary vegetation zones numbered 1–5. From Morrison and Hamilton (1974). Reproduced from the *Journal of Ecology*, **62** with permission of Blackwell Scientific Publications Ltd.

altitudinal and other environmental gradients found in montane East Africa ensure that pollen need not be transported far for it to be deposited in a vegetation type very different from that to which its parent species belongs.

A large number of variables is believed to determine the composition of pollen spectra encountered in sediments. A full discussion is given in Faegri and Iversen (1964) and is not attempted here; but contributory factors include the pollen productivity of different species, the abundance of species in the vegetation, the disposition of species relative to the sediment site, the height of the species in relation to the vegetation cover, the ease of dispersal of pollen types, the structure of vegetation growing on the sediment, the preservation characteristics of different pollen types and the relative importance at the site of atmospheric pollen rain and of pollen transported overland. Concerning East Africa, very few of these factors have been examined individually and studies have rather concentrated on the "integrative approach" of collecting samples for the determination of modern pollen deposition from a range of vegetation types; by comparing the pollen spectra of these samples with the distribution of vegetation, it is hoped that estimates can be made of the behaviour of particular pollen types and, hopefully, of the general factors governing pollen production and dispersal. Samples of recent pollen deposition may be taken from a variety of natural or experimental surfaces. Natural surfaces which have proved suitable include the superficial horizons of soils and sediments and the mats formed by epiphytic bryophytes. Judging by results from East Africa (Hamilton and Perrott, in press, a) and elsewhere in the world (Andersen, 1967; Hicks, 1977), such samples often provide a good indication of average long-term pollen deposition. Experimental surfaces include exposed slides and traps (Bonnefille, 1972; Hamilton and Perrott, in press, a).

Two strategies have been adopted in the selection of the location of sample sites. Samples have been collected from open places situated within a range of vegetation types, the idea being that such sites offer physically rather similar conditions to those from which many pollen diagrams are available, making comparisons between past and present spectra more meaningful (Hamilton, 1972). Alternatively, samples have been obtained actually from within various vegetation types, an approach which has proved valuable for pollen diagram interpretation in other parts of the world (e.g. in Scotland, Birks, 1973).

Pollen may be carried into a sedimentary basin either in the atmosphere or by overland wash, and it can be desirable to determine the relative quantities of pollen transported by these different means. Concerning lakes, Bonny (1976) has demonstrated that there is a substantial influx of river-borne pollen into lakes in the Lake District, England, and it is likely that this is also true of African lakes. Bonnefille (1979) has compared the percentages of montane pollen in surface samples from various sites in the Lake Turkana basin and has concluded that substantial quantities of montane forest pollen are transported from the Ethiopian highlands into Lake Turkana by the River Omo (Table 6). The representation of montane pollen in samples from terrestrial sites declines from 2–6% at a distance of

Table 6   Percentages of montane pollen (MP) in surface samples from the region of Lake Turkana (Bonnefille, 1979)

Samples	Sedimenta-tion	Transport	% MP
Surface–East Turkana	Aerial	Aerial 150–250 km	0·5–1·5
Surface–Shungura	Aerial	Aerial 80–100 km	2–6
River Omo	Fluviatile	Fluviatile 80–100 km	9–12
Lake Turkana	Lacustrine	Fluviatile + aerial 150 km	5–8

80–100 km from montane forest, to 0·5–1·5% at 150–200 km, giving a measure of the quantities of montane pollen transported in the atmosphere. Sediments of the River Omo are relatively rich in montane pollen (9–12%), suggesting that large quantities of montane pollen are carried by the river. The 5–8% of montane pollen encountered in surface samples from Lake Turkana is believed to have arrived by both atmospheric and water routes.

Concerning mires, it is believed that very variable quantities of pollen may be transported onto or off the surface by overland flow. Flow is thought to be less on flatter, more acidic mires, particularly those with marginal canalizing zones, than on smaller, more sloping mires. Both the type of vegetation and the mineral content of the peat may be taken as guides to the likely past importance of the overland component in pollen accumulation.

An important discovery is that pollen can be transported in the atmosphere in large quantities away from areas of production (Hamilton, 1972). The proportion of exotic pollen in surface samples varies widely with vegetation type, surface samples from the Ericaceous and Afroalpine Belts, for example, being often rich in montane forest pollen, but little Ericaceous and Afroalpine pollen being present in samples from the Montane Forest Belt. Part of the reason for this is believed to be that vegetation types vary greatly in pollen productivity, with the result that a pollen type of long-distance origin, which is being deposited at an even rate over a wide area, will be better represented in relative terms in surface samples from vegetation types of lower pollen production. That vegetation types show major differences in pollen productivity has been confirmed by determination of pollen deposition rates in pollen traps over a 5-month period of Mt Elgon (Fig. 36). This trap survey indicates that pollen production is much higher in montane forest than in either lower altitude agricultural land (maize/*Combretum*) or higher altitude Ericaceous and Afroalpine vegetation.

A decline in pollen production in the Ericaceous and Afroalpine Belts is believed to be a general feature of the East African mountains, but not all lowland communities are thought to have as low a pollen production as those examined around Mt Elgon. Surface samples and pollen diagrams from high altitudes on Ruwenzori contain large quantities of Gramineae and *Celtis* pollen, derived, respectively, largely from secondary savanna and lowland forest communities (Hamilton, 1972), and it is also noteworthy that much of the Lake Victoria pollen diagram (Kendall, 1969) is rich in lowland forest pollen types. Undoubtedly many variables influence the amount of

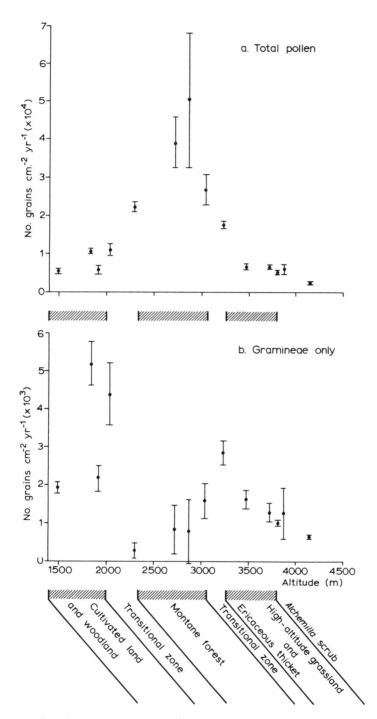

Fig. 36 Pollen deposition rates in pollen traps on Mt Elgon. (a) Total pollen; (b) Gramineae only. From Hamilton and Perrott (in press, a) and reproduced from "Pollen et Spores" with permission of Mme van Campo.

pollen produced by lowland vegetation types; judging by evidence available to date, it seems that one tendency is for lowland vegetation in climatically moister places to produce relatively large quantities of pollen.

Surface sample analysis shows that much pollen is deposited very close to source and that there is a tendency towards great differences in the abundance of locally produced pollen types at closely situated sites (Hamilton and Perrott, in press, a). Also, pollen types which have originated at some distance from sample sites tend to be represented in roughly constant proportions to one another in surface samples from the same general area (Hamilton, 1972; Hamilton and Perrott, in press, a). These findings are in agreement with those for other parts of the world (Andersen, 1967, 1974; Janssen, 1973). Excluding from consideration cases of high representation due to local origin, there is great variability in the relationship between the abundance of pollen types in pollen spectra and the abundance of their parent taxa in the vegetation of the source area. Flenley (1972) has suggested the use of the concept "relative export ability" (= relative dispersal ability of Hamilton, 1972) as a measure of this variation. Hamilton and Perrott (in press, a) have proposed the following definition of relative export ability—

$$\text{relative export ability} = \frac{\begin{array}{l}\text{\% contribution of a pollen type in}\\ \text{the long-distance component of pollen}\\ \text{spectra}\end{array}}{\begin{array}{l}\text{\% cover (or basal area) of parent}\\ \text{taxon in the source area}\end{array}}$$

For a number of reasons, especially concerning difficulties of delimitation of the source area, precise determination of relative export ability is very difficult. Quantification of relative export ability has been attempted for Mt Elgon (Hamilton, 1972; Hamilton and Perrott, in press, a) and a three-category scheme is thought to be realistic. Pollen types with high relative export ability are *Acalypha*, *Juniperus*, *Podocarpus* and Urticaceae; pollen types with moderate relative export ability include *Dodonaea*, *Hagenia*, *Myrica*, *Olea* and *Stoebe*; and there are many pollen types of low relative export ability, for example Acanthaceae, *Afrocrania*, Meliaceae, *Prunus* and *Schefflera*. Measurement of the relative export ability of a pollen type obtained for different montane areas are usually in agreement with one another, but three pollen types, which have apparently higher relative export abilities on Ruwenzori than Mt Elgon, are *Dendro-*

senecio-type, Ericaceae and *Rapanea*. It is possible that the increased vigour of the parent species on Ruwenzori is partly responsible for this contrast.

Concerning non-montane vegetation types, surface pollen spectra have been published for *Acacia/Commiphora* sub-desert savanna to the east of Lake Turkana (Bonnefille and Vincens, 1977) and in the vicinity of Olduvai Gorge (Bonnefille, 1979), and for a lake situated in *Brachystegia* woodland in northern Zambia (Livingstone, 1971). In addition, trap samples from *Brachystegia* woodland in Malawi have been obtained by Meadows (personal communication), who has also examined pollen trap and surface samples from montane communities on the Nyika Plateau. All samples from *Acacia*, *Commiphora* and *Brachystegia* savannas are rich in Gramineae, but those from *Acacia/Commiphora* differ from those from *Brachystegia* woodland in often being rich in Chenopodiaceae/Amaranthaceae. High Chenopodiaceae/Amaranthaceae (especially Chenopodiaceae) percentages are commonly found in dry environments world-wide (Livingstone, 1971; Schultz, 1979). *Acacia* and *Commiphora* are poorly represented in these samples, even when their parent taxa are abundant in local vegetation, and this poor representation of dominant species could lead to problems in recognizing the past presence of different savanna types from pollen diagrams. *Brachystegia* percentages of up to 21% have been obtained by Meadows for trap samples from *Brachystegia* woodland, contrasting with the very low values found by Livingstone in the Zambian lake. The explanation may be partly that, while produced in fair quantity, *Brachystegia* pollen is poorly dispersed from its site of origin and partly that high pollen production of fringing vegetation such as sedge swamp around the lake causes a great reduction in the proportion of pollen originating from dryland environments. Montane forest pollen types, such as *Hagenia*, *Juniperus*, *Olea* and *Podocarpus* are present in all surface samples examined from savanna.

Pollen Diagram Interpretation: Some Concluding Remarks

Most pollen diagrams from East Africa are relative pollen diagrams, in which pollen abundances are expressed as percentages of a pollen sum. Various means of defining the pollen sum have been used in the construction of pollen diagrams and, revising an earlier call for uniformity (Hamilton, 1972), I now feel that different definitions of the pollen sum can be appropriate to particular problems or to particular sites. In the case of pollen diagrams which have been previously published, the pollen sums used here are usually as in the original presentations. With regard to the desirability of excluding very well dispersed pollen type from the pollen sum as recommended in a previous paper (Hamilton, 1972), my current view is that this is generally undesirable, mainly because exclusion of such pollen types can reduce the number of grains included in a pollen sum to an unacceptably low figure.

It is usually advantageous to omit from the pollen sum pollen types which are likely to have been derived wholly or largely from local vegetation, particularly if such pollen types are abundant. One reason is that the history of wetland vegetation can be very different from that of vegetation on freely-draining soils, being to some degree under the control of different factors. Another consideration is that pollen types derived from local vegetation are liable to great fluctuations in abundance from level to level up a diagram, even in the absence of significant change in the general environment of the area; the inclusion of local pollen types in the pollen sum might well hide important changes in the abundance of other pollen types. This having been said, there remains the difficulty of determining which pollen types in a diagram have been derived to a significant degree from local vegetation. A pollen type can be of local origin in one diagram and of more distant origin in another, and, indeed, different modes of origin may have been important for the same pollen type in different parts of the same diagram. Aids to the classification of pollen types into local or non-local categories include the ecology of the parent species, the lithology of the sediment and the shapes of the pollen curves themselves. A pollen type with an irregular trace is more likely to have been derived from local vegetation than one whose values are either rather constant or systematically variable from level to level. Whatever the final decision, it must be remembered that the construction of a pollen diagram is a different process from its interpretation. The principal objective in defining a pollen sum should generally be the exclusion of pollen types which are common and which could be of local origin in at least parts of the diagram.

Zones on pollen diagrams in the present book have been recognized solely to aid description. I have often not adhered to the zonal schemes of previous authors. The zones are usually equivalent to pollen assemblage zones, in the sense that each consists of a number of contiguous pollen spectra relatively similar to one another and different from those of adjoining zones, but this is not necessarily the case. Zones of the same alphabetic designate in different diagrams are not necessarily temporally equivalent. No attempt has been made to erect a system of pollen zones applicable over a wide area, such as those proposed for Ireland by Jessen (1949).

Two inter-related approaches are usually used in the interpretation of a pollen diagram. One is an analysis of change in the diagram and the other involves attempts to reconstruct vegetation and environment from the actual presence or absence, or degree of abundance of pollen types. In the latter case in particular, it is very valuable to have surface samples from the site, as the present is the one point in time for which the relationship between vegetation composition and pollen spectra can be directly established.

It is sometimes possible to match a modern pollen spectrum with a similar fossil spectrum. Analogy, however, cannot be used uncritically and there is a likelihood that some pollen spectra can result from more than one set of environmental conditions. The normal first stage in the reconstruction of past vegetation from a pollen diagram is to try to establish which taxa were likely to have been growing close to the sample site, either in local or adjacent vegetation. Accordingly, interest is focused on pollen types which are relatively abundant and which are of low or moderate relative dispersal ability. This, in turn, may lead to an estimate of the general vegetation type present in the area, for instance the vegetation zone present. Pollen types of long-distance origin may then be recognized and further deductions made concerning past vegetation.

It has been noted that the upper altitudinal limits of many taxa are more constant from area to area than lower altitudinal limits and that this constancy is believed to be related to the greater importance of temperature as a determinant of upper than lower limits. If temperature in the past had been much higher than now (which is believed actually not to have been the case), then such higher temperatures should be readily detectable from the pollen record. This is because they would sometimes have resulted in pollen types of low relative export ability becoming common in pollen diagrams for sites above those at which the parent taxa of the pollen types grow today. Unfortunately, temperature depression (which did indeed occur during the Quaternary) is more ambiguously recorded in the pollen record, since other factors apart from temperature decrease can significantly depress the altitudinal ranges of species. In determination of past temperatures from pollen diagrams, the absence or rarity of one pollen type can be as useful as the presence of another (Hamilton, 1972). Not all pollen diagrams are equally valuable as indicators of temperature change; for this purpose, the most valuable pollen diagrams are generally those from areas in which other variables, particularly climatic moistness, have remained relatively constant.

Chapter 6

Upper Quaternary Pollen Diagrams from Montane Eastern Africa

Introduction

There has been a concentration of palynological studies in the highlands of eastern Africa and today pollen diagrams extending back to a few thousand or tens of thousands of years before the present are available for a number of montane localities (Fig. 22). According to Morrison (1968), one of the principal attractions of montane sites to the palynologist is the differentiation of altitudinal zones of vegetation along steep climatic gradients and the possibility of determining past climatic changes through the movements of these zones. In particular, he contended that even small temperature changes would have created substantial altitudinal movements in the vegetation and thus it should be possible to use pollen diagrams from highland sites as thermometers. This reason for selecting montane localities for palynological work has to some extent been vindicated by the results, although it is now realized that changes in moisture availability and, during relatively recent times, human disturbance have sometimes been more important causes of vegetation change than temperature shifts.

High altitude sediment types which have yielded abundant pollen include peat, lake mud and some largely inorganic deposits such as valley infill. Within eastern Africa peat is virtually confined to the highlands and, since peat deposits can be sampled cheaply and with lighter equipment than, for example, sediments beneath lakes, the concentration of peat deposits at high altitudes has proved an attraction to some investigators. Lake sediments at all altitudes contain pollen, and pollen diagrams are available for both highland and lowland sites. But the problems of interpreting pollen diagrams for lowland lakes, particularly for large lowland lakes, have hardly been studied (cf. Morrison, 1968); this lack of knowledge has also helped to focus attention on the highlands where the problems of pollen diagram interpretation are, if not well understood, at least better understood than in the case of the lowlands. It should be noted, however, that the few pollen diagrams which have been prepared for lowland lake sediments are very interesting.

Upper Quaternary pollen diagrams for highland eastern Africa show much variation, more so than is displayed, for example, by an average selection of pollen diagrams from the British Isles. This diversity is not surprising, considering the huge range of environments present in montane eastern Africa. The pollen diagrams are for sites at different altitudes and for a variety of mountains, differing from one another in climate, floristics, land-use and ruggedness.

In the past there has been considerable controversy over the interpretation of some pollen diagrams for highland eastern Africa (e.g. Coetzee, 1967; Livingstone, 1967) and, although many uncertainties remain, the new information on vegetation distribution and pollen dispersal outlined in the last chapter allows more confident interpretation today. A greater number of diagrams is now available and this provides increased opportunities for comparison, leading to many useful insights. I have here adopted a discursive approach to pollen diagram interpretation, discussing the diagrams from different mountains in turn, but referring to pollen diagrams from other mountains and to other evidence as seems useful to the discussion. Because of the uncertainties in interpretation, I have concentrated on the main features of the diagrams and the diagrams certainly contain additional information to that dealt with here.

Pollen diagrams for Mt Elgon

Pollen diagrams are available for four sites on Mt Elgon (Fig. 23). The samples were collected by R. A. Perrott and myself in 1976; the counts for Lake Kimilili were the work of R. A. Perrott. From the point of view of vegetation and climate, Mt Elgon is a classic East African mountain, changes in vegetation with altitude and aspect being clearly defined on the regularly-shaped mountain. An atypical feature is the local presence of pastoralists near the Ericaceous

Belt/Montane Forest boundary. These people have undoubtedly been responsible for increasing the area of high altitude grassland and it is probable that soil erosion following burning has also increased the area of rocky ground communities.

The first two pollen diagrams considered are for Lake Kimilili and Koitoboss Bog, both situated in the Afroalpine Belt. These high altitude sites were selected partly to provide evidence of the history of montane forest on the mountain. Studies of modern pollen deposition have shown that much of the long-distance pollen rain in the Afroalpine and Ericaceous Belts of the East African mountains originates in the montane forest. Moreover, its composition tends to be remarkably constant within any given high altitude area. Changes in the composition of the long-distance component in pollen diagrams from high altitude sites should therefore provide a good guide to the general history of montane forest vegetation, due notice being taken of the relative export abilities of pollen types. Given the general constancy, there is some variation reported for both Elgon and Ruwenzori in the composition of the long-distance component related to aspect. It was originally intended to attempt a detailed reconstruction of forest history on Elgon by obtaining pollen diagrams for high altitude sites situated on several different aspects of the mountain. Unfortunately, the political situation in Uganda precluded work on the western slopes in 1976 and only two Afroalpine sites were sampled. The pollen diagrams for these sites show interesting similarities and differences and undoubtedly the approach would be worth pursuing further both on this and other mountains.

Lake Kimilili is *c.* 100 × 50 m in area. It lies on the southern slopes of the mountain at 4150 m, occupying a cirque-shaped hollow which is cut into the outer rim of the caldera wall and forms the head of a glaciated valley (Figs 37 and 38). The vegetation in the catchment is predominantly *Alchemilla* scrub containing frequent giant groundsels; unvegetated cliffs are common and other vegetation types present include tussock grassland, which is frequent on thin soils, rocky ground communities, the extent of which has probably been enlarged by human disturbance, and a small *Carex* bog. The only plant growing in the lake water is *Callitriche stagnalis*.

At the time of our visit to sample the sediments in March 1976, the lake had fallen 47 cm below that of its outlet. (Overflow was observed in August 1976 and had also been seen in 1967.) Lake sediments covered by a mat of *Subularia monticola* were exposed along the western side of the lake and the stratigraphy of the sediments was examined at three places (Fig. 37). Samples were

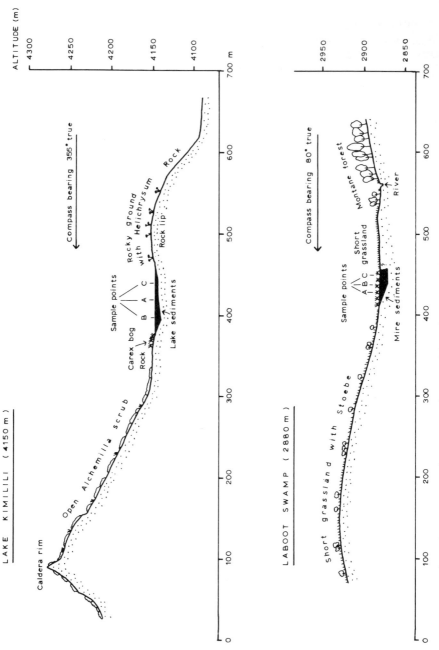

Fig. 37 Surveyed sections on Mt Elgon. (a) Lake Kimilili and its glacially eroded catchment; (b) Laboot Swamp in rounded unglaciated topography.

Fig. 38   Lake Kimilili, Mt Elgon, 4150 m. The samples for pollen analysis were collected from the exposed lake sediments on the right.

obtained for laboratory analyses from 0–410 cm at Sample Point A and from 405–655 cm at Sample Point B. Nine ^{14}C determinations are available.

The most conspicuous lithological change, recorded at all sites, is from green lake mud to brown or grey mud (Fig. 39) and this is dated to *c.* 3500 B.P. at Sample Point A, where it occurs at a depth of 175 cm. The sediment tends to be richer in clay and to have accumulated more rapidly above the boundary, suggesting that erosion in the catchment was proceeding at a faster rate. The green colour of the lower sediments is presumed to be due to the presence of chlorophyll and, since chlorophyll in sediments is rapidly degraded under oxidizing conditions, it is presumed that the lake must have remained relatively deep and well stratified up to *c.* 3500 B.P. In addition to the sediment colour and the increased inorganic content, other indications of drier conditions during more recent times are fossil roots in the upper 92 cm of sediment, orange mottles above 23 cm and a pan at 16–18 cm; changes in the concentration of pollen in the sediment are also suggestive (Fig. 40). At Sample Point A there is a gradual and regular decline in pollen concentration in the green mud followed by great variability in pollen concentration in the brown/grey muds. The initial steady decline is assumed to be

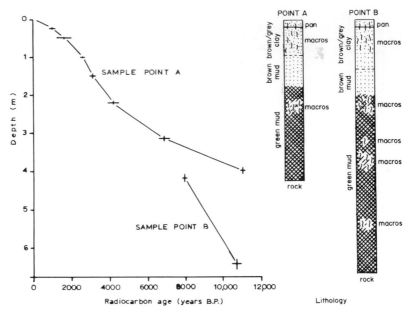

Fig. 39   Lake Kimilili sediments: lithology and radiocarbon chronology.

associated with the gradual shallowing of the lake as sediment accumulated and is a phenomenon known from elsewhere (Battarbee, personal communication). The variability in the upper sediments suggests an unstable sedimentary environment, presumably caused by a fluctuating water level. There are, then, various signs of drier conditions after *c.* 3500 B.P. Increased dryness of the sedimentary environment may have been partly due to the autogenic process of sediment infilling, but some of the strands of evidence, particularly the higher inorganic content of the sediment, suggest that a change to drier climate may also have been involved.

The results of pollen analysis are presented in two different forms, the pollen sum being in one case the sum of total pollen (Fig. 41), and in the other the sum of the long-distance pollen types (Fig. 42). Total pollen, as the pollen sum, has the advantage of simplicity, but has the disadvantage that trends shown by pollen types of relatively long-distance origin may be obscured by changes in abundant, locally-produced pollen types. This problem is less serious with lacustrine sediments than with peat, which often includes much pollen of mire taxa such as Cyperaceae. The long-distance component comprises pollen types produced by plants which are confined to montane

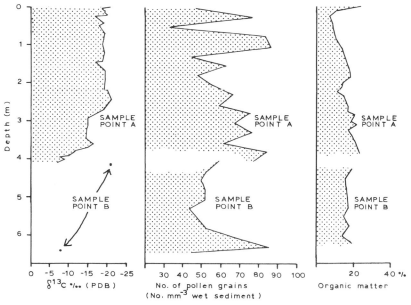

Fig. 40 Lake Kimilili sediments: some sediment properties. Pollen concentration estimated by the method of Battarbee and McCallan (1974). Organic matter determined by percentage loss in dry weight on oxidation with H_2O_2. The $\delta^{13}C‰$ (PDB) values show the relative proportions of the two stable carbon isotopes ^{12}C and ^{13}C in organic matter (i.e. excluding carbonate) in the sediments. The more negative the value, the lower is the proportion of ^{12}C. These measurements are of interest because of the exceptional degree of ^{13}C enrichment in the lowermost sediments at both sample points. The reasons for these exceptional values are unclear, but they could be related to the organic matter having been derived largely from plants possessing the C4-photosynthetic pathway (Troughton, 1972). $S^{13}C‰$ determinations by courtesy of D. D. Harkness.

forest or other lower altitude vegetation types; the excluded pollen types (the local component) are therefore those derived from taxa present in the Ericaceous and Afroalpine Belts: many of these taxa do, of course, also occur at lower altitudes. Use of the long-distance component as the pollen sum not only helps in the detection of changes in the abundance of long-distance, particularly montane forest pollen types, but also permits easier comparison between pollen diagrams for different high altitude sites, either on the same or different mountains. It should immediately be pointed out that it is certain that neither Lake Kimilili nor Koitoboss Bog has ever been surrounded by Montane Forest Belt vegetation; the pollen types included in the long-distance component have certainly always been of long-distance origin.

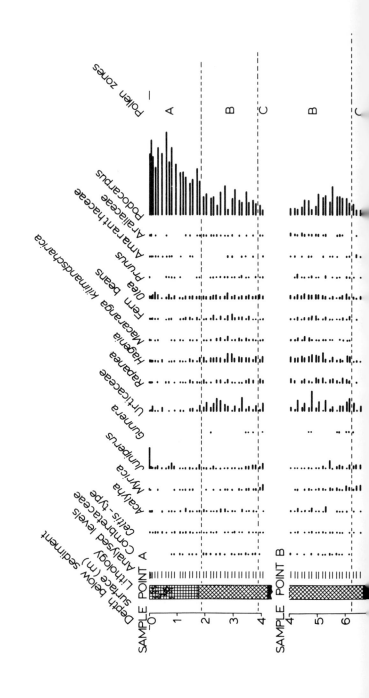

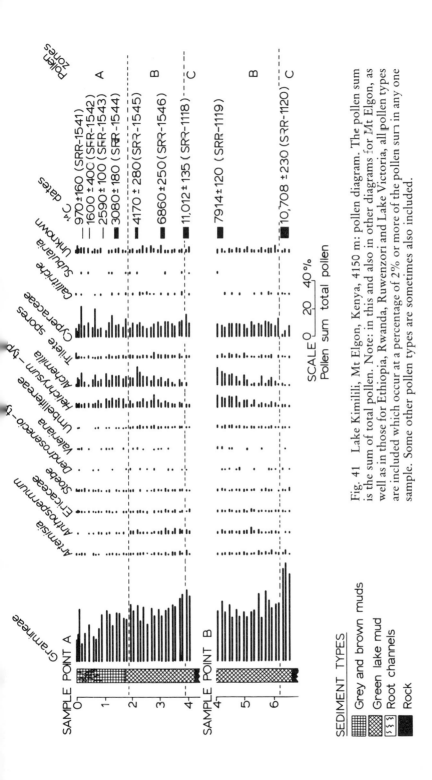

Fig. 41 Lake Kimilili, Mt Elgon, Kenya, 4150 m: pollen diagram. The pollen sum is the sum of total pollen. Note: in this and also in other diagrams for Mt Elgon, as well as in those for Ethiopia, Rwanda, Ruwenzori and Lake Victoria, all pollen types are included which occur at a percentage of 2% or more of the pollen sum in any one sample. Some other pollen types are sometimes also included.

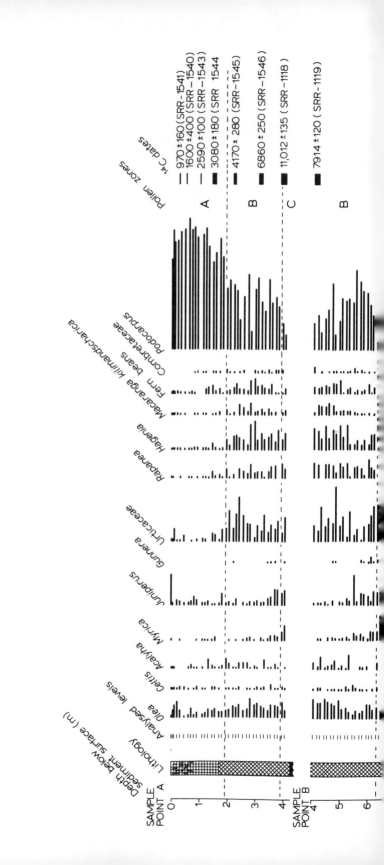

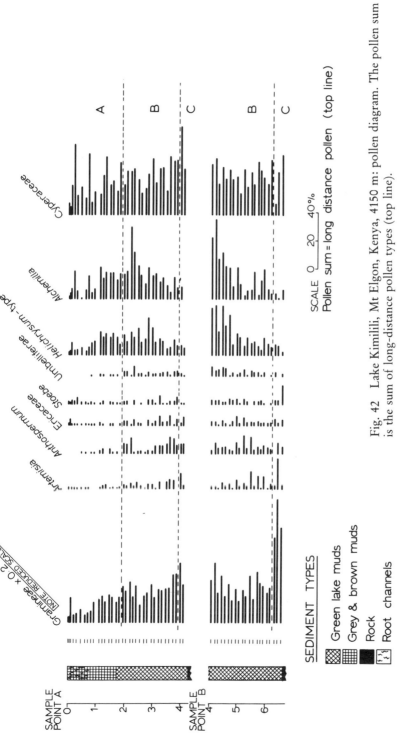

Fig. 42 Lake Kimilili, Mt Elgon, Kenya, 4150 m: pollen diagram. The pollen sum is the sum of long-distance pollen types (top line).

Comparison of the pollen diagrams from Sample Points A and B, backed up by the ^{14}C evidence, shows that the sediment sequences from the two points overlap in time and that a single pollen zone terminology can be employed for the two cores. Three pollen zones, A–C, are recognized. Zones B and C are more sharply distinct from one another at Point B than Point A; blurring of the Zone B/C boundary at Point A is believed to be associated with the slower sedimentation rate, allowing greater opportunities for sediment mixing. It is concluded that the diagram from Sample Point B gives a clearer picture of the early vegetation than that from Sample Point A.

Zone C (*c.* 11 000–10 500 B.P.) is distinguished by a very high proportion of Gramineae, both in relative terms (Figs 41 and 42) and in terms of numbers of grass grains per mm^3 of wet sediment (refer to Fig. 40). An indication of the origin of this pollen is provided by the investigation of modern pollen deposition on Mt Elgon (Hamilton and Perrott, in press, a) which has shown that, over the altitudinal range 1400–4000 m, the percentage of grass pollen in modern spectra is related to the abundance of grassland in the vicinity of the sample site. Grassland was almost certainly widespread in the catchment and it also seems likely, given the rather low quantity of tree pollen, that the area of montane forest may have been much less on the mountain than now, with some replacement by grassland. It may be recalled that this zone dates to approximately the end of the Pleistocene arid period marked by low lake levels. *Alchemilla* occurs only with low percentages and is completely absent from the basal sample at Sample Point A. Nevertheless, it is likely that some *Alchemilla* scrub was present in the catchment (Appendix). The rarity of *Dendrosenecio*-type pollen does not imply that giant groundsels were necessarily absent from the area (Appendix). The most abundant pollen types derived from montane forest trees are *Podocarpus, Olea, Juniperus* and *Myrica*, a combination which suggests the existence of a drier forest type than is found on Mt Elgon today. Various pollen types, such as *Macaranga kilimandscharica*, fern beans (monolete fern spores) and Combretaceae, indicative of moister types of forest or woodland, are relatively rare. The evidence for dry conditions in Zone C is not, however, unequivocal. In particular, two indicators of moistness are the abundance of Urticaceae and the presence of *Gunnera* at some levels, though not the two lowest at Sample Point B. High values of Urticaceae pollen are today associated with moist montane forest (Hamilton, 1972; Hamilton and Perrott, in press, a). *Gunnera perpensa*, the only East African species of *Gunnera*, is a wind-pollinated plant which grows on the edges of bogs over the altitudinal range 1560–3800 (–4000 m) (Boutique and Verdcourt, 1973); it is not recorded from Mt Elgon today. It is perhaps significant that *Gunnera* and, to a large degree, Urticaceae are herbaceous taxa, which might be particularly responsive to climatic change.

In Zone B (10 500–3700 B.P.), higher values of *Alchemilla* and lower values of Gramineae suggest expansion of *Alchemilla* scrub in the catchment at the expense of grassland. Occasional grains of *Valeriana* also point to the same conclusion since the high altitude Elgon species, *V. kilimandscharica*, is strongly associated with *Alchemilla* scrub today. Montane forest pollen types, such as *Hagenia, Olea, Podocarpus, Rapanea* and Urticaceae are common and montane forest must have been widespread on the mountain. All this indicates a moister climate than during Zone C times. It is interesting to note that *Myrica* and *Juniperus* show gradual declines in abundance from the beginning of the zone, suggesting that the species adjusted themselves rather slowly to the new climatic regime.

Zone A is marked by a dramatic increase in *Podocarpus* pollen. The probable cause was the onset of a drier climate (Appendix) and this is also suggested by disproportionate decreases in pollen types, such as Urticaceae, *Rapanea, Macaranga kilimandscharica*, fern beans and *Hagenia*, all more or less good indicators of moister forest types. Taken together with the lithological evidence previously noted, it seems that there must have been a major climatic change to increased dryness, towards a climate similar to that of today; on the basis of the *Podocarpus* curve, this can be rather precisely dated at c. 3700 B.P. A *Podocarpus* rise is a feature of several other pollen diagrams from eastern Africa and it is likely that it was roughly contemporaneous throughout the area. The diagram from Lake Kimilili is important, because it is for this diagram that the rise is most precisely dated.

Some pollen changes within Zone A might have been due to human activities. Lower values of Gramineae above 75 cm (post c. 2100 B.P.) could have been caused by the suppression of grass pollen production by the grazing of domestic stock and burning (Appendix). The very large quantities of *Juniperus* in the uppermost sample could have been derived partly from planted *Cupressus* trees.

Koitoboss Bog, the second Afroalpine site on Mt Elgon for which a pollen diagram is available, is situated at 3940 m inside the eastern rim of the caldera. (A similar bog is shown on Fig. 43.) The bog is dominated by *Carex runssoroensis* forming tussocks 10 cm high and 40 cm apart. *Scirpus fluitans* and *Swertia* cf. *crassiuscula* grow between the tussocks and *Alchemilla johnstonii* is abundant on the

Fig. 43   *Carex* bogs inside the caldera of Mt Elgon; altitude about 3900 m. These bogs are surrounded by *Alchemilla* scrub rich in *Senecio* trees and are very similar to Koitoboss Bog.

tussocks themselves. There are occasional specimens of *Lobelia elgonensis* and *Senecio johnstonii*. The vegetation in the catchment is largely *Alchemilla* scrub, containing frequent *Senecio johnstonii* trees; there is virtually no tussock grassland. The weather was exceptionally bad at the time of our visit and only one core, with a depth of 204 cm and consisting uniformly of *Carex* peat, was obtained from the bog. A basal ^{14}C date of 6505 ± 65 B.P. suggests that the deepest peat on the bog was not sampled. The pollen diagram (Fig. 44) shows a well marked *Podocarpus* rise and, in view of the fact that *Podocarpus* is such a well dispersed pollen type, this is highly likely to have commenced at the same time as at Lake Kimilili, i.e. *c.* 3700 B.P. If this is so, then the rate of sediment accumulation was reduced after 3700 B.P.

The pollen sum used for the diagram is the long-distance component and the diagram can be compared directly with that for Lake Kimilili shown on Fig. 42. Two pollen zones, A and B, are recognized, the boundary between them being defined by the *Podocarpus* rise. These zones are taken to be correlated temporally with Zone A and upper Zone B, respectively, at Lake Kimilili. They are also generally distinguished by the same differences in abundance in long-distance pollen types, with higher percentages of Urticaceae, *Macaranga kilimandscharica, Hagenia* and fern beans in Zone B and a higher percentage of *Podocarpus* in Zone A. *Olea* pollen in this diagram has been divided into two types, one with a small-celled reticulum attributed to *Olea hochstetteri/welwitschii* and the other with a large-celled reticulum assigned to *Olea africana. Olea hochstetteri*-type pollen is rather constant in abundance throughout the diagram, while *O. africana* is more abundant in Zone A than Zone B. Since *Olea africana* is a characteristic component of drier types of montane forest, the increase in *O. africana* pollen in Zone A provides further evidence for a relatively dry climate.

It was originally thought that Koitoboss Bog would receive a greater quantity of pollen derived from drier forest types than Lake Kimilili; geographically, Koitoboss Bog is closer to the dry forests of the eastern slopes. This is not, however, the case; both surface samples and the pollen diagrams show that it is Koitoboss Bog which receives and has received a greater proportion of pollen from the wetter forests. This is shown, for instance, by the higher percentages of *Podocarpus* and the lower amounts of Urticaceae in the diagram from Lake Kimilili. It is postulated that patterns of wind movement on the upper slopes are not as simple as previously believed; in particular, winds sweeping up from the south-west and west are thought (and have been observed) to frequently enter the caldera, resulting in a greater quantity of pollen, derived from moist forest types, being deposited in the caldera than would otherwise be the case.

Compared with Lake Kimilili, Koitoboss Bog has a much greater proportion of local pollen. This consists principally of Cyperaceae pollen and has presumably been derived largely from *Carex runssoroensis.* There is a tendency for Cyperaceae to decline and for *Alchemilla* to increase up the sediment column. Possibly, drier climate caused a reduction in the vigour of the *Carex* and a concomitant increase in the abundance of *Alchemilla johnstonii* growing on the *Carex* tussocks. Gramineae values are relatively low, at *c.* 50% of the pollen sum, and show little change over the diagram. This is a contrast to Lake Kimilili where Gramineae is generally much more abundant and where there is a considerable decline in the upper part of Zone A. There are no grasses growing actually in Koitoboss Bog or in Lake Kimilili and the differences in the grass curves are attributed to differences in adjacent and long-distance vegetation. The higher values, in general, at Lake Kimilili suggest that grasses

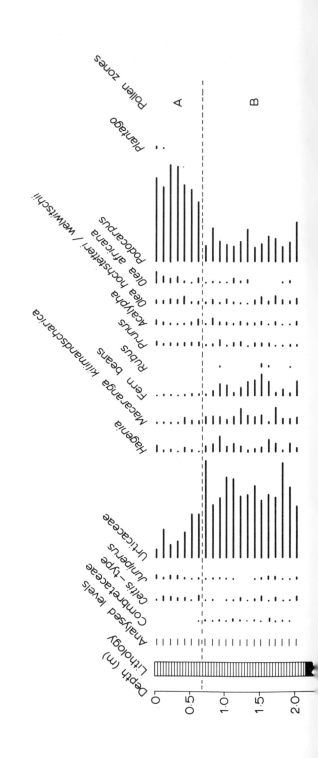

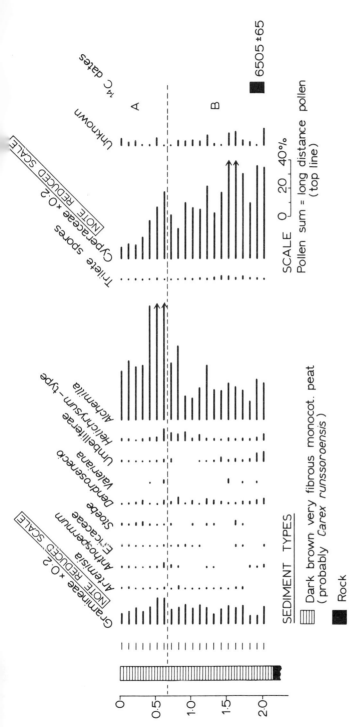

Fig. 44 Pollen diagram for Koitoboss Bog, Mt Elgon, Kenya, 3940 m.

have been a more prominent component of the vegetation on the drier slopes of the mountain; this is interesting, since it suggests that high altitude grassland was fairly widespread before the arrival of pastoral man. The lack of a decline in upper Zone A at Koitoboss Bog is attributed to the relative unimportance of human disturbance in its general vicinity.

The Koitoboss diagram contains higher values of *Dendrosenecio*-type, and lower values of *Artemisia, Anthospermum,* Ericaceae and *Stoebe* than does the diagram for Lake Kimilili. The higher *Dendrosenecio*-type values could be a consequence of a wetter climate at Koitoboss Bog increasing the vigour of giant groundsel trees (Appendix). In the case of the four Ericaceous Belt pollen types the lower values at Koitoboss Bog might have been caused by the parent species being on average situated at a greater distance. This assumes that much of the Ericaceous Belt pollen at Koitoboss Bog will have originated on the southern or western slopes and been carried not only upslope, but right across the caldera as well. These Ericaceous Belt pollen types are of low or moderate relative export ability and, with increasing distance from source, they are expected to assume lower and lower percentages in cases, such as this, where well dispersed pollen types are abundant in the pollen sum.

The third site sampled on Mt Elgon is Laboot Swamp situated at 2880 m near to the Kimilili Track on the southern slopes of the mountain (Figs 45 and 46). The vegetation of the catchment is mostly closely-grazed grassland, containing numerous *Stoebe* bushes. Forest occurs at varying distances on all sides of the swamp; the nearest patch is *c.* 100 m away and is a small secondary forest containing *Dombeya, Hagenia* and *Juniperus,* and smaller *Olea africana* and *Rapanea.* Settlements of pastoralists are present within 0·5 km and there is no doubt that the landscape has been much modified by man. Cattle frequently wander across the swamp, presumably causing some disturbance to the uppermost sediments. The swamp measures 750 × 50 m, follows the N–S run of a valley and has a gently-sloping surface. The dominant plant is *Pycreus nigricans* and this is accompanied by *Alchemilla ellenbeckii, Eriocaulon volkensii, Hydrocotyle* sp., *Lobelia aberdarica, Panicum* sp. and *Scirpus fluitans.*

Sediment stratigraphy was examined at three points along a transect and it can be seen from Fig. 37 that sediment has infilled a valley which had been previously incised into a rounded landscape. The commonest sediment type is clay, usually grey in colour and of various degrees of grittiness; there are a number of peat bands, including one at the surface. A bright orange layer, reminiscent of

Fig. 45   Laboot Swamp, Mt Elgon, 2880 m: general view. The swamp is surrounded by *Stoebe*-rich grassland.

that in the Lake Kimilili sediments is present at 38–49 (–52) cm and this suggests a fluctuating water table during more recent times. Samples were obtained for pollen analysis from 0–620 cm at Sample Point A and from 720–920 cm at Sample Point B. Four ^{14}C dates are available and two of these, 13 776 ± 80 and 23 073 ± 120 B.P., are for samples from close to the base of the sediments at Sample Points A and B, respectively. The disposition of the two sample points, and the stratigraphy of their sediments, makes it virtually certain that all samples collected from Sample Point B antedate 13 776 B.P. The rate of sediment accumulation has been very uneven, with sedimentation more rapid, on average, during the period 13 776–7385 B.P., when slightly over 4 m of largely inorganic material accumulated in the basin, than either after 7385 B.P. or between 23 073 and 13 776 B.P.

The pollen diagram has been divided into three zones, A–C (Fig. 47). Zone B (35–250 cm at Sample Point A) is recognized, not by the characteristics of its pollen spectra, as is usual with pollen zones, but rather by the state of preservation of its pollen. In contrast with the other zones, many samples from this zone proved to possess little pollen or else to have pollen in a very poor state of preservation. Detailed interpretation of the pollen spectra of Zone B is regarded as unwarranted and attention is concentrated on Zones A and C. Pollen preservation in many samples of Zone C is exceptionally good.

Fig. 46 Laboot Swamp, Mt Elgon, 2880 m: close-up of the mire showing the *Pycreus* tussocks and scattered dead inflorescences of *Lobelia aberdarica*.

At Lake Kimilili and Koitoboss Bog, it is reasonable to suppose that all montane forest and Ericaceous Belt pollen types are of long-distance origin throughout the diagrams and it is evident that the contribution of long-distance pollen to total pollen has always been high. It is thought that two factors will have helped to ensure that long-distance pollen will often have constituted a lower percentage of total pollen at Laboot. First, the mineral content of the sediment is usually very high and it is thought that much pollen is likely to have been transported along with the mineral matter into the basin from surrounding slopes by surface wash. Much of this pollen will have originated from adjacent vegetation. Second, this is a narrow mire lying within the Montane Forest Belt and montane forest has a high pollen productivity. Nearby vegetation is likely to have provided most of the pollen deposited, at least at times when montane forest occurred close to the bog. A surface sample from the swamp gives a reasonable image of present vegetation. Forty-five percent of pollen is derived from montane forest trees, particularly *Podocarpus* (33%), *Juniperus* (5%) and *Hagenia* (2%); Gramineae is 27% and both *Stoebe* and Cyperaceae have the rather low value of 6%.

In comparison with Zone C, Zone A, which dates to a period later than 5800 B.P., is marked by high values of *Podocarpus*, the frequent occurrence of various other montane forest pollen types and relatively low values of Gramineae. It is difficult to gauge the relative extents of grassland and forest in the vicinity of the swamp, but forest was clearly always present and the increase in *Stoebe* towards the surface was probably due to replacement of forest by *Stoebe* thicket as a consequence of man's activities. The cause of the decline in *Pteris*-type spores near the surface is uncertain. *Pteris*-type has a restricted distribution in surface samples from Mt Elgon, being encountered in some quantity only in those from grassland or mires surrounded by grassland at 2880–3400 m (Hamilton and Perrott, in press, a, in which the spore type is referred to as *Pteridium*). So far as is known, *Pteris*-type spores are produced only by *Pteris* and *Pteridium* among Elgon plants and, since *Pteris* is confined to forest and *Philippia* thicket and *Pteridium* to dense *Stoebe* or open *Philippia* thicket, much remains to be discovered concerning the indicator value of the spore type.

The most conspicuous feature of Zone C, which dates from before 23 073 B.P. to some time between 13 776 and 7385 B.P., is a very high percentage of Gramineae, always over 55% and in some cases exceeding 90% of the pollen sum (which is total pollen minus

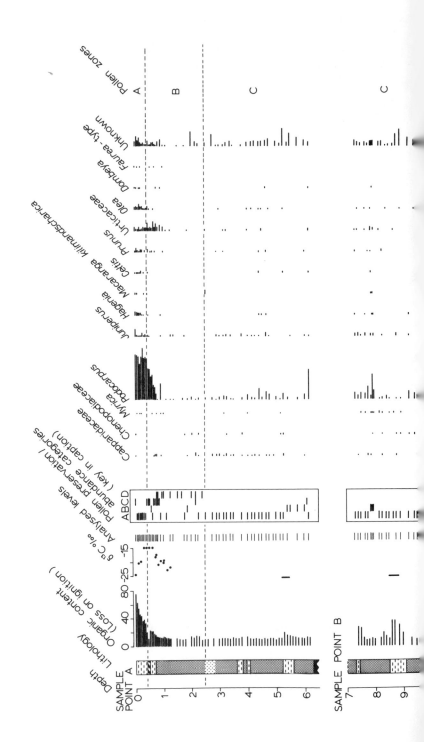

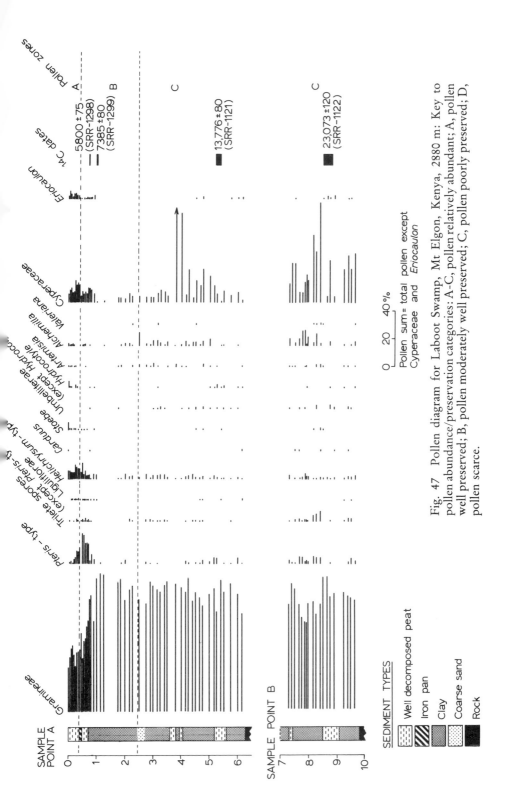

Fig. 47 Pollen diagram for Laboot Swamp, Mt Elgon, Kenya, 2880 m: Key to pollen abundance/preservation categories: A-C, pollen relatively abundant; A, pollen well preserved; B, pollen moderately well preserved; C, pollen poorly preserved; D, pollen scarce.

Cyperaceae and *Eriocaulon*). Grassland must have been very wide-spread in the general vicinity of the swamp (Appendix). It is possible that grasses may also have been common on the swamp surface at times of clay-rich sediment accumulation; a tendency for Cyperaceae pollen to peak during peat-accumulating periods indicates dominance by sedges at those times. Montane forest types are rare at most levels and in some virtually absent. As much of the montane forest pollen consists of types with high relative export ability, it seems that forest must have been of restricted distribution on Mt Elgon.

In contrast to Zone A, it is possible to estimate the general composition of forest on Mt Elgon during Zone C times. This is because the abundance of Gramineae pollen suggests that much of the tree pollen is likely to have been of long-distance origin. From the point of view of montane forest pollen deposition, the situation of the swamp is believed to have been analogous to that of a modern mire at high altitude on the mountain, the montane pollen being derived from a wide area and not being subject to bias in its composition as a result of juxtaposition of forest to the site. Table 7 is a comparison of the composition of the long-distance component of surface samples from the upper slopes of Mt Elgon with that in samples from a depth of 7·35–9·0 m at Sample Point B at Laboot. The same definition of the long-distance component is used for both sets of samples. The samples selected at Laboot date to somewhere within the period 23 073–13 776 B.P. It can be seen that the two spectra are remarkably similar. However, it is believed that the area covered by montane forest at this time was much reduced and there are some differences between the spectra that indicate that the forest was of a relatively dry type during Zone C times. *Juniperus*-type values tend to increase greatly in the uppermost parts of pollen diagrams from Mt Elgon, undoubtedly as a consequence of human activities, and thus the high *Juniperus*-type values of surface samples could be said to over-emphasize the aridity of the modern climate. It follows that the high *Juniperus* values of the Zone C sediments indicate greater aridity than now. The higher *Myrica* (Appendix), Capparidaceae and Chenopodiaceae values are other pointers to a drier climate.

Values of *Alchemilla* in Zone C are probably sufficiently high to show the presence, at least at times, of shrubby species of *Alchemilla* close to the site (Appendix) and this is also suggested by the scattered presence of *Valeriana* pollen. Shrubby Alchemillas do not grow at this altitude on Elgon now, being found only down to c. 3200 m and then only in the understory of Ericaceous thicket, and temperature depression is indicated. Pollen of Ericaceous trees and shrubs is very

Table 7   Comparison of the composition of the long-distance component of samples dating to between 23 073 and 13 776 B.P. from Laboot Swamp, Mt Elgon, with that of surface samples from the upper slopes of Mt Elgon

Pollen type	Samples from 7·30–8·95 cm at Laboot Swamp (a) % of total	Surface samples from upper Mt Elgon (b) % of total
Podocarpus	60·5	66·5
Juniperus-type	10·5	10·2
Urticaceae	6·6	7·6
Myrica	5·9	0·4
Olea	2·7	5·2
Prunus	2·7	0·8
Capparidaceae	2·7	0·0
Chenopodiaceae	2·3	0·2
Hagenia	2·0	2·9
Macaranga kilimandscharica	0·8	0·5
Thalictrum	0·8	0·0
Acalypha	0·4	1·2
Rapanea	0·4	0·7
Fern beans	0·4	0·5
Myrtaceae	0·4	0·2
Others	1·2	3·5
Total	100·3	100·4

(a)   Percentages based on the total numbers of grains encountered in all samples between the stated depths.
(b)   Mean percentages for all samples collected from >3500 m in 1976 (Hamilton and Perrott, in press, a). Counts standardized to Σ each count = 100. Most of the pollen in these samples is believed to be derived from forest on the drier aspects of the mountain.

rare: for example, out of 4795 pollen grains counted for the depth range 7 30–8·95 cm at Sample Point B, only two were *Anthospermum*, 38 *Artemisia*, three Ericaceae and eight *Stoebe*. The most obvious explanation is that the climate was too arid to permit much growth of microphyllous thicket and the greater importance of *Artemisia*, originating from the most drought-tolerant of the above Ericaceous Belt taxa, provides added support for this hypothesis.

There are similarities between Zone C at Lake Kimilili and Zone C at Laboot Swamp. In both, Gramineae values are high and *Podocarpus*, *Juniperus* and *Myrica* are the most abundant tree pollen types. The upper boundary of Kimilili Zone C is more precisely dated (at *c.* 10 500 B.P.) than the Zone B/C boundary at Laboot. In this context, it is worth noting that the greater part of Laboot Zone B is characterized by high Gramineae, very low tree pollen values and the presence of *Alchemilla, Helichrysum*-type and *Pteris*-type and this combination suggests that most of the sediments assigned to Zone B were actually deposited prior to 10 500 B.P. The period of very high sedimentation rate at Laboot is thus narrowed down to sometime between 13 776 and 10 500 B.P. and it is possible that a transition to moister climate allowed a rapid rate of soil erosion from a sparsely vegetated surface. Some of the samples in the upper part of Zone B contain quite high values of Urticaceae, as well as much Gramineae and Cyperaceae, and it is possible, though by no means proven, that bamboo forest was growing on the slopes around the swamp.

The fourth pollen diagram from Mt Elgon is for Scout Hut Swamp, a mire dominated by *Pycreus nigricans* and also containing much *Agrostis*. This small valley mire is only *c.* 20 m wide and lies at 3380 m close to the Kimilili Track. The vegetation of the catchment is burnt tussock grassland, containing frequent *Stoebe* bushes, as well as scattered individuals and groves of *Philippia excelsa*, particularly in rocky places. A pit was dug to a depth of 50 cm and the sediment was observed to consist uniformly of well-decomposed peat. Pollen was reasonably well preserved above 30 cm, but absent or very corroded between 30 and 50 cm, and in this there is a resemblance to Laboot Swamp. The pollen diagram (Fig. 48) shows comparatively little change, suggesting relative constancy in the vegetation. Neither Ericaceae nor *Stoebe* is abundant, but their percentages are more or less the same at depth as near the surface and the parent species have probably always been present in the catchment. The biggest change in the diagram is a big fall in *Pteris*-type spores above 5 cm. Since the parent species of *Pteris*-type are believed to grow in denser types of Ericaceous Belt vegetation, or in forest, but not in grassland, this could have been a consequence of an increase in the area of grassland through human activities. This explanation receives support from a slight increase in *Artemisia* in the upper few centimetres of peat.

Pollen Diagram for the Cherangani Hills

The Cherangani Hills (3370 m) lie along the western shoulder of the Eastern Rift, *c.* 120 km to the east of Mt Elgon. Judging by the account in Coetzee (1967), the vegetation has many similarities to that at appropriate altitudes on east Mt Elgon. Montane forest is of a dry type and there are only small patches of bamboo. Coetzee (1967)

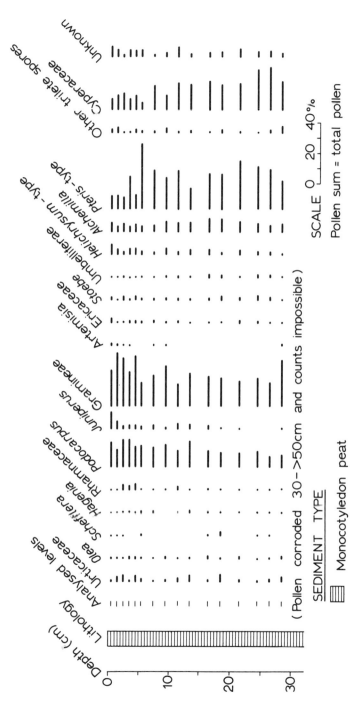

Fig. 48 Pollen diagram for Scout Hut Mire, Mt Elgon, Kenya, 3380 m.

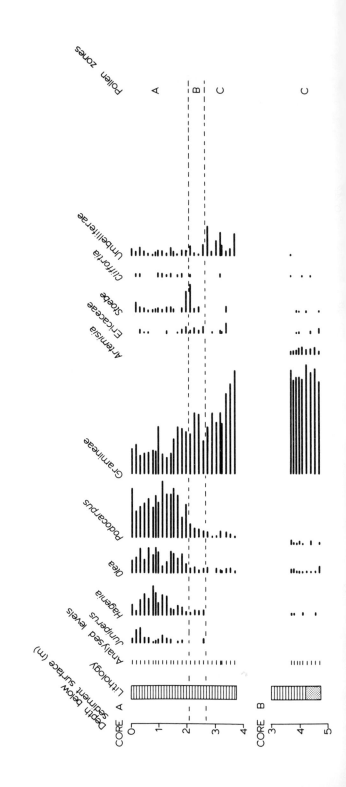

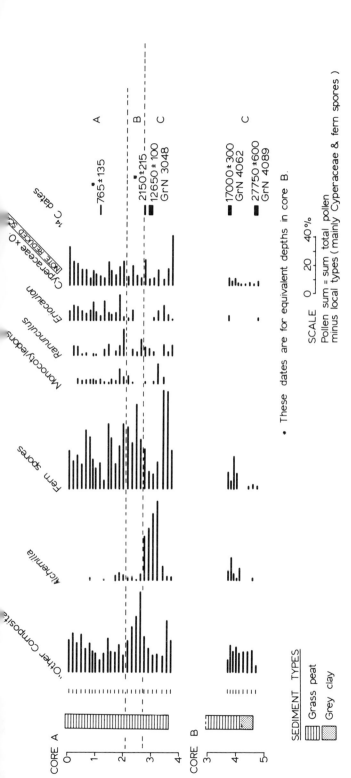

Fig. 49 Pollen diagram for Kaisungor Swamp, Cherangani Hills, Kenya, 2900 m. After Coetzee (1967). Redrawn from "Palaeoecology of Africa," with permission from A. A. Balkema and E. M. van Zinderen Bakker.

maintains that, at one time, bamboo would have extended to the top of the mountain and that it has been replaced by grassland through human activities, but it is debatable whether the climate is sufficiently moist to permit extensive development of bamboo forest. There is no proper development of Ericaceous thicket.

The pollen diagram is for Kaisungor Swamp (2900 m) in the south-west of the hills and covering long ramifications of a valley. The site is similar to Laboot Swamp on Elgon, both in altitude and general morphology. Van Zinderen Bakker (in Coetzee, 1967) includes the following species as occurring on the swamp: *Alchemilla ellenbeckii, Anagallis serpens, Carex* sp. nr. *elgonensis, Cyperus denudatus,* two Ericaceae species, *Eriocaulon schimperi, Kniphofia thomsonii, Lobelia aberdarica* and *Senecio johnstonii.*

Two cores were taken in the swamp, Core A having a length of 3·70 m and Core B of 4·70 m. The sediments are described as grass peat (really sedge peat?) throughout Core A and down to a depth of 4·17 m in Core B, with grey clay at 4·17–4·70 m. Pollen samples are available for Core A and for 3·70–4·70 m in Core B. The five ^{14}C dates obtained are shown on Fig. 49, on which it can be seen that the rate of sediment accumulation has apparently been very uneven. Coetzee (1967) maintained that the upper two dates for Core B are unreliable, the samples having been contaminated by more recent root material, and she based her temporal interpretation of the pollen diagram solely on the remaining dates. It is unclear why she regards contamination as having been significant in the case of the upper ^{14}C samples, but not the lower. The spatial relationship of the two cores is uncertain.

The pollen sum is total pollen, excluding, most importantly, Cyperaceae and fern spores. Three zones are recognized: Zone A has high tree pollen, particularly *Podocarpus*, Zone C has high Gramineae, sometimes high *Alchemilla* and low tree pollen, and Zone B is more or less intermediate, lacking such distinctive features as the other zones. In my opinion, Zone A, with its high *Podocarpus* values, is more or less equivalent to Zone A in the Mt Elgon diagrams. The high *Podocarpus* values of Zone A on Mt Elgon as compared with Zone B have been attributed to the effects of a drier climate. Mt Elgon and the Cherangani Hills are closely situated geographically and major climatic events at one locality would undoubtedly have also been experienced at the other. If this interpretation is correct, then the upper two ^{14}C dates for Core B, which were rejected by Coetzee, may indeed give a reasonable guide to the age of the sediments. We do not know the exact stratigraphic relationship between the cores, but we may note that the ^{14}C date of 2150 ± 215 B.P. is for 2·7–2·75 m in Core B and the *Podocarpus* rise occurs at depth *c*. 2·05 m in Core A.

Cherangani Zone C has many similarities to Laboot Zone C, suggesting vegetational similarities. The low tree pollen values indicate that there must have been little forest vegetation on Cherangani, as on Elgon, confirming that this was a period of marked aridity in the region. At Cherangani, the dates of the dry period are given as from at least 27 750 to later than 12 650 B.P. "Other Compositae" (*Helichrysum*-type), *Ranunculus* and, in some samples, Cyperaceae and *Alchemilla* are more abundant at Cherangani than at Laboot. These differences could have been due to wetter conditions or a more organic substrate on the swamp surface. The Cherangani mire is larger than Laboot and any increase in inorganic sedimentation may have been largely restricted to the margins.

Zone B is not considered at length here. If my view of the age of the sediments is correct, then sediment failed to accumulate or accumulated very slowly over a period roughly corresponding to that of Zone B at Lake Kimilili (*c*. 10 500–3700 B.P.). The reasons for this are discussed in a later chapter.

Cherangani Zone A is generally similar to Zone A of the high altitude Elgon diagrams. *Hagenia, Juniperus* and *Olea* are rather more common, and *Podocarpus* rather less common than in Kimilili Zone A: these differences could be due to the lower altitude of the site and its relative proximity to forest containing *Hagenia, Juniperus* and *Olea*.

Pollen Diagrams for Mt Kenya

Pollen diagrams have been published for two sites on the north-east slopes of Mt Kenya, Sacred Lake and Lake Rutundu (Coetzee, 1967). Sacred Lake, at 2400 m, is the lowest altitude site so far considered. It has a diameter of *c*. 250 m, with forest extending right up to the water's edge. The forest near the lake is classified as moist montane forest (Coetzee, 1967), though it is noted that the site is not on the wettest aspect of Mt Kenya. Trees found near the lake include *Afrocrania volkensii, Albizia gummifera, Chrysophyllum gorungosanum, Dombeya goetzenii, Macaranga kilimandscharica, Neoboutonia macrocalyx, Polyscias kikuyensis, Prunus africana, Strombosia scheffleri* and *Syzygium guineense*. Aquatics include *Cyperus articulatus, Nymphaea, Ottelia* and *Utricularia*.

The coring was made in the centre of the lake under a water depth of 3·5 m. The core has a length of 15·4 m (all depths measured from the water surface) and, excluding the upper 1 m, which was too soft to sample, consists of lake mud (4·5–13·3 m), organic-rich clay with some sand, gravel and tuff bands (13·3–14·92 m) and loam (14·92–15·4 m) (Fig. 50). Four ^{14}C dates are available, the oldest being 33 350 ± 1000 B.P. for the basal sediments. The pollen sum is total pollen excluding, most importantly, Cyperaceae, *Nymphaea* and fern beans. Four zones, A–D, are recognized.

The boundary between Zones B and A is marked by a sharp rise in *Podocarpus* pollen and considering the ^{14}C dates this could well be correlated with the *Podocarpus* rise on Mt Elgon. This is added evidence that there was an important change to drier climate in East Africa soon after 4000 B.P. Other tree pollen types present in Zone A include *Celtis, Macaranga kilimandscharica, Neoboutonia, Olea*, Proteaceae (perhaps *Faurea*) and *Prunus*: all but *Celtis* have moderate or low relative export ability and the parent trees of some of these pollen types were probably growing close to the lake. The forest may have had a similar floristic composition to that which occurs near the lake today.

Zone B (*c.* 11 000–3700 B.P.) is characterized by much lower values of *Podocarpus* than Zone A, and by higher values of *Afrocrania*, *Galiniera* and *Hagenia*. Taken together, these differences indicate increased rainfall. Gramineae values are higher than in Zone A, possibly due to the presence of extensive stands of bamboo somewhere near the lake (Appendix). Urticaceae pollen is surprisingly scarce, but this is true of all of Coetzee's pollen diagrams and perhaps this inconspicuous pollen type has been under-recorded.

Zone C, with a lower date lying somewhere between just after 33 350 and 14 050 B.P. and an upper date of *c.* 11 000 B.P., differs from the more recent zones in having substantial quantities of pollen derived from the following taxa characteristic of Ericaceous Belt vegetation: *Anthospermum, Artemisia, Cliffortia*, Ericaceae and *Stoebe*. Studies of modern pollen deposition show that little pollen is carried downwards from the Ericaceous Belt and deposited in the Montane Forest Belt. Values of the Ericaceous Belt pollen types as high as those encountered in Zone C must indicate the presence of the parent taxa close to the lake. Today the boundary between forest and the Ericaceous Belt on north-east Mt Kenya lies at an altitude of *c.* 3100 m (Coetzee, 1967). There was then apparently a lowering of the altitude of the upper forest boundary by at least 700 m, equivalent to a temperature at least 4·4°C below the present. It should be noted however, that none of these species is strictly confined to the Ericaceous Belt and the possibility that factors other than temperature change were responsible for this increase in Zone C merits serious consideration. This type of question is a recurrent one in the interpretation of East African pollen evidence. In this case, a number of features of the pollen diagram suggest that temperature is the main factor. First, the presence of one or two of the Ericaceous Belt taxa near the lake could fairly readily be accounted for by non-temperature factors, but the co-existence of all five is less easily explained in this way. Second, pollen types such as *Afrocrania* and *Neoboutonia*, which are of low relative export ability and which are produced by relatively low altitude taxa, are insufficiently abundant to indicate the presence of their parent taxa close to the lake. Third, all tree pollen types which are relatively well represented, for instance *Hagenia, Olea* and *Podocarpus*, have high or moderate relative export ability and their presence could easily have been due to long-distance dispersal from plants growing at altitudes below that of the lake.

It is thought that Sacred Lake Zone C is of comparable age to Zone C in the diagrams from Laboot Swamp (Elgon) and the Cherangani Hills. Compared with these other diagrams, Gramineae is less abundant and Ericaceous Belt and montane forest pollen types are more abundant, suggesting a denser vegetation cover. This, in turn, is attributed to a wetter climate, further evidence for which is provided by the constant presence, admittedly in low percentages, of *Macaranga kilimandscharica* and *Neoboutonia*. Both of these pollen types belong to species of moist montane forest and both are virtually absent from Zone C at Laboot and Cherangani. There are, however, some signs of drier conditions than at present at Sacred Lake during Zone C times; among these, we may note the relatively high quantities of *Artemisia* pollen (Coetzee, 1967).

Zone D, which includes the ^{14}C date of 33 350 ± 1000 B.P. towards its base, has many similarities to Zone C, suggesting similar environmental conditions. The principal distinguishing feature is higher *Hagenia* and there are slightly higher percentages of several other tree pollen types. Values of the Ericaceous Belt pollen types are such as to indicate the growth of their parent plants around the lake, and temperatures are believed to have been depressed compared with today. Possible explanations for the higher *Hagenia* compared with Zone C are slightly higher temperatures or a somewhat wetter climate.

The second pollen diagram (Fig. 51) is for Lake Rutundu, a 300 m diameter lake lying at 3140 m in the Ericaceous Belt. The adjacent

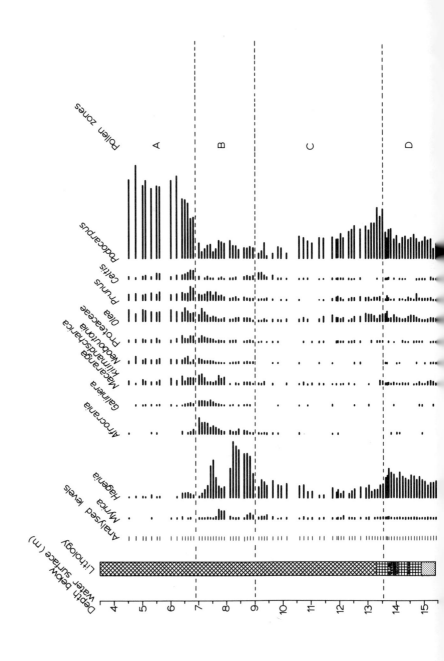

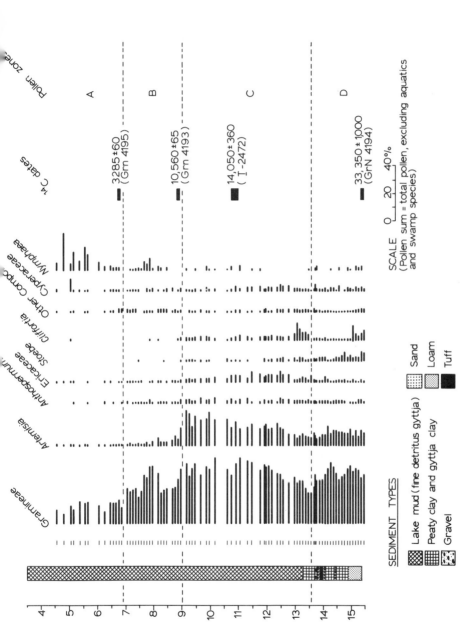

Fig. 50 Pollen diagram for Sacred Lake, Mt Kenya, 2400 m. After Coetzee (1967). Redrawn from "Palaeoecology of Africa," with permission from A. A. Balkema and E. M. van Zinderen Bakker.

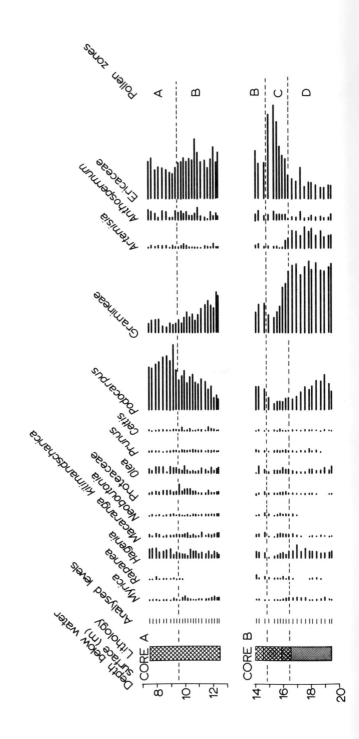

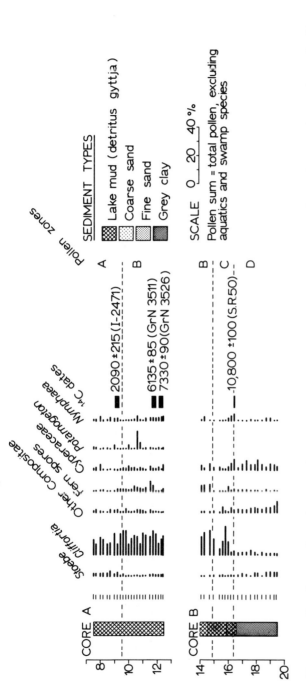

Fig. 51 Pollen diagram for Lake Rutundu, Mt Kenya, 3140 m. After Coetzee (1967). Redrawn from "Palaeoecology of Africa", with permission from A. A. Balkema and E. M. van Zinderen Bakker.

vegetation is grassland, containing shrubs of *Artemisia, Cliffortia*, Ericaceae and Proteaceae. Montane forest appears at a slightly lower altitude. Two cores were taken, Core A, collected 25 m from the bank and under a depth of 7·5 m of water, and Core B, extracted further from the shore and under 12·35 m of water. Core A extends to 12·5 m (depths from the water surface) and consists entirely of lake mud and Core B reaches 19·50 m and is composed of lake mud (to 14·5 m), detritus mud containing sand (14·5–16·55 m) and grey clay (16·55–19·5 m). Four ^{14}C determinations are available, the oldest being 10 800 ± 100 B.P. for the base of the sand-rich detritus mud. Pollen analysis has been carried out on samples from Core A and from 14–19·5 m in Core B. The pollen sum is total pollen, excluding, most importantly Cyperaceae, *Nymphaea, Potamogeton* and fern spores. Four pollen zones, A–D, are recognized.

Values of the pollen of Ericaceous Belt shrubs, *Anthospermum, Artemisia, Cliffortia*, Ericaceae and *Stoebe*, are probably sufficiently high to indicate the presence of shrubby Ericaceous Belt vegetation around the site throughout the period represented. The commonest montane forest tree pollen types in all zones are *Hagenia, Olea* and *Podocarpus* and these are likely to have always been of long-distance origin.

Zone D, which extends back from just before 10 800 B.P. to an unknown date, differs from the upper zones in having higher quantities of Gramineae and *Artemisia* and lower quantities of Ericaceae and *Cliffortia*. As with Sacred Lake Zone C, which is believed to be of comparable age, these differences are thought to be due to a somewhat drier climate than at present, and this interpretation is supported by the clay-rich sediment, this being attributed to a relatively high rate of soil erosion under a decreased vegetation cover in the catchment. Values of montane forest and Ericaceous Belt tree and shrub pollen are higher than in zones of equivalent age on Mt Elgon and the Cherangani Hills and this backs up the Sacred Lake evidence that Mt Kenya was relatively wet. It is difficult to read temperature changes from this diagram, but the record is thought to be quite compatible with temperature reduction during Zone D, as inferred for the correlated Zone C at Sacred Lake. The problem at Lake Rutundu is that the changes in adjacent vegetation consequent on increased aridity are so great that they mask any possible changes in vegetation due to lower temperatures which might have occurred.

Zones C and B, dating together from *c.* 11 000 B.P. to somewhere between 6135 and 2090 B.P., are similar to one another in most respects. The reduced values of Gramineae and *Artemisia* and the increased values of Ericaceae and *Cliffortia*, compared with Zone D, are believed to be the results of a moister climate. Forest tree pollen types, including those of the moisture-loving plants *Macaranga kilimandscharica* and *Neoboutonia*, are generally more abundant. The main difference between the two zones is that Zone C has a marked Ericaceae peak. Ericaceae pollen is rather poorly dispersed in the atmosphere (Appendix) and it is suggested that the high Ericaceae values, and also the sand present in the lake mud of this zone, are the consequences of a high rate of inwash. A possible explanation is that the change to a wetter climate at *c.* 11 000 B.P. produced a brief period of rapid erosion before the vegetation cover became adjusted to the new climatic regime.

The boundary between Zones B and A is marked by a rise in *Podocarpus* and judging by the ^{14}C dates this could be correlated with the *Podocarpus* increase at Sacred Lake and, indeed, also with those recorded for Mt Elgon and the Cherangani Hills.

Pollen Diagram for Kilimanjaro

The pollen diagram is for a small crater lake, 30 × 50 m in area, at 2650 m in the Montane Forest Belt on the south-east side of the mountain (Coetzee 1967). The forest type near the site is inadequately documented, but *Ilex* and *Podocarpus* are present though infrequent, and *Dombeya*, *Dracaena* and *Erica arborea* have also been noted. There is much *Juncus* cf. *effusus* growing in the crater, suggesting that the lake is ephemeral. The core has a length of 2·5 m and consists of fine detritus gyttja above 1·27 m and clay below. The two ^{14}C dates available are shown on Fig. 52. The pollen sum is total pollen minus, most importantly, Cyperaceae and fern spores. Two pollen zones, A and B, are recognized.

Zone B extends downwards from 1·75 m and is characterized by high values of *Ilex* and fern spores. *Ilex* pollen is believed to have low relative export ability and it seems certain that the single East African species, *Ilex mitis*, must have been common around the lake. I agree with Coetzee (1967) that the abundant *Ilex* and fern spores of Zone B can probably be attributed to a wetter climate than in Zone A and it is of interest that, according to the ^{14}C dates, the Zone B/A boundary falls somewhere between 1530 and 4620 B.P. and this could be of the same age as the *Podocarpus* rises noted in many of the other diagrams.

Hagenia and *Podocarpus* are abundant in both zones and *Dombeya, Galiniera, Mimulopsis* and *Newtonia* are all present at low

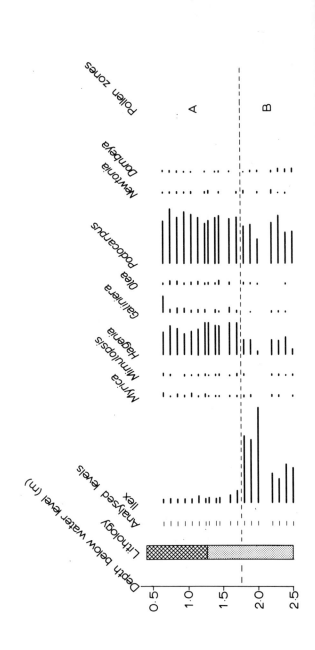

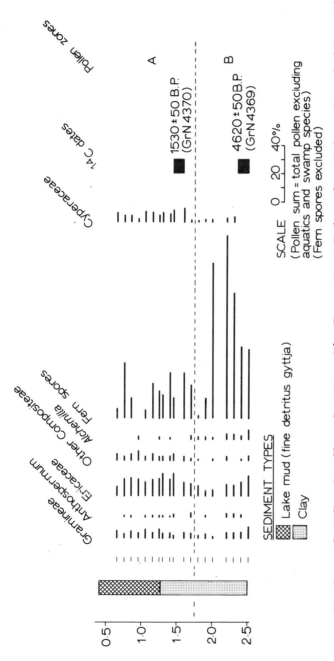

Fig. 52 Pollen diagram for Kilimanjaro, Tanzania, 2650 m. After Coetzee (1967). Redrawn from "Palaeoecology of Africa," with permission from A. A. Balkema and E. M. van Zinderen Bakker.

percentages. The last four pollen types are believed to have low relative export abilities and their parent taxa may well have been growing close to the lake. The Ericaceae pollen present throughout the diagram may have originated from *Erica arborea*, which still occurs in the proximity of the lake.

Pollen Diagrams for Ethiopia

Two Upper Quaternary pollen diagrams are available for montane Ethiopia. Both are for high altitude mires dominated by tussock-forming species (probably Cyperaceae) and lying within formerly glaciated valleys. One site is at 4040 m on Mt Badda, Arussi Mountains, and the other is at 3830 m in the Danka Valley, Bale Mountains (Fig. 53). Cores were collected by A. T. Grove and F. A. Street.

No detailed description of Ethiopian vegetation is available, but general accounts (Beals, 1969; Bonnefille, 1972; Hedberg, 1971, 1975; Logan, 1946; Lundgren, 1971) show that it is similar in many ways to the vegetation of East Africa, which is better known. At lower altitudes, deserts and bushlands with *Acacia* and *Commiphora* predominate, with *Acacia* and *Combretum* woodlands becoming common above 1000 m. Before clearance by man, forest must have covered much of montane Ethiopia. Surviving patches can be classified into five types, the distributions of which are related by authors to moisture availability and altitude. In wetter areas, that is mainly in south-west Ethiopia (Fig. 53), a forest type, similar to the Moist Lower Montane Forest Zone of East Africa and containing, *inter alia*, *Aningeria adolfi-friederici*, *Ekebergia capensis*, *Prunus africana* and *Syzygium guineense*, is found between 1200 and 2000 m and an *Arundinaria* Bamboo Zone is present at higher altitudes. Two types of gymnosperm-dominated forest are recorded in drier areas, one dominated by *Podocarpus gracilior* (the only species of *Podocarpus* known from Ethiopia) and the other by *Juniperus procera*, usually with abundant *Olea* spp. Gymnosperm forests are common in northern and eastern Ethiopia and extensive patches survive on both the Arussi and Bale Mountains. *Juniperus* forest is said to occur in drier regions than *Podocarpus* forest, but it is also likely that the fire- and grazing-resistant *Juniperus* has locally replaced *Podocarpus* as a consequence of human activities. Finally, between 2700 and 3300 m, in both moist and dry areas, these various forest types are succeeded by a forest type with much *Hagenia* and *Hypericum revolutum*.

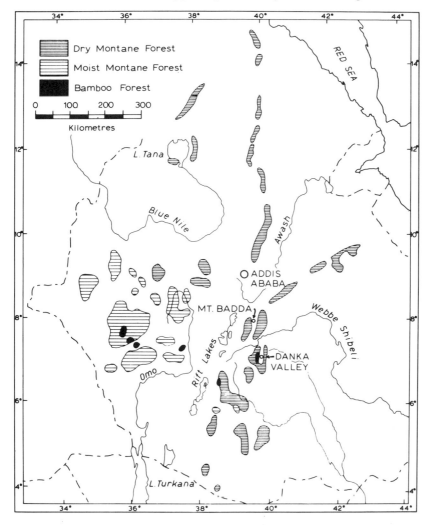

Fig. 53   Map showing forests and sites of pollen diagrams in Ethiopia. Forest distribution and types based on Logan (1946).

Ericaceous and Afroalpine vegetation is found above 3300 m. Badda Bog is surrounded by *Alchemilla* scrub and the lower altitude Danka site by burnt-over Ericaceous scrub. The latter is probably similar to that described by Hedberg (1971) for Mt Galama, Arussi Mts, where the most important dominant is *Philippia keniensis* and common associates are *Erica arborea* and *Helichrysum* spp.

There is great human pressure on all natural and semi-natural vegetation types in Ethiopia. Woodland is deteriorating rapidly, forest is being heavily exploited for timber and shrinking fast, and high altitude scrub is being replaced by grassland. Cultivation is practiced on very steep slopes and in some places extends up into the Ericaceous Belt. Most of the land which would naturally be occupied by gymnosperm forest is today taken up by grassland or montane scrub, the latter with *Carissa edulis, Dodonaea viscosa, Euclea schimperi*, etc. (Beals, 1969).

The core from Badda has a length of 3 m and consists entirely of peat. The five ^{14}C dates available for Badda show that the rate of sediment accumulation has been very uneven (Fig. 54). The three upper dates fall on a straight line, when plotted against depth, and this suggests a regular rate of sediment build-up between 4000/ 3500 B.P. and the present. Below the 3430 B.P. date for 183–200 cm, the dates obtained increase far more rapidly with depth to 7490 B.P. at 232–250 cm and 11 500 B.P. at 290–300 cm. Pollen spectra from 250 cm to the base of the core suggest a period of great aridity, such as is known from other evidence to have existed in Ethiopia prior to *c.* 10 000 B.P. The basal ^{14}C date is thus conformable with the pollen evidence. Pollen spectra between *c.* 250 and 200 cm are very variable and at some levels a large proportion of the pollen is corroded. The general impression is of slow and irregular deposition, perhaps with breaks in sedimentation and periods of erosion. This period of slow sediment accumulation is very roughly dated at 10 000 to 4000/ 3500 B.P. In my opinion the 7490 B.P. date for level 232–250 cm cannot be used uncritically in the calculation of sedimentation rates for this profile.

An investigation of diatoms in the peat has revealed an extremely rich flora, a testament to environmental heterogeneity, and a remarkable cyclic pattern of alternation between two quite different diatom assemblages (Gasse, 1978; Fig. 54). One assemblage is characterized by species indicative of relatively acidic and terrestrial conditions and the other by species of more base-rich and wetter environments. Large numbers of diatom valves in samples assigned to the first assemblage were found to be corroded. Gasse (1978) believes that the most likely explanation for the pattern is that there have been cyclic changes in climate, leading to alternate flooding and drying-up of the bog. She maintains that the rate of sediment accumulation at the site is shown by linear extrapolations between the top three, and the basal three, ^{14}C dates, an approach which reveals a sudden increase in sediment accumulation rate at 3500 B.P. (Fig. 54).

I find it difficult to accept Gasse's climatic explanation of the cyclic

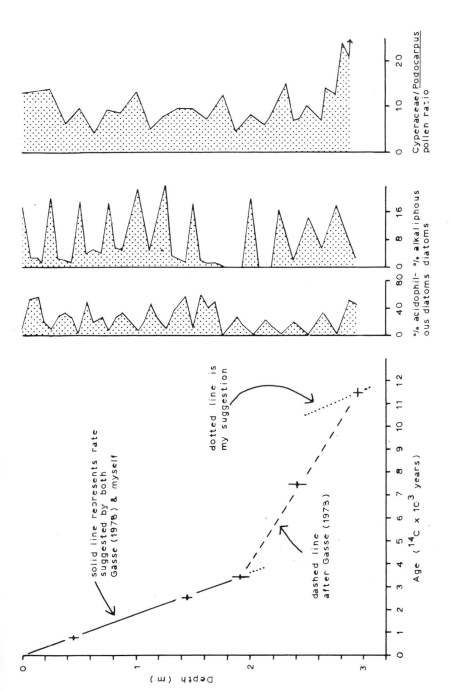

Fig. 54 Some properties of a peat profile of a bog on Mt Badda, Ethiopia. The diatom curves are after Gasse (1978) and are reproduced with permission of the editor of Revu Algologique.

changes in the diatom curves for the following reasons. First, the theory of regular climatic alternations is not supported by other evidence from eastern Africa. Second, it ignores the pollen evidence that level 2·5 m must predate *c.* 10 000 B.P. Although the shape of the bog has not been studied in detail, it is probably a sloping valley mire similar to those which are common on the East African mountains. In my view, the most likely cause of the diatom changes is a cyclic pattern of bog growth, related to the alternation at any one place of the tussocks and hollows of the dominant bog plant. The tops of the tussocks could have offered a suitable environment for diatoms of Gasse's first assemblage, and the inter-tussock hollows, enriched by nutrients carried by flowing water, could have constituted the environment of her second assemblage. It might be expected that there would be cyclic changes in the abundance of some pollen types, paralleling the diatom changes, and that these actually occur is suggested by a general correlation between changes in the Cyper-aceae/*Podocarpus* pollen ratio at Badda and changes in the diatom flora (Fig. 54). These pollen types were chosen to illustrate this point because of their abundance and different modes of origin. But Badda Bog has probably accumulated peat in two phases, separated by a period of no or little growth. During each phase of peat accumula-tion, the cycle of tussock growth and decay could have had about the same periodicity of *c.* 400 years.

The pollen sum is the long-distance component. Four pollen zones, A–D, are recognized (Fig. 55). A conspicuous feature of Zone D, which in my view antidates *c.* 10 000 B.P., is values of Chenopo-diaceae-type which are much higher than those which have been recorded in any other diagram from montane eastern Africa. Most of this pollen is of a distinctive type which, after a thorough search, has only been found in two eastern African species, *Chenopodium procerum* and *Suaeda monoica*. Pollen of *Suaeda* is the more similar. In Kenya, *Chenopodium procerum* is known as a herb of upland grassland and a weed of cultivation below 2600 m (Agnew, 1974) and *Suaeda monoica* is a bush which occurs on the landward side of mangroves and on the edges of salt pans (Dale and Greenway, 1961). High values of *Suaeda* pollen are recorded by Bonnefille and Vincens (1977) in some surface samples from arid *Acacia-Commiphora* savan-na to the east of Lake Turkana. Since Zone D easily predates the known age of cultivation in tropical Africa, the abundance of *Suaeda*-type pollen is taken to indicate grassland or, more probably, the widespread occurrence of salt pans. A much drier climate in Zone D times than in the other zones is suggested. Relatively high

Chenopodiaceae values are a feature of the zones dating to the pre- *c.* 10 000 B.P. arid period in many other pollen diagrams from eastern Africa; the exceptionally high values at Badda could have been due to relative proximity to extensive areas of exposed lake sediments in the nearby rift.

The most abundant montane forest pollen types in Zone D are *Podocarpus*, *Juniperus*, *Olea* and *Myrica*, together indicating that some dry montane forest was present on the Arussi Mountains. The high Cyperaceae/*Podocarpus* ratios towards the base of the zone (Fig. 54) suggest that *Podocarpus* was less common than at later times. Other signs of aridity are the low values of pollen types indicative of wetter environments, such as *Alchemilla*, Ericaceae, *Hagenia*, *Macaranga kilimandscharica* and Urticaceae, especially in the lower part of the zone. The high *Acacia* at some levels is very striking, especially in view of the poor representation of *Acacia* pollen in surface samples from *Acacia*-dominated communities. These high values may be due to both the widespread occurrence of *Acacia* woodland, perhaps in part replacing lower montane forest, and the presence of vegetation of very low pollen productivity around Badda Bog. Montane *Acacia* woodland could have been an early phase in forest development from montane savanna, as it is in the Lower Montane Forest Zone on Mt Elgon today. In contrast with pollen spectra of similar age from other mountains, values of Gramineae are low and Cyperaceae, *Alchemilla*, *Helichrysum*-type and Umbelliferae are very abundant. Either the effects of recent deglaciation or a somewhat drier climate could have favoured the development of *Helichrysum* scrub rather than grassland on the slopes around the mire; *Helichrysum* scrub is today a characteristic vegetation type of rocky ground in the Afroalpine Belt of the East African mountains. High values of Umbelliferae pollen have been found in surface samples from high altitude rocky ground communities on Mt Elgon (Hamilton and Perrott, in press, a).

Zone C is not interpreted in detail here. Only 50 cm, at most, of sediment were deposited during a period lasting an estimated 6000–7000 years, and the irregular pollen curves and the large numbers of eroded grains point to a very variable depositionary environment. A peak in Urticaceae suggests a moist climate.

The most abundant tree pollen types in Zone B (*c.* 3700–1850 B.P.) are *Podocarpus*, *Juniperus* and *Olea*, together indicative of dry montane forest. The pollen spectra have many similarities to temporally equivalent spectra for Mt Elgon and the Cherangani Hills, but *Juniperus* is more abundant at Badda, presumably as a result of

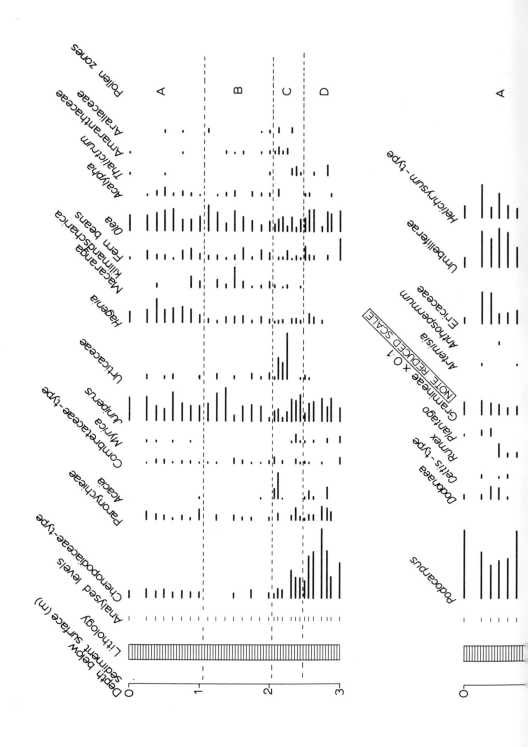

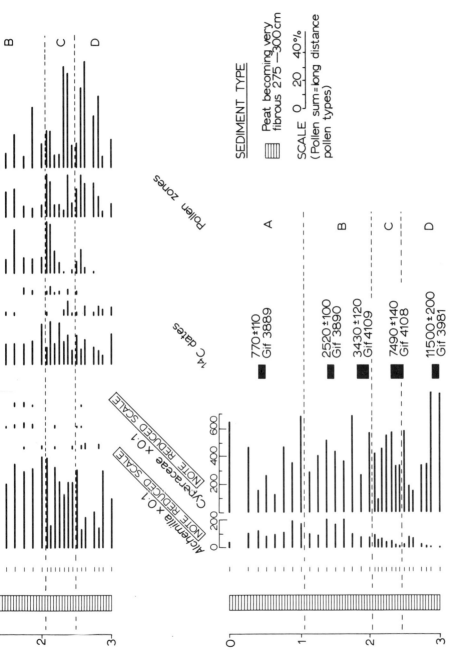

Fig. 55 Pollen diagram for Mt Badda, Arussi Mts, Ethiopia, 4040 m.

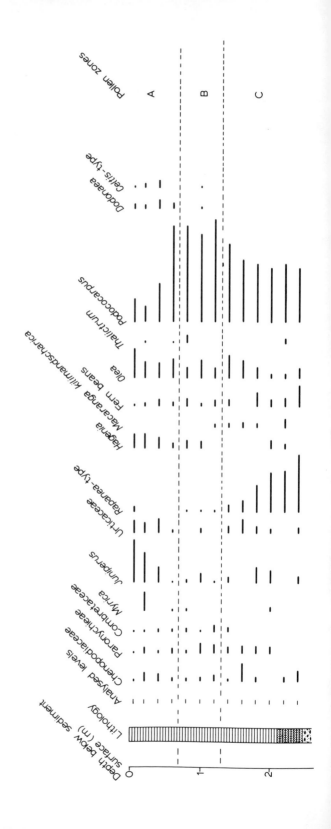

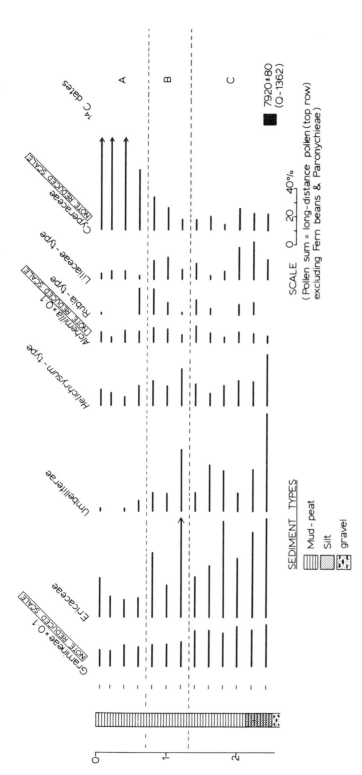

Fig. 56 Pollen diagram for Danka Valley Bog, Bale Mts, Ethiopia, 3830 m.

greater abundance of the driest type of montane forest on the Arussi Mountains. The existence of some moist montane forest is shown by the presence of *Macaranga kilimandscharica* pollen.

Changes in the diagram between Zones B and A can be interpreted largely in terms of human disturbance of the vegetation. There is believed to have been widespread destruction of *Podocarpus* forest (shown by the decline in *Podocarpus* pollen) and its replacement by secondary forest (with *Celtis* or *Chaetacme*), montane woodland (with *Dodonaea*, *Hagenia*, *Myrica*) and grazed and cultivated land (with Chenopodiaceae, *Plantago*, *Rumex*). The estimated age of the B/A boundary is 1850 B.P. This is the first pollen diagram so far described in this chapter which shows such massive vegetation changes consequent on human activity and the reason for this could have been a greater density of settlement from an early date on the Arussi Mountains than on many of the mountains of Kenya. On Mt Elgon, for example, a complete and fairly undisturbed montane forest girdle above *c.* 2100 m survived into the present century, but this was certainly not the case on some of the Ethiopian mountains, where vegetation degradation and soil erosion in the highlands has proceeded much further than in East Africa.

The core from Danka is 2·5 m long and comprises mud-peat, with much silt at 2·1–2·4 m, and a gravel floor (Fig. 56). A ^{14}C date of 7920 ± 80 B.P. has been obtained for basal sediments. The pollen sum is the long-distance component. Three pollen zones are recognized, A–C: A and B are believed to be correlated with Badda Zones A and B. Zone C at Danka dates to the period marked by a hiatus or very slow rate of sediment accumulation at Badda. The presence of dry montane forest on the Bale Mts throughout the period covered by the diagram is suggested by the continued presence of *Podocarpus* and *Juniperus*.

Signs of human disturbance in Zone A are taken to be the relatively high values of *Celtis*-type, *Dodonaea* and *Hagenia* and the relatively low values of *Macaranga kilimandscharica* and *Podocarpus*. A decrease in Ericaceae over the Zone B/A boundary may be a consequence of human disturbance at high altitude. The increase in Urticaceae could be associated with the opening-up of the forests. A contrast with Badda is a marked rise in *Juniperus*, reminiscent of that encountered in Scout Hut mire on Mt Elgon; again, human disturbance is taken to have been the cause.

The C/B boundary is marked by a rise in *Podocarpus*. This could be correlated with the *Podocarpus* increase seen in pollen diagrams from East Africa and have had a similar cause, namely a switch to drier climate. Moister conditions in Zone C, compared with Zone B, are also indicated by higher *Macaranga kilimandscharica* values and also by the large quantities of *Rapanea*-type pollen. *Rapanea* is said to be common in bamboo forest in Ethiopia (Lundgren, 1971).

Pollen Diagrams for Ruwenzori

Following exploratory work by Osmaston (1958), Livingstone (1967) has published pollen diagrams for three sites on Ruwenzori, Lake Mahoma in the Montane Forest Belt, and Lakes Bujuku and Kitandara, both in the Afroalpine Belt. Ruwenzori is the wettest montane locality to be discussed so far in this chapter. Montane forest grades down into the lowland forest of the Congo basin on the north-west part of the mountain range and there are extensive patches of lowland forest, remnants of a once more extensive lowland forest cover, lying close to Ruwenzori to the east.

Lake Mahoma occupies a kettlehole at 2960 m on moraines of the Mahoma Lake Glaciation. The vegetation around the lake is mainly bamboo forest, containing scattered Ericaceae, *Podocarpus* and *Rapanea* trees. The 6 m core was taken under 9·5 m of water and, except for a basal silt stratum slightly over 60 m thick, consists of lake mud. The base of the lake mud has been ^{14}C dated at 14 700 ± 290 B.P. Within the mud there is a sharp rise in organic content at 12 700 ± 120 B.P. and a slight decline over the upper 2·5 m. A band of volcanic ash at 2·3 m has a date of 4670 ± 80 B.P. The pollen sum used for the diagram is total pollen. Four pollen zones are recognized (Fig. 57).

The basal zone, D (*c.* 15 500–12 500 B.P.), differs radically from the upper zones. Tree pollen, as a group, is relatively scarce and the most abundant tree pollen types are *Myrica, Dendrosenecio*-type and *Hagenia*, with less frequent *Podocarpus, Olea* and Myrsinaceae (actually *Rapanea*, according to Livingstone, personal communication). Common non-tree pollen types include Gramineae, *Artemisia, Anthospermum* and *Alchemilla*. The abundant *Dendrosenecio*-type pollen is taken to indicate the occurrence of giant groundsel forest close to the site (Appendix) and, since dense groundsel forest is today found only above 3660 m, this seems to imply a temperature fall of at least 4·4°C compared with the present. *Artemisia afra* is the only species of *Artemisia* found in East Africa today, but it does not grow on Ruwenzori, probably because the climate is too wet (Livingstone, 1967). The presence of *Artemisia* on Ruwenzori during Zone D

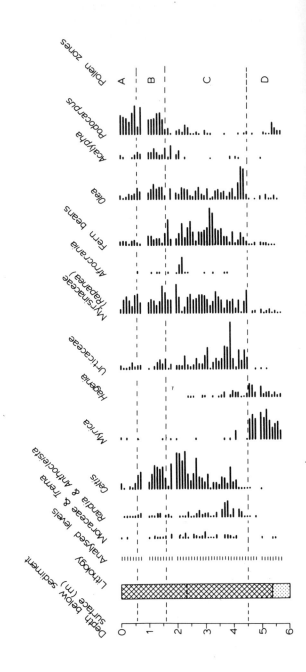

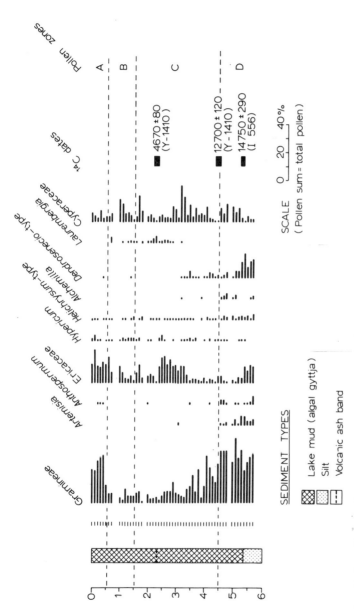

Fig. 57 Pollen diagram for Lake Mahoma, Ruwenzori Mountains, Uganda, 2960 m. Adapted from Livingstone (1967).

times, in conjunction with the relatively high Gramineae values and the relatively high inorganic content of the lake sediment, is evidence that vegetation belts were not only depressed, but also that the Afroalpine vegetation was of a drier type than is present on the mountain today.

Livingstone (1967) has argued against lower temperatures during Zone D on the grounds that the high values of *Myrica* pollen show that *Myrica* was growing in adjacent vegetation, a presence which he believed to be incompatible with a temperature fall. He proposed that the vegetation represents an early seral stage in the colonization of the fresh moraines. There are two objections to this theory. First, giant groundsels are not colonizing plants; they are slow-growing (Hedberg, 1969b) and would hardly be expected to compete well with some of the vigorous species of secondary vegetation which occur within the Montane Forest Belt of Ruwenzori. Second, the high *Myrica* pollen values do not necessarily imply that *Myrica* was growing in adjacent vegetation. Livingstone (1967) did not appreciate the low pollen productivity of high altitude vegetation, nor the fact that a pollen type with a moderate relative export ability, such as *Myrica*, can in some circumstances be abundant in a pollen diagram even in the absence of the parent taxon from adjacent vegetation. In my opinion *Myrica* and probably also *Hagenia* were growing at altitudes below that of Lake Mahoma. The abundance of *Myrica* is believed to be mainly the result of climatic dryness and the absence of some potential competitors (Appendix) and it is possible that it was also encouraged by the presence of the extensive moraines.

The pollen spectra of Zone C–A have many similarities to surface samples from the vicinity of Lake Mahoma and the vegetation is believed to have been approximately similar to today ever since 12 500 B.P. *Celtis*-type, which is common in Zones B and C, is believed to have originated largely from lowland forest growing around the mountain. Its rarity in Zone D is a sign of absence or rarity of lowland forest near the mountain, again indicating a dry climate before 12 500 B.P. (Appendix). High values of Urticaceae pollen are today associated with moist montane forest and it is interesting to note that Urticaceae is one of the first pollen types to increase around the Zone D/C boundary. As has been suggested for Lake Kimilili Zone C, the largely herbaceous parent species of Urticaceae may have been capable of rapid response to increased rainfall. *Olea* probably originated partly from *Olea hochstetteri*, growing in montane foest, and partly from *O. welwitschii*, in lowland forest. The *Olea* peak at the base of Zone C could reflect an early seral stage in lowland forest spread (Appendix). The bed of ash at 2·3 m may have been derived from an eruption in the nearby rift. *Afrocrania* pollen increases transiently just above the ash band, probably due to a positive response of the parent species to the ash fall (Livingstone, 1967; Appendix).

The main feature differentiating Zone B from Zone C is much higher *Podocarpus* and, extrapolating from the ^{14}C dates, the *Podocarpus* rise could well have occurred at about the same time here as on Mt Elgon (*c.* 3700 B.P.) and elsewhere in eastern Africa. In the case of most previously mentioned localities, the increase in *Podocarpus* pollen has been attributed to an increase in the population of *Podocarpus gracilior*. But *Podocarpus milanjianus* is the only species of this genus growing on Ruwenzori today. It is likely that in the past it occupied a similar position to the present, growing primarily on ridge tops where the effects of the slightly diminished rainfall would have been most marked. Just prior to the *Podocarpus* rise there is an increase in *Acalypha*. The *Acalypha* pollen was almost certainly derived from plants growing at lower altitudes than the lake, probably either in lower montane forest or lowland forest. Unfortunately, the indicator value of *Acalypha* pollen is poorly understood, but I suspect that a shift towards drier forest types is more likely to have been the cause of the *Acalypha* increase than human disturbance, as was suggested by Livingstone (1967).

Zone A (*c.* 1000 B.P.—present) is marked by high Gramineae, low *Celtis* and increased quantities of *Anthospermum* (probably here derived from the weed species, *A. herbaceum*). The most likely explanation is clearance of forest around the foot of the range by man and the consequent spread of grassland. Pollen diagrams from mountains further east in East Africa do not show any comparable evidence of changes in the abundance of pollen types following the presumed date of arrival of agricultural man and it is believed that the clear changes observed here reflect the higher pollen productivity of lowland vegetation in moister areas.

The two other pollen diagrams for Ruwenzori, both for sites in the Afroalpine Belt, are not illustrated here. The diagram for Lake Kitandara (3990 m) dates back to *c.* 7000 B.P. *Dendrosenecio* values are high and this and other evidence shows that the lake has lain within the Afroalpine Belt throughout the period. The diagram contains a *Podocarpus* rise, at a time roughly corresponding with the Zone C/B boundary at Mahoma, and a Gramineae increase and *Celtis* decrease, at about the time of the Mahoma B/A boundary. The diagram thus confirms the widespread nature of the vegetation events which gave rise to these changes. The diagram for Lake Bujuku (3920 m) extends back *c*. 3000 years. A surprising feature is that lake sediment extends down only *c*. 1 m from the mud/surface interface and is underlain by gravelly peat; Livingstone (1967) has suggested that the lake originated by blocking of the valley by a landslide. *Alchemilla*, Cyperaceae and *Dendrosenecio* are generally abundant pollen types. A Gramineae rise and a *Celtis* fall are present as at the other Ruwenzori sites.

Pollen Diagrams for the Rukiga Highlands (S.W. Uganda)

Four pollen diagrams have been published for the Rukiga Highlands of south-west Uganda (Morrison, 1961, 1968; Morrison and Hamilton, 1974). These hills form part of the eastern shoulder of the Western Rift and are composed predominantly of Precambrian mudstones, shales and phyllites (Combe and Simmons, 1933). The topography is rugged and slopes are steep; valleys lie at 1800–2256 m and ridges at 2250–2500 m. Many of the valleys contain mires and lakes, and there is great potential for palynological work. The topographic relationships of the four sites for which diagrams are available are illustrated on Fig. 58. The Rukiga Highlands lie close to

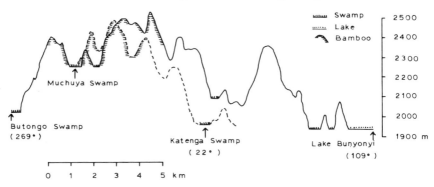

Fig. 58   Topographic relationships of sites used for pollen analysis in south-west Kigezi, Uganda. The transects drawn are from the sample site on Muchoya Swamp to the other sample sites. The deviations of the transect lines from north are indicated. After Morrison and Hamilton (1974). Redrawn from The Journal of Ecology, **62**, with permission from Blackwell Scientific Publications Ltd.

the Virunga Volcanic Field and themselves contain a few volcanic outliers in the form of ash cones, ash fields and lava flows. Indeed, three of the sedimentary basins for which pollen diagrams are available (Bunyonyi, Butongo, Katenga) are partially or completely blocked by lava flows. Unfortunately, only three ^{14}C dates have been obtained and these relate to only one of the sites, Muchoya Swamp. Two of the diagrams are perhaps chiefly of interest for their evidence of human disturbance and are mentioned in a later chapter.

The highest altitude site is Muchoya Swamp, a long mire lying at 2256 m within Echuya bamboo Forest (Fig. 59). The mire is dominated by *Pycreus nigricans* and there are scattered bushes of *Erica*

Fig. 59 Muchoya Swamp, Kigezi, Uganda, 2256 m. Most of the swamp is covered with *Pycreus* tussocks. It is surrounded by bamboo forest (Echuya Forest), with some grassland along the swamp margins.

kingaensis and, very locally, *Myrica kandtiana* (Hamilton, 1969; Morrison, 1968). The sedimentary sequence was investigated at several points by Morrison (1968) who showed that at one time the valley contained a lake which later became overgrown by mire vegetation. Fossil wood in the peat shows the former presence of a fairly dense cover of woody plants (Ericaceae and *Myrica*, according to the pollen diagram). Unfortunately, the diagram itself ends at a depth of 1 m below the sediment surface and from surface samples (Hamilton, 1972) and from comparisons with the Bunyonyi and Katenga diagrams it is certain that there must be major changes in pollen spectra associated with human disturbance within the upper 1 m of sediment. The pollen sum used for Fig. 60 is the same as in Morrison (1968) and includes a selection of both arboreal and herbaceous pollen types. Four pollen zones, A–D, are recognized. The diagram shows many similarities to that for Sacred Lake, Mt Kenya. The two sites are at comparable altitudes and are believed to have experienced similar environmental histories. Notice particularly the shapes of the *Hagenia* and Gramineae traces.

The uppermost zone, A, differs from the others in containing larger quantities of a variety of forest tree pollen types, including *Alchornea hirtella*, *Anthocleista*-type, *Ilex mitis*, *Macaranga kilimandscharica*, *Nuxia congesta*, *Olea* and *Podocarpus*. Some of these pollen types have low or moderate relative export abilities and it is likely that the mire was surrounded by moist lower montane forest. The vegetation was probably similar to that present today at the altitude of Muchoya Swamp in Bwindi Forest, a few miles to the north. Revising an earlier opinion, I now think that the bamboo forest present at Muchoya is a secondary vegetation type induced by human disturbance (see previous chapter). The base of Zone A is rather imprecisely ^{14}C dated at 6570 ± 95 B.P. and it is possible that the rises in *Podocarpus* and some other tree pollen types which occur within the zone may be correlated with the *Podocarpus* rises seen elsewhere in pollen diagrams from eastern Africa.

According to Morrison and Hamilton (1974), temporal equivalents of all or parts of Zone A are present in the Katenga and Butongo diagrams. As at Muchoya, these other sites were once surrounded by moist lower montane forest. Many of the differences in forest composition around the three mires, as indicated by the diagrams, are believed to have been due to the different altitudes of the sites. Morrison (1968) has suggested that high *Polyscias fulva* at Butongo may have resulted from human disturbance, but, both in the view of Robyns (1948) and also in my own experience, *Polyscias fulva* can be common in undisturbed montane forest: in Bwindi Forest, for example, the species is abundant on steep slopes very similar to those which surround Butongo Swamp. The greater abundance of *Afrocrania* pollen at Butongo and Katenga, compared with Muchoya, may be due to the proximity of volcanic outliers (Appendix).

Muchoya Zone B, extending very approximately from 10 000 to 6500 B.P., is characterized by high *Hagenia*. High values of *Hagenia* are also found in the basal zone at Butongo and Katenga and, while these may be of the same age as Muchoya Zone B, this is uncertain in the complete absence of ^{14}C dates from these other sites. Small porate grains (probably mainly Urticaceae) are abundant in Muchoya Zone B and tree pollen types present, in addition to *Hagenia*, are *Olea* and *Macaranga kilimandscharica*. *Hagenia* must have been common around Muchoya during Zone B times, but the environmental significance of this is uncertain. Today, *Hagenia* can be abundant in upper montane forest, in the Bamboo Zone, on volcanic soils, and under conditions of reduced competition in the Moist Lower Montane Forest Zone. Temperatures may not necessarily have been depressed compared with now during Zone B times and, considering other evidence for East African climates at *c*. 10 000–6500 B.P., the most likely cause of the abundant *Hagenia* was a very wet climate, perhaps with slight temperature reduction. High rainfall is also suggested by the abundance of small porate grains. It is of interest that a major change in vegetation apparently occurred at Muchoya at *c*. 6500 B.P., which is not known to be a date marked by large-scale vegetational change at other sites in montane eastern Africa. Further investigation is required in the Rukiga Highlands, with better dated pollen diagrams.

Zone C at Muchoya, which extends from *c*. 10 000 B.P. back beyond 12 890 B.P. to an uncertain date, is distinguished partly by the presence of *Stoebe* and *Anthospermum*, the latter presumably derived, in this case, from *A. usambarensis*. *Stoebe* is absent today from the Rukiga Highlands, though recorded from some of the Virunga Volcanoes outside Uganda; its presence, with *Anthospermum*, in Zone C suggests a colder and drier climate than now. Other signs of dry climate are high Gramineae, low numbers of small porate grains and fairly abundant *Myrica* (in these lower, lacustrine sediments, this is believed to have been derived from *Myrica salicifolia*). There are obvious parallels with zones of comparable age in diagrams from sites elsewhere in eastern Africa. The climate, though drier than now, was clearly not as arid as that which prevailed on Mt Elgon and the Cherangani Hills. The tree pollen types, *Hagenia*, *Olea* and *Podocarpus*, are fairly common and *Hagenia*, at any rate, was probably growing within the catchment, perhaps on upper slopes.

Zone D is not well dated. There is an increase in *Hagenia* and decreases in Gramineae, *Stoebe* and *Anthospermum*. There is considerable similarity with Zone D at Sacred Lake and, as with Sacred Lake, warmer or wetter conditions than Zone C are suggested.

Discussions of the history of wetland vegetation at the four Rukiga Highland sites are given in Morrison (1968) and Morrison and Hamilton (1974). The change to wood peat occurs at approximately

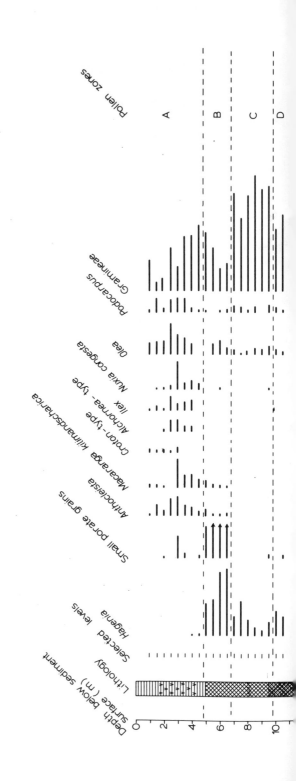

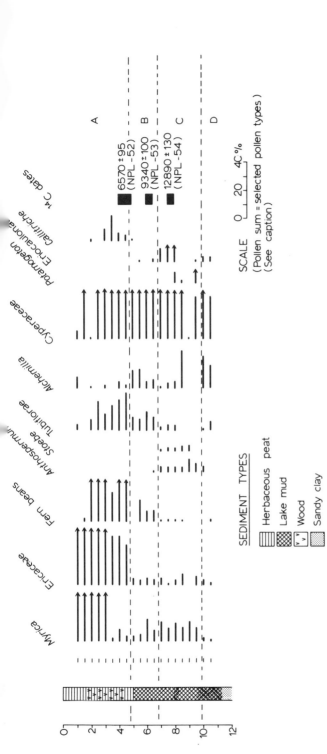

Fig. 60 Pollen diagram for Muchoya Swamp, Rukiga Highlands, Kigezi, Uganda, 2260 m. Adapted from the *Journal of Ecology*, **56** and reproduced by permission of Blackwell Scientific Publications Ltd. The pollen sum is total pollen minus pollen types regarded by Morrison as originating principally from plants growing in swampy or aquatic habitats. (Morrison, 1961, 1968).

the Zone B/A boundary, providing further evidence for a shift to drier conditions at this time (*c*. 6500 B.P.).

Pollen Diagrams for Rwanda

Pollen diagrams are available for two swamps in Rugege Forest in south-west Rwanda. One is the very large flat swamp at 1950 m known as Kamiranzovu Swamp and the other is a small sloping valley mire, Kuwasenkoko Swamp, at 2340 m (Fig. 61). The samples were collected by R. A. Perrott and myself in 1976, a year when it was becoming clear that during the last period of generally arid climate in tropical Africa there must have been an important forest refuge in East Zaire, probably with extensions into Rwanda and south-west Uganda. One of the objectives of working in Rwanda was to obtain fossil evidence of this refuge.

Rugege Forest and the forest on the Virunga Volcanoes in the north are the only two extensive forests remaining in Rwanda, a country with a very high population density and much land-hunger. Rugege Forest lies between (1700–) 1900 m and just under 2800 m and is situated on very rugged terrain similar to that found in Bwindi Forest, Uganda. Geologically, the area is dominated by schists and phyllites, containing occasional quartzite bands (Carte Lithologique du Rwanda). The forest is of a moist type, with a rainfall of *c*. 220 cm year^{-1} at 1950 m (Bouxin, 1976), and is floristically similar to Bwindi Forest, though richer in species. Deuse (1966) lists the following trees as being characteristic of montane rain forest in Rwanda generally: *Carapa grandiflora, Galiniera coffeoides, Podocarpus usambarensis, Symphonia globulifera* and *Syzygium parvifolium*, with *Hagenia* and bamboo at higher altitudes. Bouxin (1976, 1977) has made a detailed study of a small part of Rugege Forest situated in a flat-bottomed valley at 1950 m close to Kamiranzovu Swamp. In this area, where soils vary in depth from "several metres" close to the swamp to only 20–30 cm nearer the hills, floristic variation is related principally to soil moisture. *Anthocleista zambesiaca* and *Syzygium staudtii* are characteristic of the wettest places, *Balthasaria schliebenii, Begonia meyeri-johannis* and *Podocarpus milanjianus* are found on intermediate sites and *Carapa grandiflora, Impatiens* spp., *Isoglossa runssorica, Memecylon bequaertii* and *Olea welwitschii* grow on the driest ground.

According to my own observations, trees present in Rugege Forest at 2200–2400 m on the slopes above Kamiranzovu Swamp include

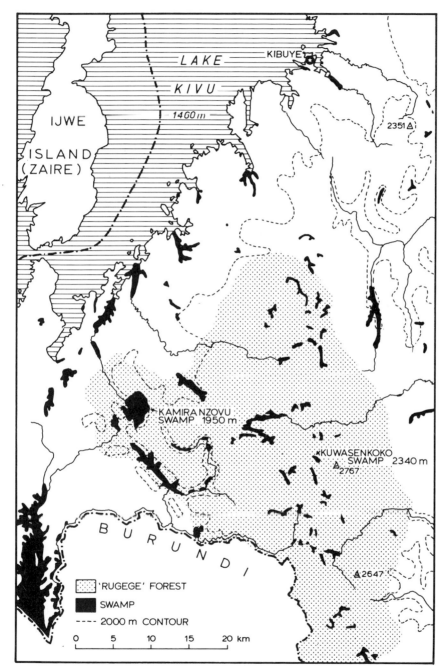

Fig. 61   Map of south-west Rwanda showing Rugege Forest and the localities of the
sites used for pollen analysis. Note: parts of neighbouring Burundi are also forested.

Alchornea hirtella, Allophylus sp., *Ficalhoa laurifolia, Harungana madagascariensis, Macaranga kilimandscharica, Maesa lanceolata, Parinari excelsa, Polyscias fulva, Schefflera* sp. and *Symphonia globu-lifera. Faurea saligna, Rapanea rhododendroides* and *Syzygium* cf. *guineense* grow on ridges and *Hagenia abyssinica, Neoboutonia macrocalyx* and tree ferns are abundant in gullies. Vegetation near Kuwasenkoko Swamp, at 2300–2400 m, shows inverted zonation, with lower montane forest containing much *Macaranga kilimandscharica* on upper hill-slopes and a zone of *Hagenia* below. Tree heathers to 5 m tall are locally present below the *Hagenia.* I did not see any bamboo in Rugege Forest and, according to informants, the plant is of very local occurrence in the forest.

Kamiranzovu Swamp (Figs 62 and 63) is considered first. The swamp itself contains one of the largest peat bodies in Africa and has a surface area of *c.* 13 km² (Bouxin, 1974; Deuse, 1966). According to Bouxin (1974) and Deuse (1966) the swamp is occupied by a central swamp forest with *Syzygium cordatum* and *Erica kingaensis,* an intermediate *Erica* zone and an extensive outer *Cyperus latifolius* association. There is a peripheral zone, with *Cyperus platycaulis.* According to my observations, the central *Syzygium* zone is domin-ated almost exclusively by *Syzygium,* growing to 7 m, and is rich in both shrubby and herbaceous species. Among others, I collected various Rubiaceae, *Begonia meyeri-johannis, Hypericum humbertii, Laurembergia tetrandra* and *Vaccinium stanleyi.* A small area of distinctive vegetation, with much *Hypericum revolutum, Lobelia gibberoa* and *Xyris capensis,* as well as many sedges and ferns, was present near the *Syzygium* forest. The *Cyperus latifolius* zone was seen to be wetter and poorer in species than the *Syzygium* zone; *Crassocephalum* sp., ferns and *Polygonum* were abundant. Near the margin of the swamp, close to the area of dense valley forest examined by Bouxin (1976, 1977), a number of trees and shrubs were seen growing in very wet conditions. These included *Anthocleista, Brillantaisia kirungae, Dichaetanthera, Podocarpus milanjianus* and *Schefflera.*

The sediments beneath Kamiranzovu Swamp were examined at one point, just within the margin of the central *Syzygium* zone. The upper 11·75 m of the 17·5 m core consisted of peat, generally very low in mineral matter, but with increases in inorganic material below 10·5 m and near the surface (Fig. 64). Sand was seen in a few samples above 50 cm and also occurred very rarely elsewhere. The peat itself was predominantly dark brown or red-brown, well-decomposed and usually containing abundant fossil wood (*Erica,* judging by the pollen

Fig. 62 Kamiranzovu Swamp, Rwanda, 1950 m. The swamp lies in the basin in the background and is surrounded by Rugege Forest. Lake Kivu lies over the hills in the distance.

Fig. 63 Kamiranzovu Swamp, Rwanda. This photograph was taken in a sedge-dominated area containing abundant *Lobelia*.

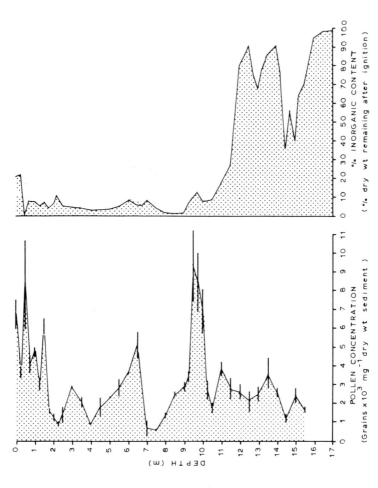

Fig. 64 Kamiranzovu Swamp, Rwanda: pollen concentration and inorganic content of sediments. Pollen concentration estimated by the method of Battarbee and McCallan (1974).

diagram). Monocotyledon fossils were scattered throughout, but only became abundant at *c.* 2·10–3·25 m and at 10·50–11·75 m, in the latter case to the exclusion of wood. It was thought that the material below 16 m was rotten rock.

Ten ^{14}C dates are available (Fig. 65). Two of these dates are for the lowermost organic band and are >43 040 B.P. for 14·65–15·00 m and 39 838 B.P. for the deeper layer of 14·9–15·25 m. The apparent reversal of these dates is probably because the samples are from parallel cores and I am inclined to accept both dates. All the other ^{14}C dates are internally consistent and are thought to provide an excllent dating framework for the sediments. It is thus of exceptional interest that sediment accumulated rather regularly from *c.* 40 000 B.P. to somewhere between 12 600 and 11 000 B.P., after which the mire surface apparently stagnated. It is noted that removal of peat by surface water flow is unlikely to be a significant factor in the central part of this huge and virtually flat mire with its well developed marginal wet zone. The cessation of peat growth must have been due to a climatic event and, since there is very widespread evidence (including from nearby Lake Kivu) of a major change to wetter climate in eastern Africa at *c.* 12 000/10 000 B.P. (which, in itself, would have resulted in inhibition of peat decomposer activity), it is inferred that when the peat was accumulating it must have been colder. The period of this temperature reduction extended from at least *c.* 37 630 B.P., marking the beginning of the formation of organic-rich peat, to sometime between 12 600 and 11 000 B.P.

Except for some samples from the basal clays and some from the upper 50 cm, pollen was found to be in an excellent state of preservation. Most of the pollen (Fig. 66) belongs to taxa thought to have been growing on the surface of the swamp; a low contribution of pollen from plants at greater distances is to be expected, in view of the huge expanse of the Kamiranzovu basin and the probably high pollen productivity of some of the wetland vegetation types. Dealing first with non-swamp vegetation, there is evidence of forest persistence throughout the period represented, but few signs of changes in forest composition. Pollen types derived from forest plants probably include *Acalypha, Hagenia, Macaranga kilimandscharica, Olea, Myrica, Podocarpus* and Urticaceae. A proportion of the latter three could have been derived from plants growing on the swamp. The lack of evidence for floristic change does not mean that such change did not occur. This large swamp is unsuitable for a detailed examination of forest history. Pollen of many taxa common in the forest today are

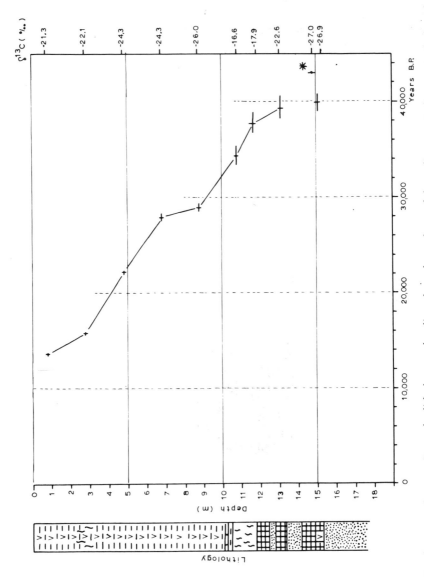

Fig. 65 Kamiranzovu Swamp, Rwanda: lithology and radiocarbon chronology of the sediments. Sediment symbols as for Fig. 66. The starred sample is older than 43 040 B.P.

clearly poorly dispersed and are unrepresented in the surface sample from the swamp.

Artemisia and *Stoebe* occur at low percentages in some samples and are taken to indicate the presence of dry types of higher altitude montane communities somewhere in the vicinity of Rugege Forest. *Stoebe*, although rare, was only recorded from samples between depths of 1·75 and 4·5 m, inclusive. This depth range dates to 14 500–21 000 B.P., which could well correspond with the poorly-dated phase marked by high *Stoebe* at Muchoya, south-west Uganda. The lowermost sample at Kuwasenkoko Swamp, with its single *Stoebe* grain, could well also belong here.

Five pollen zones, A–E, are recognized. Zones A (post *c.* 13 000 B.P.), C (*c.* 37 500–38 500 B.P.) and E (pre *c.* 39 500 B.P.) are very similar to one another. High Myrtaceae (*Syzygium*) and fern beans, and the presence of *Anthocleista, Begonia, Ilex* and *Impatiens* show the presence at the site of *Syzygium* swamp, such as is found at Kamiranzovu today. In Zones C and E, the existence of swamp forest is not surprising, in view of the inorganic nature of the substrate. Higher *Podocarpus* in Zone E suggests a drier swamp forest type than in the other zones. The presence of swamp forest in Zone A is presumably associated with cessation of growth of the mire surface, with perhaps better drainage and a greater availability of nutrients through decomposition processes. The latter would have been due to a greater recycling of nutrients and the steady accumulation of nutrients being recruited from outside the mire, either through surface water flow or in the atmosphere.

Zone D, lasting no longer than 39 500–38 500 B.P., is outstanding for its high values of *Cliffortia nitidula* and there is no doubt that the species must have been growing locally. From the point of view of substrate, conditions appear to have been favourable for development of *Syzygium* swamp forest and there must have been some other cause for the peculiar vegetation. *Cliffortia* is not known today in the vicinity of Kamarinzovu, but grows at the side of Kuwasenkoko Swamp (2340 m), a low altitude occurrence for the species, presumably related to temperature inversion. To account for the absence or rarity of *Syzygium* and the presence of *Cliffortia* in Zone D, it seems that there must have been a short cold spell and, since *Cliffortia* is not today regarded as a mire species, it must also have been rather dry. Dryness would also explain the higher Gramineae of Zone D, in comparison with Zones A, C and E. Possibly the deposition of the upper clay-rich band, just after the *Cliffortia* phase, was due to enhanced erosion following the onset of a moister climate. A similar

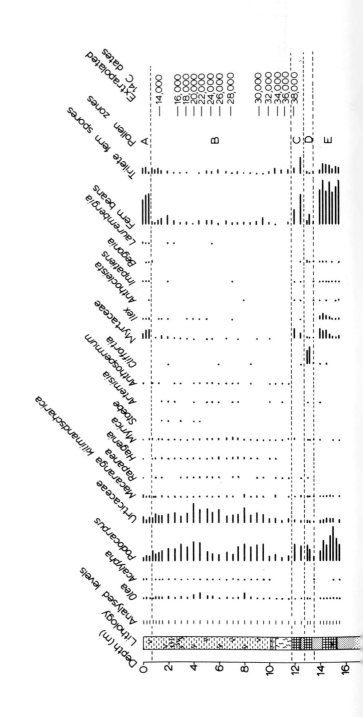

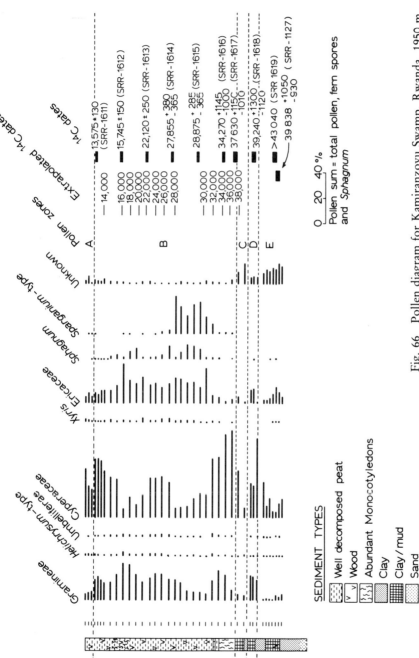

Fig. 66 Pollen diagram for Kamiranzovu Swamp, Rwanda, 1950 m.

explanation has been given for the high rate of inorganic deposition recorded in several basins during the period *c.* 12 000–10 000 B.P.

Herbaceous vegetation types, sometimes with *Erica*, were present at the sample site throughout Zone B (*c.* 37 500–13 000 B.P.), but big changes in the abundance of Cyperaceae, Ericaceae, *Sphagnum* and *Sparganium*-type show that substantial changes in mire vegetation did occur. Five subzones can be recognized. In the basal Subzone, Be (*c.* 37 500–32 300 B.P.), sediment lithology shows that the site was occupied by monocotyledons and this accords with high Cyperaceae in the diagram. During the remainder of Zone B, the sediment is rather uniform and it is likely that a community with *Erica*, *Xyris* and *Sphagnum* stood over the sample site for most of the period. The transition from *Syzygium* swamp forest in Zone C, to sedge swamp in Zone Be and then to the *Erica* community could have been due to increased wetness (greater rainfall or lower temperature) or perhaps to the process of vegetational succession, operating under constant external environmental conditions.

Subzone Bd (*c.* 32 200–28 000 B.P.) is characterized by high values of *Sparganium*-type and *Sphagnum*, and by an exceptionally rapid rate of sediment accumulation. Non-organic material is at a minimum (Fig. 64) and the site was clearly exceptionally wet and oligotrophic. *Sparganium*-type pollen is produced by the genera *Sparganium* and *Typha*, but *Sparganium* is not recorded from tropical Africa today and the pollen type at Kamiranzovu is not exactly matched by modern eastern African species of *Typha*. The palynologist, I. K. Ferguson of the Royal Botanic Gardens, Kew (England), is of the opinion that the pollen is probably *Sparganium* (personal communication). For a photograph of *Sparganium*-type, see Fig. 93.

Subzone Bc (*c.* 28 000–20 000 B.P.) contains high Cyperaceae and shows a return to a lower sediment accumulation rate. Judging by the lithology, the immediate vegetation of the sample site was still an *Erica* community and it is thought that much of the Cyperaceae pollen must have blown over from an expanded peripheral sedge zone. The sedge zone is thought to have a much higher pollen productivity than the *Erica* zone and this helps to explain a big increase in pollen concentration in the sediment (Fig. 64). The expansion of the sedge zone was rapid and cannot be explained by autogenic processes. The immediate cause is likely to have been an increase in nutrient inwash into the swamp. Cyperaceae values are lower, and *Sphagnum* values higher, in Subzone Bb (*c.* 20 000–15 800 B.P.) and there is a return to high Cyperaceae values in Subzone Ba (*c.* 15 800–13 000 B.P.), though, once again, the vegetation at the sample site remained the *Erica* community. Under the theory that expansion of the sedge zone is likely to have been induced by increased penetration of water from the periphery towards the centre of the mire, then the climates of Subzones Bc and Ba are likely to have been warmer or drier than Subzones Bd and Bb. Warmer or drier climates are also expected to increase the nutrient content of inwash water. It is suggested that climatic changes during the 32 200–13 000 B.P. period have been as follows: 32 200–28 000 B.P., wetter and/or colder; 28 000–20 000 B.P., drier and/or warmer; 20 000–15 800 B.P., wetter and/or colder; 15 800–13 000 B.P., drier and/or warmer. Since 20 000–15 800 B.P. is known from other evidence to have been a dry period in eastern Africa, this must have been a time of great temperature reduction, and likewise, since 28 000–20 000 B.P. is thought to have been relatively moist, then it can be postulated that this period was relatively warm.

A fairly extensive area of tussock grassland is present on the slopes around Kuwasenkoko Swamp. This is the only patch of tussock grassland seen in Rugege Forest and it is suggested that it has originated, at least in part, as a consequence of forest clearance, followed by repeated burning, during construction and subsequent use of a road which passes nearby. Plants seen in the grassland include abundant *Pteridium* and also *Anthospermum usambarensis*, *Blaeria* and *Lycopodium*. *Hagenia* trees, accompanied by *Hypericum revolutum*, are abundant near the swamp and marginal swamp species include *Cliffortia nitidula*, *Erica arborea* and *Osmunda regalis*.

The swamp is a sloping valley swamp c. 250 m long and c. 75 m wide. It is covered by large tussocks of *Pycreus nigricans*, c. 20 m tall, and contains *Xyris capensis* and species of *Alchemilla* (cf. *ellenbeckii*), *Anagallis*, *Carduus*, *Epilobium*, *Geranium*, *Helichrysum*, *Hydrocotyle*, *Kniphofia* and giant *Lobelia*.

The sediments at Kuwasenkoko Swamp were examined at three places along a transect; all points showed similar stratigraphy, with four conspicuously distinct horizons. The upper horizon, from 0 to 84 cm (depths relate to the sample point illustrated in Fig. 67), consisted of black well-decomposed peat containing some monocotyledon fibres. Earthworms were seen down to 30 cm. The second horizon (84–169 cm) was a grey loam, containing abundant angular sand and gravel particles of quartz and mica and also frequent large brown monocotyledon fragments. The third horizon (169–305 cm) was highly decomposed black mud, containing a few small monocotyledon fragments, some sand and a pebble band at 280 cm. The basal horizon (305–450 cm) consisted of sandy clay and rotting rock.

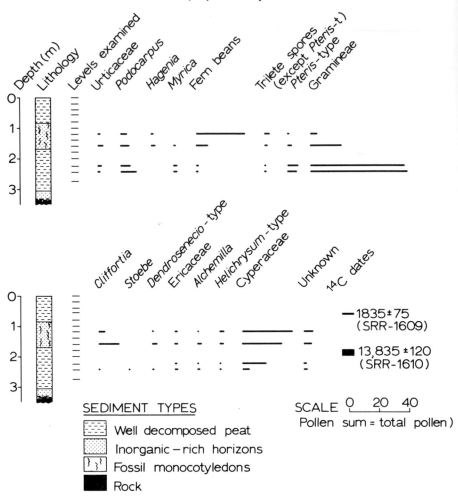

Fig. 67   Pollen diagram for Kuwasenkoko Swamp, Rwanda, 2340 m.

Two ^{14}C dates are available: 1838 ± 75 B.P. for 60–65 cm and 13 835 ± 120 B.P. for 180–200 cm.

A number of separate attempts were made to prepare slides for pollen analysis, but, in the event, only four levels could be satisfactorily counted (Fig. 67). Pollen at many levels was found to be scarce or badly preserved; the upper peat layer contained large quantities of fragmented grains. The four spectra which are available, however, are of considerable interest. Two of the spectra are for the lower peat and date to before 13 835 B.P. They are distinctive, mainly because of high Gramineae, and in this they resemble many spectra of presumed equivalent age from other parts of eastern Africa. It is thought that grassland must have been widespread on the slopes around the swamp and the climate was presumably drier than now. *Podocarpus* and *Myrica* are the two most abundant montane forest tree pollen types, another indication of dryness. The presence of *Stoebe*, albeit by only a single grain, is of interest, since this is a genus which is unrecorded from Rwanda today, but which is found in sediments of equivalent age both at Muchoya Swamp and at Kamiranzovu Swamp, the *Stoebe*-containing phase at Kamiranzovu being rather well dated at 21 000–14 500 B.P. The presence of Urticaceae, fern beans and a number of other pollen types suggests that the climate was not as dry as it was, say, on Mt Elgon.

The upper two spectra are for the sand-rich loam. The spectra resemble those from the basal peat in the types of pollen present, but have increased quantities of some pollen types produced by relatively high altitude species and which have low or moderate relative export abilities, for example, *Cliffortia nitidula*, *Dendrosenecio*-type and *Hagenia*; Gramineae is reduced. A possible explanation is that vegetation was similar at the time of deposition of all four samples, but that the upper two benefitted from an increased input of pollen by surface wash. That such wash occurred is, of course, clearly shown by the inorganic-rich sediment. *Dendrosenecio*-type is thought to have originated from giant groundsels growing in the catchment and this suggests a very extended range of *Dendrosenecio* in this part of eastern Africa, requiring considerably lower temperatures than at present. Judging by better dated evidence for the time of temperature depression in other diagrams, it is thought that deposition of the sand-rich loam must predate *c.* 12 000/10 000 B.P. The large sizes of many mineral particles in the loam suggests a catastrophic event, or events.

Putting together the various strands of evidence, it is postulated that, before 13 835 B.P., vegetation in the vicinity of the swamp consisted predominantly of tussock grassland, with some giant groundsels, *Cliffortia* and *Hagenia*, the latter probably on upper slopes. A change to moisture climate resulted in a short period of rapid sediment inwash into the basin. Deposition of sediment in the basin has proceeded very slowly since *c.* 12 000/10 000 B.P. and, judging by the upper ^{14}C date, it is possible that peat accumulation recommenced only during the last few thousand years, as is thought to have been the case at Cherangani and Badda.

Pollen Diagrams for Nyika Plateau, Malawi

The Nyika Plateau (2606 m) lies to the west of Lake Malawi and stands in a region with a single rainy season, November–March. Much of the plateau consists of rolling, grass-covered country at an altitude of over 2135 m. Forest probably covers less than 5% of the total area and is stunted and confined to valleys, hollows and rocky places (Chapman and White, 1970). Genera recorded include *Afrocrania, Hagenia, Ilex, Myrica, Podocarpus, Prunus* and *Rapanea*. Other forest types are known at lower altitudes on the slopes and escarpments which surround the plateau. The extent to which the Nyika Plateau was forest covered when there was less human disturbance than now has been debated; Chapman and White (1970) postulate that much of the grassland is secondary. There is no evidence of past permanent settlement on the plateau, but there are numerous old iron-smelting works and the area must also have been visited by hunters and occasional herders.

Meadows (personal communication) has carried out palynological studies of sediments on the Nyika Plateau and has also investigated modern pollen deposition (his diagrams are unpublished). Cores were collected from two marshes, three from Mwala Dambo (maximum depth sampled, 620 cm) and one from Chelinda Bridge Dambo (maximum depth sampled, 220 cm). All four cores contain exceptionally high quantities of deteriorated pollen, 30% of the grains examined overall being unrecognizable. The significance of this high content of deteriorated pollen is uncertain, though physical damage during transportation and chemical damage, perhaps under oxidizing conditions or through burning, are regarded by Meadows as possible causes.

The marsh at Chelinda Bridge is *c.* 300 m wide and contains a stream for which there is strong evidence of past changes in channel route. The vegetation of the marsh is dominated by tussock-forming species of sedges and grasses. Grassland clothes the surrounding slopes, there is a zone of *Pteridium* on lower valley slopes, and the stream is lined by *Philippia benguelensis*. No forest patches occur in the immediate vicinity, but several large forest stands can be seen within 1 km in positions where they are protected from fire.

Sedge pollen, grass pollen and fern beans are the most abundant pollen types throughout the diagram and other relatively common pollen types include *Cliffortia*, Ericaceae, *Helichrysum*-type, *Rubia*, Umbelliferae and trilete spores. Forest pollen forms only *c*. 10% of total pollen in the lower part of the diagram and an even lower percentage above *c*. 80 cm. Meadows considers that grassland has dominated the surrounding landscape throughout the period recorded, which is dated by a ^{14}C determination of 2467 ± 97 B.P. for level 210–219 cm, near the base of the 220 cm long diagram.

Mwala Dambo is one of the largest swamps on Nyika. The vegetation is similar to that at Chelinda, with the exception that there are three small forest patches, with *Hagenia, Myrica* and *Podocarpus*, at the head of the valley only 100 m from the coring sites. The pollen diagram contains abundant Gramineae, Cyperaceae and fern beans, and Ericaceae, *Helichrysum*-type, Umbelliferae and trilete spores are fairly common. Tree pollen is generally less than 10% of total pollen and Meadows thinks that forest could never have been widespread in the region. The diagram is not well dated, but, judging by a ^{14}C date for a core from the swamp, the sediments extend back several thousand years.

An interesting feature of the diagrams for both sites is an increase in the Cyperaceae/Gramineae ratio near the surface. This is regarded as a consequence of maintained pollen production by sedges, which are abundant in the (largely unburnt) marsh, and reduced influx of Gramineae, due to an increased frequency of burning of the grassland around the marshes. The increase in the ratio is thus taken to mark an intensification of human disturbance at Nyika.

Meadows provides some further insight into the vegetation history of Nyika. Charcoal has been found in an organic clay horizon, which has been shown by two ^{14}C dates to have been deposited between 11 678 ± 165 B.P. and 9432 ± 135 B.P. Pollen in the clay is in poor physical condition, but the pollen spectra obtained are rich in Gramineae and Cyperaceae, suggesting that forest was not abundant.

Finally, in the context of this Nyika study, mention is made of palynological research by Tomlinson (1974) in the Inyanga Mountains of Zimbabwe. This is a plateau area, similar to Nyika in possessing a vegetation pattern consisting of a forest/grassland mosaic. Five cores of mineral-rich peat were obtained at altitudes between 2200 and 2400 m. Two ^{14}C dates show that sedimentation has occurred since *c*. 11 800 B.P. Tomlinson concludes from his studies that, as at Nyika, grassland communities have existed in the area for a long time.

Summary of Evidence for Upper Quaternary Vegetational and Climatic Changes in Eastern Africa Derived from Montane Pollen Diagrams

Taken together, the pollen diagrams available for montane eastern Africa provide a largely coherent picture of vegetation and climatic events during the Upper Quaternary. Working from the present back, we may note the following main stages:

(1)   Some diagrams show a phase marked by great human disturbance of the vegetation. The dating of this stage, which is hardly likely to be synchronous right across eastern Africa, is poor, but in no case is there evidence of much human disturbance before very roughly 2000–1000 B.P. Forest clearance can readily be seen in pollen diagrams from three localities: south-west Uganda, where slopes around some sites were stripped of a forest cover, high altitude Ruwenzori, thanks to the high pollen production of moist lower altitude vegetation types and high altitude Ethiopia, a country in which destruction of montane forest has been on an exceptionally large scale. Pollen diagrams from montane Kenya and Tanzania show rather little evidence of human disturbance, and this is attributed to a combination of relatively low pollen production by drier types of lower altitude vegetation and to the retention, to a large degree, of a forest cover on many mountains up to modern times. A decrease in grass pollen in some pollen diagrams from relatively dry areas is attributed to reduced grass pollen production with domestic stock grazing and more intensive burning.

(2)   The second stage was characterized by the widespread occurrence of forest and extends back to *c*. 3700 B.P. The climate appears to have been approximately the same as during stage 1. The base of this stage is distinguished in particular in many diagrams by an increase in *Podocarpus* pollen, which is attributed to the onset of drier climatic conditions.

(3)   The third stage is marked by a wet climate and an extensive development of moister vegetation types. It extends back from *c*. 3700 B.P. to *c*. 12 500–10 000 B.P. It is thought that at about the beginning of this stage there was an increase in rainfall to levels higher than the present and that this was accompanied by a temperature rise up to roughly modern conditions. There is

some evidence that major forest spread occurred earlier (12 500–12 000 B.P.) in the climatically moister areas of Ruwenzori and northern Lake Victoria (see next chapter) than in the drier areas of Mt Elgon, Mt Kenya and Mt Badda (11 000–10 000 B.P.). This is perhaps as might be expected (Livingstone, 1975), given the same percentage increase in rainfall in all areas, superimposed on moisture differences between the areas similar to those which pertain today. There is some evidence of a shift towards greater dryness in the climatically moist areas of south-west Uganda and Lake Victoria (see next chapter) at *c.* 6500–5000 B.P.

(4) The fourth stage is the driest and coldest, for which there is detailed evidence, and which extends back from 12 500–10 000 B.P. It includes a period of maximum world glaciation. According to the evidence from Kamiranzovu, maximum coldness dates to 21 000–14 500 B.P. Forest was greatly reduced in extent. Mt Elgon, Cherangani and the Arussi Mts were particularly arid, but fairly extensive forest persisted on Mt Kenya and in south-west Uganda and Rwanda. There was considerable depression of the upper limits of vegetation zones. The time of the beginning of this dry period is not well dated from the pollen diagrams. There was apparently little forest on Mt Elgon back to at least 23 000 B.P. and on Cherangani back to before 27 750 B.P.

(5) The fifth stage appears to have been slightly warmer and considerably wetter than stage 4. This stage probably came to an end at roughly 20 000 B.P. and includes the ^{14}C date of 33 350 B.P. from Sacred Lake. The period preceding 28 000 B.P. at Kamiranzovu was very moist and it is noted that there is evidence for a reduction in temperature in Lake Abhé at *c.* 30 000 B.P. Together this suggests that rainfall was higher before *c.* 30 000–28 000 B.P. than later.

(6) Judging by the evidence from Kamiranzovu, there was a brief cold, dry spell between 39 500 and 38 500 B.P.

It would be worthwhile studying the pollen diagrams further to investigate the lag which taxa show in response to climatic events. Certainly, there is evidence that *Juniperus* and *Myrica* populations only gradually declined during the moist third stage on Mt Elgon, and *Dendrosenecio* seems to have persisted for some time after the presumed date of temperature increase at Lake Mahoma.

Chapter 7

Other Palynological Evidence and the Plant Macrofossil Record

In this chapter, a miscellany of pollen analytical and plant macrofossil evidence relating to lowland environments is presented.

Upper Quaternary Pollen Diagram for Lake Victoria

A pollen diagram has been published for Pilkington Bay close to the northern shore of Lake Victoria at 1130 m (Kendall, 1969) (Fig. 68). The present vegetation around this side of the lake consists of a mosaic of forest, savanna (mostly derived from forest) and cultivated patches. The core is 18 m long and has been very well ^{14}C-dated with 28 determinations. The base of the core is c. 15 000 years old. The sedimentation rate, which is well established, has been rather constant throughout. Four zones are recognized.

In Zone D, dating to c. 14 500–14 000 B.P., pollen preservation is poor. At this time chemical and other evidence shows that the lake lacked an outlet and was much more chemically concentrated than it is today. The most abundant pollen types are Gramineae and *Podocarpus* and it is possible that these relatively large and robust grains may have been differentially preserved (Kendall, 1969). It is thought that the high grass values are probably due to the presence of savanna vegetation around the lake; forest was seemingly rare or

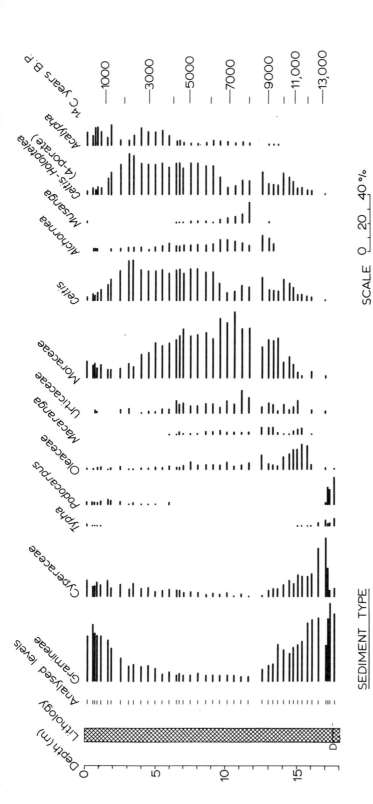

Fig. 68 Pollen diagram for Pilkington Bay, Lake Victoria, Uganda, 1130 m. Drawn from data in Kendall (1969). Note: The increase in *Podocarpus* and declines in Urticaceae and *Macaranga* are paralleled in several montane pollen diagrams and are probably attributable to increased aridity.

absent. The origin of the *Podocarpus* pollen is uncertain. *Podocarpus* spp. do grow in swamp forest near the north-west shore of Lake Victoria at the present time, but the aridity of the climate and the alkaline nature of the lake water would have been unfavourable factors for swamp forest development at 14 500–14 000 B.P. Aridity would also have precluded extensive montane forest spread in lowland Uganda. Perhaps a parallel can be sought with modern River Omo, which flows from a catchment in Ethiopia containing montane forest into Lake Turkana surrounded by arid savanna and which transports large quantities of *Podocarpus* pollen (Bonnefille, 1979). Highland areas to the east or, more likely, to the west of Lake Victoria are suggested as the source of the *Podocarpus* pollen.

Zone C extends from *c.* 13 500 to 9500 B.P. According to the chemical record, the lake started to overflow at *c.* 12 000 B.P. and, with the exception of a brief closed spell at *c.* 10 000 B.P., has remained open ever since. In the pollen record, there is a switch at *c.* 12 200 B.P. from high Cyperaceae and *Typha*, produced by swamp species, to abundant *Nymphaea*, implying higher water levels. Grass values are at first high, but from *c.* 12 000 B.P. these decline as tree pollen increases. There is a brief resurgence in grass pollen at *c.* 10 000 B.P. The most abundant of the early tree pollen types; is *Olea*, *Trema*, *Diospyros*, *Myrica*, Rhamnaceae and Rutaceae are also present. It is thought that a substantial amount of forest became established around Pilkington Bay.

Zone B (*c.* 9500–2000 B.P.) shows high quantities of tree pollen and it is believed that forest was the dominant terrestrial vegetation type around the northern Lake Victoria shore. Common pollen types include Moraceae, *Celtis*, Oleaceae, *Alchornea* and Urticaceae. Beginning at *c.* 6000 B.P., there are major shifts in the abundance of some pollen types, for example both *Celtis* and *Holoptelea* increase in abundance. Kendall (1969) interprets these changes as indicating the spread of semi-deciduous forest at the expense of evergreen forest, suggesting a somewhat drier climate.

Zone A (*c.* 2000 B.P.–present) is marked by an increase in the relative abundance of Gramineae and a decline in that of forest pollen. In terms of absolute pollen deposition rates, the decline in tree pollen actually begins earlier, at 3500–3000 B.P. It is difficult to ascertain the extension to which the decline in tree pollen could have been the result of human disturbance or of the onset of drier climatic conditions.

Pollen Analysis of Samples from Kalambo Falls

Kalambo Falls (1150 m), close to the south end of Lake Tanganyika, is one of the most important archaeological sites in eastern Africa, with a continuous record stretching from an Acheulian industry ^{14}C-dated at *c.* 60 000 B.P. to the present (Clark, 1969). The archaeological material is from sediments deposited in a basin just upstream from the falls themselves, the sediments consisting mostly of sands, with some clay bands, pebble horizons and fossil leaves and wood. Pollen analysis of samples from two of the excavations, Sites A and B, each of which is a few metres in depth, has beeen undertaken by van Zinderen Bakker (1969a). The vegetation near the site is mostly *Brachystegia* (miombo) woodland, with some riparian/swamp forest in the valley. Small patches of montane forest occur on hills at distances of over 10 km from the site and, very locally, lower altitude forest types can be found within the *Brachystegia* woodland (e.g. Siszya Forest).

The pollen spectra are generally rich in Gramineae and Cyperaceae and often contain frequent *Syzygium* and, less abundantly, *Myrica*. *Uapaca* is common in some samples and *Brachystegia* is regularly present at low percentages. Ericaceae can be common. An unusual feature is the abundance of Podostemaceae pollen in some samples (produced by specialized riverine plants). Montane forest pollen types are present, but never abundant: *Podocarpus*, for example, is always less than 7% of the pollen sum (which, *inter alia*, excludes Cyperaceae and Podostemaceae) and it is unlikely that montane forest ever occurred close to the site.

Van Zinderen Bakker (1969a) has classified the spectra into six zones, the same zonal sequence being recognized at Sites A and B, and has published a climatic curve showing a detailed correlation of temperature changes at Kalambo Falls with those reconstructed for Europe for the post-60 000 B.P. period. There seems now to be no justification for this early interpretation which predates nearly all work on pollen dispersal which has been carried out in East Africa. To mention just one problem, the climate of Zone Y is said to have probably been warmer and wetter than now, but the evidence for a warmer climate is based largely on the presence of *Alchornea*, *Combretum* and *Parkia* pollen and none of these is present in either of the two samples assigned to this zone at a percentage in excess of 1%.

In my opinion, the depositional environment at Kalambo has been too variable to allow a really good palynological record of climatic change, but, so far as it goes, the pollen evidence shows that the vegetation has not changed greatly during the period represented. Adjacent vegetation has probably usually consisted of *Brachystegia* woodland and there has generally been herbaceous and arboreal (*Syzygium, Uapaca, Myrica*) swamp vegetation in the valley. Perhaps the only indication of temperature change is the relatively high Ericaceae (8·7–12·2%) in the uppermost zone, Z, which, according to van Zinderen Bakker (1969a), may date to the Würm glacial maximum of Europe.

Upper Quaternary Pollen Diagram from Ishiba Ngandu, Northern Zambia

Ishiba Ngandu is a lake *c.* 1 × 5 km in area and lying at an altitude of 1400 m in northern Zambia. The lake is surrounded by *Brachystegia* woodland and there is an extensive fringing papyrus swamp. The maximum depth of the lake is *c.* 7 m and the core was taken under 6·5 m of water. The core consists of 3·5 m of lake mud underlain by slightly over 1·5 m of organic-rich sand, the latter considered to be a fluviatile deposit predating lake impoundment. A single ^{14}C date of 21 600 ± 400 B.P. relates to the base of the lake mud.

The pollen diagram shows comparatively little change throughout its length and contains high values of Gramineae and Cyperaceae. The Cyperaceae is probably derived largely from swamp and riparian species. The high Gramineae probably shows that the lake has been surrounded by some sort of savanna throughout the period represented. There is no evidence that either lowland forest or very arid savanna has ever been present extensively in the area. The diagram does contain considerable quantities of montane forest pollen, particularly towards its base, but, considering the abundance of Gramineae, it is unlikely that montane forest or scrub was ever of widespread occurrence in the area.

A difficulty in interpreting this diagram in detail is that many common savanna trees such as *Acacia, Brachystegia* and *Commiphora* are believed to have pollen of low relative export ability and therefore their former presence outside the extensive fringing swamp zone might not be well recorded in the lake sediments. In spite of this and given the general uniformity of the diagram, it is possible to distinguish three zones. The upper zone, A, extending from 0 to 0·5 m and believed to correspond very roughly to the period since *c.*

3000 B.P., is richer in Combretaceae, Myrtaceae, *Brachystegia* and *Acalypha* than the rest of the diagram and also contains reduced quantities of various forest and Ericaceous Belt pollen types, the former including *Alchornea, Celtis, Chlorophora, Hymenocardia, Holoptelea, Macaranga,* Meliaceae, *Myrica, Olea, Podocarpus* and *Rapanea,* and the latter including *Anthospermum, Cliffortia* and Ericaceae. Much of this forest and Ericaceous pollen is believed to be of long-distance origin and, taken together, the changes over the B/A boundary may indicate a reduction in the extent of wetter environments. This interpretation is certainly in accordance with much palynological evidence from eastern Africa, indicating a switch to drier climate soon after 4000 B.P. An alternative explanation (Livingstone, 1971) is that the changes may have been consequent on the arrival of iron-age farmers in the area; further research, perhaps involving smaller sedimentary basins in which the source of the pollen is better defined may help to resolve this matter.

Below 2·6 m and particularly in the basal sand (deposited prior to 21 600 B.P.), there are a number of changes in the diagram, most noticeably increased quantities of *Cliffortia*, which achieves > 15% total pollen in several samples. It is likely that *Cliffortia* was present in the neighbourhood, perhaps growing as a riparian shrub along the stream. This could have been partly a consequence of temperature reduction, an explanation consistent with other evidence from eastern Africa and which is believed to also have been a factor in the presence at one time of *Cliffortia* on Kamiranzovu Swamp, Rwanda.

Pliocene/Lower Pleistocene Pollen Spectra

Bonnefille (1970, 1976, 1979) and Vincens (1979) have investigated the pollen contents of Pliocene/Lower Pleistocene rocks in the Omo/Turkana basin (altitude *c.* 500 m) and in the Olduvai basin (altitude *c.* 1500 m). These investigations were inspired by the importance of these sites as localities for hominid fossils. Unfortunately, few of the samples collected have proved to contain sufficient pollen for adequate counts; for instance, only four samples from the Shungura Formation in the Omo valley and six samples from the Koobi Fora Formation on the eastern side of Lake Turkana have so far yielded spectra (Bonnefille, 1979).

Only the four samples giving pollen spectra from the Shungura Formation, ranging in age from just before 2·35 to *c.* 1 million years, are discussed here. The lithology varies, but all are from sedimentary deposits indicating fluvio-deltaic to lacustrine conditions. According to Bonnefille, the spectra are "composite", the pollen being derived from several different vegetation types. Gramineae is the most abundant pollen type in all samples and, considering this and other features of the pollen spectra, Bonnefille contends that the vegetation in the sample area was roughly similar at 2·35–1 million years to now, with montane forest at a distance in the highlands and tree/shrub savanna in the lowlands. The percentage of montane forest pollen (including *Podocarpus* and *Olea*) varies between the samples, with values ranging from 2 to 21%. Bonnefille argues that higher values are associated with wetter climates, being a consequence of either higher quantities of montane pollen transported long-distances in the atmosphere from enlarged montane forests in the highlands or else to a relatively greater input of pollen by water flow. It is noted that studies of modern pollen deposition suggest that much montane forest pollen is transported from montane forests in Ethiopia by the River Omo. The sample with only 2% montane pollen (E4; age 2·1 million years) also contains higher percentages of Chenopodiaceae/ Amaranthaceae pollen, another indication of dryness.

Two criticisms can be made about the use of montane pollen percentages as indicators of aridity in this context. First, the pollen sums include high percentages of pollen types of supposedly rather local origin, such as Cyperaceae and Gramineae, the abundance of which might be expected to vary considerably from sample to sample even under constant climatic conditions. Second, the representation of montane forest pollen in surface samples is used as a guide to palaeoclimatic interpretation, but this representation must be considerably reduced by recent widespread deforestation on the Ethiopian Highlands. Thus, it does not necessarily follow that the climate was wetter at times when the montane forest percentage in the rocks exceeds 9–12%, which is the range recorded in modern River Omo sediments.

At a level in the Shungura Formation below that of the lowermost of the pollen samples and perhaps of an age of *c.* 3 million years, fruits of *Antrocaryon* (probably *A. micraster*) have been found (Bonnefille and Letouzey, 1976). *Antrocaryon micraster* is a forest tree known from West African forests as far east as the Central African Republic and Uganda and the fossil fruits are taken to indicate the presence of tropical rain forest or galley forest in the Lower Omo valley at the time.

The Plant Macrofossil Record

There have been few studies of plant macrofossils in eastern Africa. The most thoroughly documented of the various Miocene floras which have been described (e.g. Chaney, 1933; Hamilton, 1968) is that from Rusinga Island, Lake Victoria, with identifications based on well preserved fruits and seeds (Chesters, 1957). The flora is rich in climbers and trees and the fossils are believed to have been derived from forest vegetation.

Plant macrofossils have been described from several localities within the Upper Quaternary volcanics of the Toro-Ankole field in western Uganda (Osmaston, 1965). Volcanism has been dated in the Fort Portal area to 4070 ± 120 B.P. (Osmaston, 1967). The finding of a leaf, a fruit and wood of *Parinari* in a swamp near Fort Portal in an area now used for intensive agriculture demonstrates the former presence of a forest type similar to that which still survives nearby, and Osmaston believes that forest extended continuously from Ruwenzori to Kibale Forest before clearance by man. The presence of *Celtis adolfi-fredericii* and probably also of *Uapaca guineensis* in the Fort Portal volcanics might have been due to slightly warmer and wetter conditions than pertain today. In contrast, plant macrofossils from nearby Lake George show no evidence of climatic or man-induced vegetation changes, with, for example, savanna being found in the Rift Valley near Lake George, as it is now.

Quaternary plant macrofossils have been found on Jebel Marra in western Sudan (Wickens, 1975). Identifications include *Combretum molle*, *Elaeis guineensis*, *Oxytenanthera abyssinica* and the genera *Lippia*, *Olea* and *Phragmites*. The presence of the oil palm (*Elaeis*) is of considerable interest since this is a forest species with its nearest known locality today 650 km to the south. The *Elaeis* fossils are perhaps a million or more years old and certainly do not date to the last wet climatic period as postulated by Wickens (Williams *et al.*, 1980). The fossil evidence provides little support to the theory that during the last major wet phase the climatic belts were shifted at least 400 km to the north (postulated by Wickens, 1975; see also Wickens, 1976).

Chapter 8

Distributional Evidence for Environmental Change

Introduction and Approach

The publication of "The Bird Faunas of Africa and its Islands" by R. E. Moreau in 1966 was a milestone in the development of thought concerning the environmental history of Africa. From our point of view, the outstanding significance of this work was its contention, for the first time reaching a wide audience, that Quaternary environmental events, particularly changes in climate, have been major determinants of the modern distributions of organisms in Africa. The principal model of Quaternary climatic change which Moreau used to help explain bird distributions was the pluvial theory, according to which glacial periods were marked by the existence of a cool humid climate over much of tropical Africa. Accordingly, each glaciation was said to have witnessed a great increase in the extent of montane forest, many of the now isolated patches of montane forest being connected together. Today, the pluvial theory is known to be substantially incorrect and it is a great tribute to Moreau that the many difficulties he encountered in trying to account for bird distributions in terms of the theory were frankly acknowledged.

The range within which any plant or animal species is able to survive and reproduce successfully is clearly restricted to those which possess an environment within the range of tolerance of the species. However, the distributions of species are determined not only by the present environment, but also by processes which have operated in the past, and most species consequently occupy only a part of their potential ranges. It is therefore theoretically possible to use contemporary patterns of species distributions as a source of evidence of environmental history. The clearest evidence is obtained by comparing the biota of two or more geographically distinct areas lying at present within the same general ecosystem type.

A simple model involving two areas of the same ecosystem type surrounded by other ecosystem types is considered here (Fig. 69).

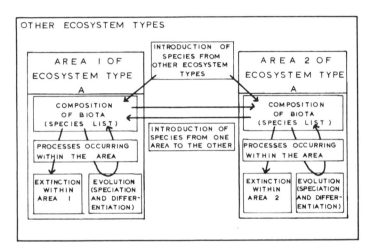

Fig. 69   Model showing some of the processes which determine biotic similarities and differences of two areas of an ecosystem type. The two areas could be geographically separated or contiguous.

This illustrates some of the processes believed to determine similarities and differences in the biota of two such areas and the general usefulness of distributional evidence for reconstructing the past. The processes concerned include introductions from one area to the other, evolution, extinctions and gains from other ecosystem types. The latter process involves a major shift in species ecology and is probably relatively unusual. As an example of the influence of environmental change on biotic composition, imagine that, as a consequence of a recent change in climate, one area of the ecosystem type, say Area 2 on Fig. 69, is much younger than the other (Area 1). Let us also suppose that it is fairly easy for species to move between the areas. Under these circumstances, it would be expected that Area 1 would be richer in species than Area 2 and that the biota of Area 2 would represent to a large extent an impoverished version of the biota of Area 1. If the determinants of the rates of the processes shown on Fig. 69 were sufficiently well known, it would be possible to estimate the dates of past environmental events from distributional evidence alone. In practice, however, some of the best evidence of these rates comes from comparisons of patterns of distribution with dated sedimentary evidence of environmental change. By itself, distributional evidence can usually only be used to erect a relative dating framework (e.g. by comparison of the degree of differentiation of taxa showing different disjunctions). Distributional evidence is valuable for providing a broad picture of general changes in past distributions of ecosystems, supplementing the more specific but much more geographically restricted evidence supplied by the fossil record.

Major changes in the distribution of an ecosystem in tropical Africa during the Quaternary would be expected to have produced similar responses in the distributions of species belonging to all taxonomic groups. However, the patterns shown by different groups are expected not to be identical, since the rates of some of the processes shown in Fig. 69 certainly differ in a gross way between at least some major plant and animal taxa. Comparative studies between patterns of distribution shown by different groups of organisms should provide many insights into the ecology and evolution of African organisms and herein undoubtedly lies a fruitful field for future research. A review of the literature (partly given in Hamilton, 1976a) shows that, to date, few distributional studies of African organisms have been inter-disciplinary. Interestingly, zoologists have shown a much greater willingness to resort to historical explanations to explain patterns of distribution than botanists, whose primary concern in studying distributions has been the erection of classificatory schemes.

Some ways in which the past can be reconstructed from distribution patterns are illustrated with reference to Fig. 70. The five cases shown all involve comparison of the distribution of a particular species with that of an apparently suitable ecosystem-type. In Cases a–c, the distribution of the ecosystem-type is continuous, while, in Cases d–e, it is disjunct. In Case a, the species occupies its entire potential range and there is no evidence to suggest either that the area of the ecsoystem-type has changed or that the species has recently evolved. In Case b, the distribution of the species does not correspond to that of its ecosystem-type. Possible causes might be recent expansion of the ecosystem-type or recent origin of the species, in either instances involving a relatively slow rate of spread of the species. In Case c, the

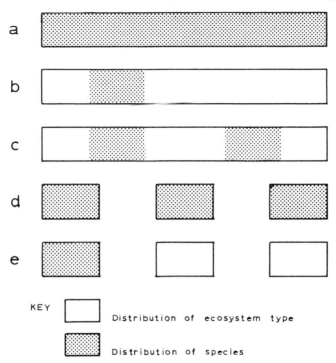

Fig. 70 Examples of distribution patterns. See text for explanation.

species not only occupies only part of its potential range, but it also shows a disjunct distribution. The origin of the disjunction could perhaps be a former contraction of the ecosystem-type into two disjunct areas, with a slow rate of expansion of the species following enlargement of the ecosystem-type. Alternatively, the species might have spread by "abnormal means" (long-distance dispersal) from one area to the other without occupying the intervening zone. In Case d, the species occupies all areas of its disjunctly distribution eco-system-type. This may be because the species has the capability of spreading from one area to another across intervals of unsuitable habitat or because the ecosystem-type itself was once continuous, allowing free movement of the species, and has later become fragmented by an environmental change. In Case e, the species is confined to only one area of a disjunctly distributed ecosystem-type. Possibly, all areas of the ecosystem-type are ancient and the species, having originated in one area, has lacked the ability to move to, or establish itself in the others. On the other hand, this distribution could also have arisen if the species is newly evolved or if the two areas of the ecosystem-type which are not occupied by the species are of recent origin: in these instances, the length of time involved may be relatively short and the species may eventually be able to spread to the other areas.

There is little observational evidence relating to the abilities of species to cross areas of unsuitable habitat. In the case of African forest birds, for example, the little evidence that exists is inconclusive (Moreau, 1966). In the absence of direct evidence, the morphology of a species or, in the case of a plant, of its dispersal organ, is sometimes used as a guide to dispersal ability. Thus, comparing the terrestrial mammals with the birds of an ecosystem type, many authors would hold that it is the birds, through their ability to fly, which are the more likely to cross areas of unfavourable habitat. Again, wind-dispersed plants possessing plumed seeds are generally regarded as more capable of long-distance spread than those with seeds which are winged (cf. Ridley, 1930).

In the great majority of instances there are many problems in determining environmental history from distributions shown by single species taken in isolation and it is usually much more reward-ing to work on patterns of distribution exhibited by large numbers of species considered together. There are several reasons for this. First, the importance of incomplete recording is generally reduced. Second, the confusing influence of "rougue" taxa is diminished. These are taxa with exceptional histories which have resulted in distributions at odds with general trends. For example, in a situation where a newly created area of an ecosystem-type stands adjacent to a long-established and biotically-rich area of the same ecosystem type, then the former might be expected to be an impoverished version of the latter. But, it is possible that the occasional species which has moved to the new area has later become extinct in the old, leading to a distribution at variance with the general pattern. Third, different taxa show different degrees of lag in their response to environmental change. Thus, in the event of an increase in the extent of an ecosystem-type, some organisms may rapidly occupy all of their potential range, while others are still confined to the old area of the ecosystem-type; considering also intermediates, the expected con-sequence of expansion of an ecosystem-type is a gradient of declining species diversity. Depending on the capacity of species for long-distance dispersal, this might occur not only when the ecosystem-type is continuously distributed, but also when it is disjunct (Fig. 71).

A critical decision in a study of distributions is the delimitation of

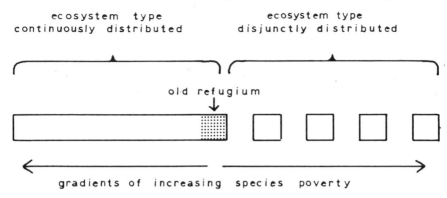

Fig. 71 Gradients of declining species diversity resulting from expansion of an ecosystem type.

the boundaries of the ecosystem type, within which the biotic lists are to be compared. Biological, physical and, particularly in the case of aquatic ecosystems, chemical attributes of the environment can all be valuable for determining whether areas should or should not be included within the same ecosystem-type. Species complements are among the most important attributes of ecosystems, but, since environmental change is believed to be a major determinant of species ranges, the degree of biotic similarity of different areas is obviously not an "absolute" guide as to whether they should be included within the same ecosystem category. It is inevitable that there frequently remains uncertainty over the best way to classify ecosystems for distributional investigations.

Three ecosystem-types have been selected for discussion here: freshwater, forest and Afroalpine. Within these, attention is directed towards groups of organisms which have been well studied. The area considered is generally tropical Africa as a whole since the explanation of local patterns often becomes more apparent in the light of features seen on a broader scale.

The Inland Water Fauna

The distributions of aquatic animals, particularly fishes, have been used to reconstruct the history of African lakes and rivers (information based largely on Beadle, 1974, with modifications after Greenwood, 1974.) Both climatic and geological changes are believed to have contributed to the present pattern. Specialized organisms are found in very saline and very oligotrophic lakes and there are biotic differences between running rivers, still rivers and lakes. These differences apart, the physical and chemical properties of water bodies are much less important than historical factors for determining distributions (Beadle, 1974).

One of the main problems in interpreting the evidence is establishing the extent to which species can migrate between water systems. Although the watersheds between many African river basins are rather flat, providing occasional water connections between opposing tributaries, it is thought that only specialized fishes are able to take advantage of this to achieve interchange, and that physical and chemical factors inhibit most species from approaching the upper reaches of streams. By far the majority of fish populations in the Nile, Congo and Zambezi basins, for example, are believed to be completely isolated from one another.

Although the matter remains controversial, Beadle (1974) believes that geographical isolation is essential for speciation in African fishes. He quotes the example of Nabugabo, a small lake isolated from Lake Victoria during the last 4000 years and containing no fewer than five endemics out of a total of nine species of *Haplochromis*. Rates of differentiation are believed to vary widely between groups of fishes. For example, compared with the non-cichlid fishes (lungfishes, catfishes, etc), cichlid genera such as *Haplochromis* and *Tilapia* are believed to be genetically plastic, speciating readily under suitable conditions. There has been some controversy over the possible role of predator differences between the lakes in promoting or resisting speciation (Beadle, 1974).

(a) *The Soudanian fish fauna*

The rivers and lakes of nearly the whole of Africa north of 5°N share a similar and relatively impoverished fish fauna known as the Soudanian (or Nilotic). Water bodies included are the Rivers Gambia, Senegal, Niger, Volta and Nile (south to and including Lake Mobutu), Lakes Chad and Turkana, and the isolated water bodies of the Sahara as far north as the Atlas Mountains (Fig. 72). This homogeneity suggests that there must have been widespread water connections during relatively recent times across the whole region from the Senegal to Lake Turkana. Increased aridity and the isolation of water bodies from one another has produced many disjunct distributions in the fish species within the region and

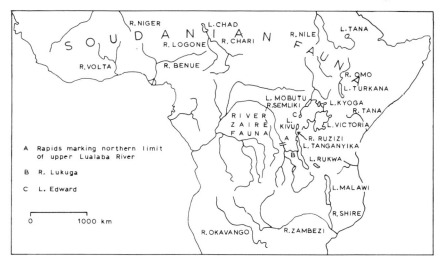

Fig. 72 Distribution of fish faunas in tropical Africa. Based on ideas in Beadle (1974).

contractions in the ranges of other aquatic or semi-aquatic organisms, such as the hippopotamus (Beadle, 1974).

In comparison with other areas, the impoverished fish fauna of the Soudanian region suggests that its water bodies as a group have been relatively unstable, probably due to past aridity. However, within the region some water bodies have apparently been more persistent than others. Thus, endemic species are particularly numerous in West African rivers flowing into the Gulf of Guinea, testifying to a greater maintenance of river flow than elsewhere. Again, there is only one endemic fish in Lake Chad, compared with 25–30 in the Chari-Logone river system flowing into Lake Chad, 13 in Lake Mobutu and 16 in Lake Turkana. It is known that Lake Chad has been subject to great fluctuations during recent times; the Chari-Logone system must have been more stable.

(b) *The Congo basin fish fauna*

The congo basin (taken as excluding Lake Tanganyika) is rich in fish species and endemics. The number of species recorded to date is 669 and it is thought that the total may exceed 1000. Of the 669 known species, 558 are endemic. These characteristics are attributed to persistence of river flow for a very long period, the existence of a wide range of habitats and prolonged isolation.

The fauna of the upper Lualaba River (Fig. 72) is largely isolated from the rest of the Congo River system by rapids. The fishes include many endemics, some Zambezian species (demonstrating previous connection with the Zambezi basin) and, surprisingly, several species which are identical with, or are subspecies of Soudanian species. The presence of the latter group, which is found elsewhere in the Nile basin but not in the remaining part of the Congo basin, suggests previous connection of the upper Lualaba River with the Nile system.

(c) *The fish faunas of the great lakes*

There are considerable differences in the numbers of fish species and endemics in the various great lakes of eastern Africa (Table 8). Lakes Tanganyika and Malawi are very rich in numbers of both species and endemics and all authorities agree that they must be long-established, probably for well over a million years. Lake Tanganyika is remarkable for the wide divergence of the non-cichlids, with no fewer than seven endemic genera, and is also renowned for extensive speciation in such non-fish groups as molluscs, crabs, planktonic copepods and Crustacea. The apparently marine character of some members of the fauna, especially some of the prosobranch molluscs, suggested to some biologists around the turn of the century that Lake Tanganyika is a remnant of a sea which during the Jurassic connected across the Congo basin with the Atlantic. Today, it is thought that the "marine" forms are all related to freshwater species found elsewhere in Africa and that their peculiarity is due in part to the great age and long isolation of the lake. Some of the "marine" features may be adaptations to the rough conditions frequent on the lake margin; high waves are often raised by strong winds funnelling along the lake between the walls of the rift and these create similar physical conditions on the shores to those found in the marine intertidal zone.

The fishes of Lake Victoria are believed to be descended from those which lived in the pre-Quaternary west-flowing rivers present in the area before the creation of the lake. Virtually all of the cichlid species are endemic, but the degree of taxonomic and morphological differentiation is lower than in the cases of Lakes Tanganyika and Malawi and the cichlid flocks appear to be of more recent origin. It is thought that environmental conditions have been less stable than in the case of Lakes Malawi and Tanganyika. The presence of species flocks of *Haplochromis*, each containing several closely related species with apparently identical feeding habits, is regarded as

Table 8 Fish faunas of various East African lakes (after Greenwood, 1974)

| Lake | Numbers of cichlids | | | | Numbers of non-cichlids | | | |
| | Species | | Genera | | Species | | Genera | |
	Total	Endemic	Total	Endemic	Total	Endemic	Total	Endemic
Victoria	c. 150–170	All but 3	8	4	38	16	20	1
Edward-George	c. 35–40	All but 5	4	0	17	2	10	0
Mobutu	10	4	2	0	36	3	21	0
Turkana	7	2	3	0	32	5	22	0
Malawi	c. 200	All but 4	23	20	42	26	19	0
Tanganyika	126	126	37	33	67	47	29	7
Nabugabo	10	5	4	0	14	0	11	0

explicable only as the result of some degree of separation of populations in the past and subsequent reunion after divergent evolution. Several theories have been advanced, including that of Kendall (1969) who suggests that high salinity during periods of low lake level may have driven fishes into inflowing streams, thus dividing species into several populations.

Lakes Edward and George, connected to each other by the Kazinga Channel, contain *c.* 100 species of cichlid fish. Many are endemic, but are related to forms in Lake Victoria suggesting early connection with Lake Victoria, followed by long isolation. The composition of the fish fauna of Lakes Edward/George suggests that the lakes are in the process of recovery and recolonization following partial extinction, possibly in part due to past aridity and in part to volcanic activity.

Lake Kivu contains only 16 species of fishes, with a further 16 species in streams and pools within the Kivu catchment. The fish fauna is mainly an attenuated version of that of Lake Edward and is practically unrelated to that of Lake Tanganyika. It is possible that the poverty of the Kivu fish fauna is due to extinction either at times of volcanism or during unusually violent storms bringing up oxygen-free and H_2S-charged water from depth.

Forest Organisms

At the present time there is usually little difficulty in deciding whether a particular tract of vegetation in tropical Africa should or should not be classified as forest. Likewise, forest plants and animals usually belong to different species from those found in non-forest communities. While undoubtedly largely a natural phenomenon, the clarity of the forest/non-forest boundary is believed to have been accentuated towards the present by certain human activities, especially regular burning in savanna ecosystems.

The possibility of distinguishing between different types of forest in tropical Africa has produced a divergence of views. In particular, there are two main schools of thought regarding the nature of altitudinal variation. According to some workers, the forest is divided into two well-defined and altitudinally-distinct ecosystems (lowland and montane) with few species transgressing the boundary between them. It is maintained that, because they are so distinct from one another, the two ecosystems should be treated as separate entities when considering the historical significance of the distribution pat-

terns shown by forest organisms. Moreau (1966) was a strong
proponent of this view, holding that the boundary between lowland
and montane ecosystems normally lay at an altitude of *c.* 1500 m. He
was impressed by the number of species which recur in patches of
montane forest geographically isolated from one another and believed
that the biotic homogeneity of montane forest was due to the spread
of species during glacial periods. An adherent of the pluvial theory,
he held that during glaciations a combination of lower temperatures
and a maintained or enhanced rainfall was reponsible for lowering the
lowland/montane forest boundary to *c.* 500 m, allowing a very great
increase in the extent of montane forest in tropical Africa (Fig. 73). A

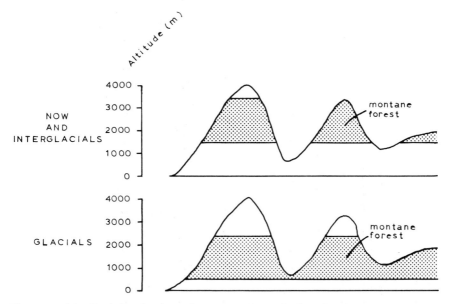

Fig. 73   Altitudinal distribution of montane forest during glacials and interglacials
according to the pluvial theory. The connections between many montane forest
pathces during glacials are envisaged to have permitted ready interchange of species.

well defined lowland/montane boundary has been accepted by a
number of other authors, e.g. Carcasson (1964), Chapman and White
(1970) and J. K. Morton (1972), many of whom also maintain that
montane disjunctions originated during pluvial (glacial) periods.
    The second school of thought concerning the nature of the
lowland/montane boundary holds that, on a broad geographic scale,
there is continuous biotic change in forest composition with increasing altitude and that, while it may be useful for some purposes to try

to classify species into lowland or montane elements, the division is to some degree arbitrary. I favour this second view for a number of reasons. First, even the most ardent believer in a well-defined lowland/montane boundary admits that some "montane" species are present in lowland forest. These lowland occurrences may be dismissed as "relicts" or otherwise be regarded as atypical, but it is striking that no fewer than 21 of the 107 passerine bird species recorded from montane forest in tropical Africa can also be found in lowland forest (based on data in Hall and Moreau, 1970). Second, according to Moreau (1966), zonation is atypical in three important montane areas, the East Usambaras, Mt Cameroon and the Angolan Highlands. With such conspicuous exceptions, the idea of a "normal" zonation becomes less easy to accept. Third, even the strongest proponent of the existence of a hard-and-fast divide between lowland and montane ecosystems often accepts a broad zone of overlap; authorities differ on the altitude of the lowland/montane boundary or on the altitudinal range of the overlap zone, but extreme opinion covers an altitudinal range of 1000 m (Carcasson, 1964; Chapin, 1932; Keith *et al.*, 1969). This range of altitude approaches the ranges said to be occupied by lowland and montane forests themselves, so the division between lowland and montane ecosystems can hardly be said to be clearly defined. Fourth, a quantitative analysis of altitudinal zonation of forest trees in Uganda, where in contrast to Kenya and Tanzania forest spans the lowland/montane boundary at several localities, indicates that forest forms a floristic altitudinal continuum (Hamilton, 1975a).

In my opinion, many authors working in East Africa have been inclined to accept a well defined division between lowland and montane forests because in drier areas forests only begin to appear on the mountains at *c.* 2000 m and in wetter areas the altitudinal band *c.* 1500–2000 m has often proved attractive to cultivators, resulting in widespread forest destruction. The result is that most modern forests belong to two altitudinally well separated groups.

I have elsewhere reviewed the literature on distributions of forest organisms in tropical Africa (Hamilton, 1976a) and, together with A. W. Diamond, have published a quantitative analysis of the distribution patterns shown by forest passerine birds in tropical Africa (Diamond and Hamilton, 1980). The latter work is based on distribution data in Hall and Moreau (1970). Considering all available evidence, it is thought that in general all groups of African forest organisms share the same pattern of distribution. The inquisitive reader may pursue the evidence relating to particular groups further by reference to the following works, all of which are discussed in Hamilton (1976a): (for plants)—Aubréville (1949), Ayodele Cole (1974), Boughey (1954/1955), Chapman and White (1970), Curry-Lindahl (1968), Exell (1953), Hall (1973), Hall and Medler (1975), Hamilton (1974a, 1975b), Keay (1954/1955), Léonard (1965), Morton (1961, 1972), Richards (1963), Polhill (1968), Weimarck (1941), White (1962), Wickens (1975), Wild (1968); (for birds)—Hall and Moreau (1970), Marchant (1954), Moreau (1966); (for mammals)—Balinsky (1962), Bigalke (1968), Booth (1954, 1957, 1958), Dandelot (1965), Groves (1971), Kingdon (1971 etc.), Misonne (1963), Rahm (1966), Tappen (1960); (for amphibians and reptiles)—Laurent (1973); (for butterflies)—Carcasson (1964); (for molluscs)—Verdcourt (1972).

The pattern of distribution of African forest organisms is illustrated on Fig. 74. The sketches show (a) the basic elements of the pattern shared by all groups, and two particular aspects of the pattern as demonstrated by passerine birds, namely (b) the numbers of species in different areas and (c) major divisions of the forest into biogeographical regions as shown by cluster-analysis. A principle feature of the pattern is that there are a number of core areas (terminology following Haffer, 1977), which are rich in numbers of species and in endemics and are the centres of the isolated populations of disjunct species. The two most important core areas are in E. Zaire (perhaps extending into W. Rwanda and S. W. Uganda) and in Cameroon/Gabon. Core areas which are somewhat poorer in numbers of species are found in West Africa (probably two or three areas, two being in Sierra Leone/Liberia and E. Ivory Coast/ W. Ghana) and eastern Tanzania (including the East Usambara and Uluguru mountains). Very much more minor centres are present in northern Angola and Ethiopia.

A second prominent feature of the distributional pattern is that gradients of increasing species poverty extend away from the core areas. Such gradients occur away from E. Zaire and Cameroon/ Gabon into the centre of the Congo basin, from Cameroon/Gabon westwards into Nigeria, from E. Ivory Coast/W. Ghana eastwards into W. Nigeria, from E. Zaire across Uganda and into western Kenya, from eastern Tanzania into Kenya, and from Kenya northwards into Ethiopia. There are remarkably few exceptions to these trends. For example, not a single forest passerine bird species is known to be confined to the central Congo basin or to Kenya.

The distributional pattern shown by African forest organisms is not wholly explicable with reference to the present-day environment

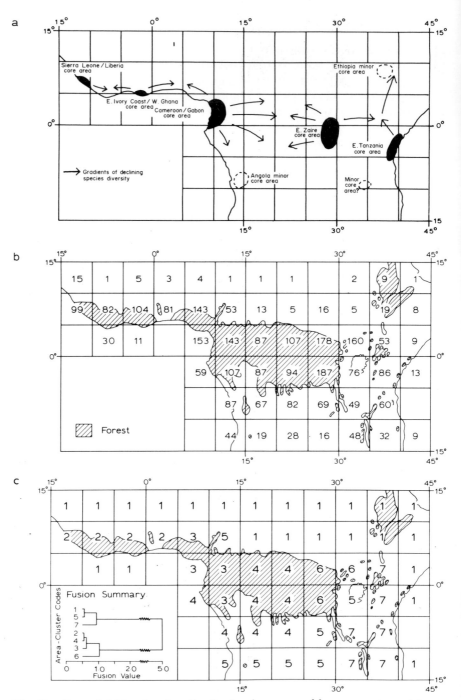

Fig. 74 Central Africa showing distributional patterns of forest organisms. (a) core areas and gradients of declining species diversity; (b) the numbers of passerine bird species in grid areas; (c) division into avifaunal regions: (b) and (c) are from Diamond and Hamilton, 1980).

alone. The most obvious explanation is that forest was confined to the core areas at a time or times when the climate of tropical Africa was generally unfavourable for forest development (i.e. it was arid) and that species have moved out of the core areas at varying rates following a change to increased humidity. There is no doubt from the body of evidence given in the previous chapters that the most recent arid period to have caused forest contraction must have been that which occurred over the few thousand years preceding 12 000/10 000 B.P. and the distributional evidence allows us to identify more closely those areas which retained a relatively moist climate during this dry episode.

Palynological evidence shows that forest was present in at least some localities outside the core areas during the pre-12 000 B.P. dry phase. Mt Kenya appears to have continued to carry some fairly moist montane forest. Also, forest, albeit of a dry type and greatly reduced in extent compared with today, seems to have persisted even on Mt Elgon and the Cherangani Hills, which were situated in a particularly arid climatic zone. There is distributional evidence from Uganda that the tree species which survived in these patches tended to be those which can grow at particularly high altitudes or in dry montane forest types (Hamilton, 1974a). It is presumed that some forest would also have persisted outside the core areas during earlier dry episodes. The explanation for the paucity of endemics outside the core areas may be first the accumulative effects of the series of arid phases and second that forest patches which survived outside the core areas during phases of climatic aridity tended to be small, species-poor and subject to relatively severe environmental stress; if populations within these patches did become differentiated from populations of the same species in climatically more favourable areas, then it is thought that in many cases these genetic differences became submerged by gene flow from the core areas during moister periods. It is noted that there are a few species of organisms endemic in the species-poor forests of Ethiopia. These forests were certainly greatly reduced during Quaternary arid phases and the presence of the endemics, contrasting with endemic-poor Kenya, can perhaps be attributed to the great isolation of Ethiopian forests.

Some of the effects of Quaternary climatic fluctuations on patterns of distribution are particularly well illustrated within East Africa. For example, it is instructive to compare distributional patterns on the mountains of north-east Tanzania and extreme south-east Kenya with those present between E. Zaire and western Kenya. According to Moreau (1966), the birds of the Usambaras and neighbouring forested massifs, some of which are within sight of one another, show an unprecedented degree of differentiation of populations. The same is probably true of some other groups of forest organisms. The pattern in E. Zaire, Uganda and western Kenya is, in contrast, one of increasing poverty from west to east and there is very little differentiation. This is particularly well shown by the mammalian fauna in which the complication of separation into lowland and montane elements is lacking (Kingdon, 1971). In the case of birds, the "lowland" element shows impoverishment to the eastern limit of "lowland" forest at Kakamega Forest and the "montane" elements shows the same west-to-east gradient, though this is broken by a disjunction of *c.* 500 km across Uganda (Diamond and Hamilton, 1980). It is suggested that the persistence of relatively species-rich forest on many of the East Coast massifs for a long time has allowed their montane avifaunas to occupy much of the available ecological space, thus reducing the opportunities for colonization by species arriving from elsewhere. In contrast, many forest species, whether lowland or montane, are thought to have moved out of the E. Zaire core area during comparatively recent times.

Judging by the distributional evidence alone, it is possible that the disjunctions of montane species across Uganda are due to the former presence of montane forest in the intervening area. (This could also be said of any montane disjunction.) This is, however, regarded as not being essential to account for these disjunctions. The altitudinal ranges of "montane" species are known to vary greatly between different localities, many plants, for example, tending to occur down to lower altitudes in wetter places or where competition is reduced. Terborgh and Weske (1975) for South America and Mayr and Diamond (1976) for northern Melanesia regard many of the divisions between lowland and montane bird distributions as not due to altitude nor to vegetation, but rather to interspecific competition among the birds. It is thought that interspecific competition must be a major factor excluding many "montane" species of all taxonomic groups from lowland forests in tropical Africa also. It is suggested that many "montane" species have been able to reach western Kenya from the E. Zaire core area through transient occupation of lowland forest in Uganda, either during particularly moist climatic periods, such as that which prevailed between 10 000 and 8000 B.P. (Livingstone, 1975) or else during the early years of forest spread, when the lowland forest would have been species-poor. It is also noted that the establishment of montane species in western Kenya, whether they arrived by long-distance dispersal or by short-term occupancy of the intervening lowland forest zone, would have been facilitated by the absence of a species-rich and well integrated fauna in western Kenya during the early stages of montane forest expansion.

Considering now the origins of disjunctions between the core areas, it is noted that the disjunct taxa show a wide variation in the degree of divergence of the separated populations (Fig. 75). In the

Fig. 75 Distribution of gorilla (map modified from Groves, 1971). This is an example of a common pattern of distribution shown by African forest organisms, with a disjunct distribution across the Congo forest basin. Western gorillas are found in lowland forest, but the eastern animals range from lowland forest up to the Afroalpine Belt. Populations of taxa sharing this disjunction show various degrees of divergence. In the case of *Gorilla gorilla*, the two populations are usually regarded as distinct subspecies, though an alternative view has been expressed by Groves (1971).

case of plants with disjunctions between the East Coast forests and the main Guineo/Congolian forest block, Faden (1974) maintains that there may have been two periods of contact, an earlier one to account for similarities at the generic level and a latter one to explain the large numbers of species common to both areas. For similar reasons, though based on birds, Moreau (1966) also argues for two connections. This line of argument seems to me to be faulty, because, even if former forest connection is believed to be necessitated by the distributions, there is no reason to suppose that the rates of differentiation of populations are the same for different taxa and that, for example, two populations regarded as belonging to different species in the same genus have necessarily been isolated from one another for longer than populations which are thought to be specifically identical. It is more likely that taxa in general vary tremendously in their rates of evolution and there is indeed evidence to show that this is so for members of the Afroalpine flora (Hedberg, 1969a; see also Hamilton, 1974b). It can, however, be argued that the much greater degree of divergence shown, on average, by taxa disjunct between the East Coast forests and the Guineo-Congolian forest block, as compared with montane taxa disjunct between the East Zaire core area and western Kenya, means that, on average, movement of biota across the former disjunction occurred at a much earlier date.

Given the probable antiquity of many of the East Coast/Guineo-Congolian disjunctions, the chance that a species will have crossed the interval by long-distance dispersal is increased. Diamond and Hamilton (1980) have pointed out that many of the rather low number of species of passerines which show this disjunction have exceptionally wide ranges in West and Central Africa, very few having even moderately restricted distributions within this vast area. This indicates that these are among the more mobile of African forest birds and the existence of the disjunctions does not perhaps necessitate former forest connections. However, in the opinion of many workers, some of the other forest taxa which share this disjunction are unlikely to have good long-distance dispersal ability. This is for instance regarded to be the case for some of the plants (Faden, 1974) and mammals (Kingdon, 1971; Tappen, 1960). Forest connection from west to east at one or more times in the past thus probably existed, but it is uncertain whether contact was by means of a broad forest band or whether connection was more tenuous, perhaps involving narrow strips of riverine forest. The former would imply very different environmental conditions from the present and this could have been either due to the existence of wetter and perhaps warmer climates in the intervening zone or, given the length of time with which we may be dealing, to tectonic movement and consequent adjustment of climatic belts.

It is reasonable to assume that many of the numerous lowland forest taxa which are disjunctly distributed on either side of the Congo basin once had continuous distributions since these populations are not separated by any major environmental barrier today. Greater doubt concerns the origin of the montane taxa which share the same disjunction, since the distribution of these corresponds to that of their ecosystem type and there is greater uncertainty as to the possible role of long-distance dispersal processes. If these montane disjunctions included many terrestrial mammals, then, given the presumed inability of the majority of such mammals to disperse by long-distance means, a sound case might be made for former montane forest connection either across the basin as a whole or, more likely, around peripheral hills. But this is not the case; no well defined division of African forest mammals into lowland and montane forms exists (Bigalke, 1968; Kingdon, 1971; Tappen, 1960). There is a parallel with E. Zaire–western Kenya, though a difference is the probably greater average degree of differentiation of the isolated populations. It seems quite possible, therefore, that many of the disjunct "montane" taxa may once have occurred in lowland forest either during wetter periods or else during initial phases of forest expansion.

It is pertinent to note that, as within the East Coast forests, the movement of a species from one core area to another will not necessarily be followed by successful establishment. Because of their species-richness, core areas might indeed be exceptionally difficult to penetrate by newly arriving species. It is possible that colonization of core areas occurred rapidly when, for one reason or another, they first appeared, and that subsequent movement of species between the core areas has proceeded at much slower rates.

Finally, mention is briefly made of a distribution pattern shown by some savanna organisms, since this provides further evidence of the former reduction of forest in tropical Africa and the parallel expansion of more arid ecosytem types. The south-west arid zone of Africa (the Kalahari region) and, to a lesser degree, the Somali arid zone both contain many endemic species (e.g. of plants: Milne-Redhead, 1954/1955) and it is likely that the two are long-established. There are many examples of disjunctions at various taxonomic levels between the two areas (Bigalke, 1968; Kingdon, 1971; van Zinderen Bakker, 1969b; Verdcourt, 1969; Werger, 1973; Winter, 1971; Winterbottom, 1967). According to Kingdon (1971) many of the disjunct species are sub-desert rather than true desert forms, and this provides a guide to the maximum degree of desiccation which once prevailed in the interval between the two areas.

The Afroalpine Flora

The flora of the Afroalpine Belt of East Africa and Ethiopia is well known, thanks to the work of Hedberg (1957, etc.). The various enclaves of Afroalpine vegetation are scattered like islands in a sea of lowland vegetation and the origin of their peculiar biota has been much discussed.

According to Hedberg (1969a), no fewer than 80% of species in the Afroalpine flora are endemic, a testimony to the environmental peculiaraty of the Afroalpine Belt and perhaps also to its long existence. The majority of Afroalpine species are not related to taxa found in lowland tropical Africa, but rather have their nearest relatives in more distant parts of the world. This might by itself be taken as evidence of direct former connections with distant eco-systems, were it not that the Afroalpine flora is believed to be of very mixed origin. Thus, according to Hedberg (1963), of the 278 vascular plant taxa in the Afroalpine flora, 6% constitute a South African element (South Africa being the area of supposed origin), 4% belong to a Cape element, 15% to a North-hemispheric temperate element, 6% to a Mediterranean element, . . . and so on. The actual number of ancestral species is thought to have been fairly small and, considering the mixed origin, a more likely explanation is that the taxa have been introduced into eastern Africa by long-distance dispersal over a very long period of time, perhaps by mountain hopping. Movement may have been easier during periods of temperature reduction.

The number of endemic species in the Afroalpine floras of the different high mountains varies, for example from 23 on Mt Elgon to only three on Mt Meru (Hedberg, 1961). Hedberg (1961) has suggested that the high Elgon figure may be a consequence of its position on the route through which the ancestors of many endemics entered from the north, this perhaps being by way of the Ethiopian Highlands, the Imatongs and intermediate ranges. It is also possible that the ages of the mountains may also be a factor. Basal lavas from Mt Elgon have been dated at 20 million years (Brock and MacDonald, 1969), while the shape of Mt Meru shows that it must have been an active volcano during relatively recent times. Summit rock from Mt Kenya has given a date of 2·7 million years (Coe, 1967) and it is regarded as significant that the mountain has the intermediate number of 13 endemic Afroalpine species.

Hedberg (1969a) has discussed the possibility that climatic changes may have allowed direct connections between the Afroalpine floras of different mountains in eastern Africa. According to illustrations in Hedberg (1969a), the depression of the lower limit of the Afroalpine Belt which would be required for it to extend continuously between mountain areas would have been at least 1500 m and, in some cases, over 2000 m. Such depression of vegetation belts is much greater than that for which there is evidence in the Quaternary palynological record. The lower limit of the Afroalpine Belt is not, however, the lower limit of the altitudinal ranges of most "Afroalpine species", many of which are found down to below 3000 m and some even beyond 2000 m (Hedberg, 1969a). Hedberg (1969a) has shown that the further the downward extension of an "Afroalpine species", the lower are its chances of being endemic to a single mountain or group of neighbouring mountains. Even so, he believes that this does not necessarily imply that Afroalpine species with wide altitudinal ranges have necessarily had access to continuous migration routes between mountains. He points out that the greater the altitudinal range of a species, the larger the areas available for production and reception of disseminules, and hence the greater the opportunities for spread, even by long-distance atmospheric dispersal. He believes that cyclones may have been important agents of dispersal.

During my vegetation survey of Mt Elgon, I had the opportunity of studying the distribution of endemic species on the mountain in relation to their occurrence in vegetation types. Four hundred and two species of plants were recorded in the vegetation as a whole (the survey extended down to the lower forest boundary) and of these eight are believed to be endemics. The distribution of endemics by vegetation type is shown on Table 9. No endemics were recorded for forest, in spite of the large number of species recorded (237), and other vegetation types lacking endemics were *Stoebe* thicket and mire communities. Grassland, which is not only the most widespread non-forest vegetation type on the mountain but is also species-rich (112 species recorded) has just one endemic, *Senecio snowdenii*. Ericaceae thicket is also rather poor in endemics, with only two species being recorded, but the remaining vegetation types, rocky ground communities and *Alchemilla* scrub, are both relatively rich in endemics, in spite of the relative poverty of their floras.

The reason for the absence of endemics in forest has been discussed in a previous section. The low endemic status of grassland may be due to former montane grassland connections with other mountains as a consequence of more arid conditions in the past. The high percentages of endemics in *Alchemilla* scrub and rocky ground communities point to long persistence of these ecosystem types on the mountain, with long isolation from similar communities on other mountains. In contrast to grassland, the isolation of *Alchemilla* scrub on Mt Elgon from that on other mountains would be expected in the absence of much colder and wetter past climates.

Table 9 Distribution by vegetation type of endemic species in sample plots on Mt Elgon

Vegetation type	Numbers of plots			Species recorded from vegetation types				
	With endemics	Lacking endemics	Totals	Endemics		Non-endemics		Totals
				No.	% of total	No.	% of total	
Mire communities	0	6	6	0	0	29	100	29
Rocky ground communities	2	2	4	3	11	25	89	28
Alchemilla scrub	4	1	5	3	10	27	90	30
Grassland	4	6	10	1	1	111	99	112
Stoebe thicket	0	2	2	0	0	44	100	44
Ericaceae thicket	2	2	4	2	3	72	97	74
Forest	0	18	18	0	0	237	100	237
Totals (for all plots)	12	37	49	14	3·5	388	96·5	402

Summary

Distributional evidence allows an appreciation of environmental change over a wide geographical scale. An aspect which is stressed is the difference in environmental stability between places, with areas which have enjoyed relatively little change over long periods of time being rich in numbers of species and endemics, and areas subject to change being impoverished. Modern ecosystems are clearly often in a state of biotic adjustment following relatively recent environmental events.

Chapter 9

Quaternary Climatic Change in Tropical Africa

The evidence presented in the foregoing chapters demonstrates that major climatic changes have occurred during the African Quaternary. The recent accumulation of records of Quaternary climatic events for the world as a whole has naturally led to speculation on the underlying causes of Quaternary climatic change, and to attempts to model general atmospheric circulation for different times in the past. Such attempts bring together individual observations and help to identify evidence requiring re-examination or re-interpretation. Models of atmospheric circulation can also be used to help predict the climatic history of the poorly dated Middle and Lower Quaternary and of areas for which no direct evidence is available.

In tropical Africa there is well-dated evidence for climatic events only for a few sites and for the last c. 40 000/30 000 years. The Quaternary record is actually fragmentary in all terrestrial regions and Africa is perhaps more fortunate than some areas in that the potential for detailed long-term investigations may exist. It is likely that lacustrine sedimentation has been continuous through all or much of the Quaternary under parts of Lakes Tanganyika and Malawi and possibly also under Lakes Kivu and Bosumtwi.

Deep-sea sedimentation can be slow and continuous and on a world scale deep-sea sediment cores provide the best long-term records of Quaternary environmental change. There are numerous links between the characteristics of deep-sea sediments and terrestrial environmental history and no doubt the information-content of deep-sea sediments is still only partly exploited. Figure 76, from a

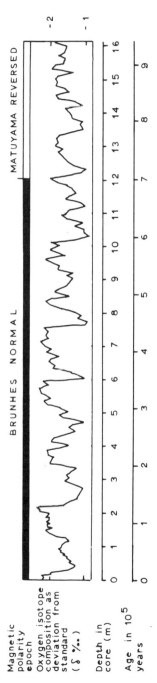

Fig. 76 Oxygen isotopic composition of tests of *Globigerinoides sacculifera* in deep-sea sediment core V28–238 from under a water depth of 3120 m in the Equatorial Pacific. In effect, the changes in the isotopic composition of the tests are believed to be a record of changes in world ice volume, the less negative the values, the greater the quantity of ice. Notice that there have been perhaps nine glacial stages since the magnetic polarity reversal (Brunhes/Matuyama) at 700 000 B.P. and that fluctuations in ice volume have been rather irregular. From Shackleton and Opdyke (1973). Reproduced from "Quaternary Research", Vol. 3, with permission.

Pacific deep-sea core, shows changes in the relative abundance down the core of the two stable oxygen isotopes ^{16}O and ^{18}O contained in fossil tests of foraminifera (Shackleton and Opdyke, 1973). Ice is isostatically light and in consequence deep-sea sediments deposited during glacial periods tend to be enriched in ^{18}O. It is indeed believed that the fluctuations in the $^{16}O/^{18}O$ ratio shown in Fig. 76 provide a record of the waxing and waning of world ice sheets over about the last 900 000 years, other factors influencing the $^{16}O/^{18}O$ ratio being relatively unimportant. Parallel changes in oxygen isotope ratios have been recorded in many other deep-sea cores.

Largely through the evidence contained within deep-sea sediments, it is today acknowledged that many models of Quaternary climatic change widely held before *c.* 1960 require great modification. These early models envisaged that there had only been about 3–5 ice ages in temperate parts of the world (e.g. the famous Günz, Riss, Mindel, Würm Glaciations of the Alps) and that, on the whole, the climate had oscillated between well defined full glacial and interglacial periods. It is now established that there have actually been many more than five major glacial phases during the Quaternary, the exact number being, however, a matter of opinion. A figure of nine important glaciations during the last 700 000 years is often quoted (cf. Shackleton and Opdyke, 1973) and cold oscillations seem to have been just as pronounced between 700 000 and 2 million years as subsequently (Faure, 1980). It is also known that ice volume has fluctuated in an apparently irregular fashion, many periods being marked by volumes of ice accumulation intermediate between the full glacial and interglacial extremes. It is also thought that the proportion of time during the last 1 million years occupied by interglacials (in the vegetational sense, i.e. with temperate deciduous forest established in north-west Europe) is rather small, probably a tenth of the total. The consequences for tropical Africa are that there must have been numerous environmental fluctuations during the Quaternary, with the likelihood that those conditions characteristic of full interglacial climates (relatively warm and wet) have occupied a relatively small proportion of at least the last 1 million years.

Despite the limitations of the evidence there are good correlations between climatic events in tropical Africa and those recorded for other parts of the world for the last *c.* 40 000/30 000 years (Fig. 77). Considering the broad picture, the climate of tropical Africa at, and following on from, the last world glacial maximum (centred at *c.* 18 000 B.P.) was cool and dry and the "postglacial period", beginning at *c.* 12 000/10 000 B.P. and extending up to the present, has

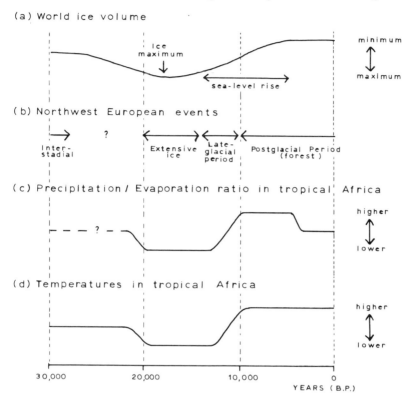

Fig. 77 Very generalized summary of some major environmental events in tropical Africa and elsewhere during the last 30 000 years. Notice in particular the associations between aridity in tropical Africa and the glacial maximum at 18 000 B.P., and between wetter conditions in tropical Africa and the Postglacial Period in north-west Europe.

been warmer and wetter. The period preceeding the glacial maximum was marked by a cool and rather moist climate in tropical Africa: this corresponds to a phase of intermediate world ice volume, with "interstadial" conditions prevailing in north-west Europe. The correlations are generally accepted as being so clear (e.g. by van Zinderen Bakker and Maley, 1979) that it is highly likely that full glacials have been marked by aridity and interglacials by wetness in tropical Africa throughout the Quaternary. There is indeed direct evidence of this from deep-sea cores from the east North Atlantic which contain peaks in atmospheric dust of presumed Saharan origin corresponding to the times of glacial maxima (Parkin and Shackleton, 1973; Parmenter and Folger, 1974).

Looking at the earth as a whole, it is likely that the primary cause of Quaternary climatic variations is change in the energy budget of the earth (van Zinderen Bakker and Maley, 1979). Coming down to a more modest scale, a number of authors have advanced models of atmospheric circulation over Africa for various times during the Quaternary (Heath, 1979; Rognon, 1976; Rognon and Williams, 1977; Talbot, 1980; van Zinderen Bakker, 1976; van Zinderen Bakker and Maley, 1979). Some of the ideas which have been put forward are incompatible with one another and clearly much remains poorly understood. Readers interested in detail are advised to consult the original papers.

The period *c.* 21 000–12 000 B.P. was marked by general aridity in tropical Africa. There is much information on palaeo-environments for the world generally for this period, particularly for 18 000 B.P., which was marked by a world ice volume maximum, and which has been selected as a study date by many workers for modelling the Quaternary climate (the CLIMAP project). A massive ice-sheet spread over northern North America and there were also smaller, but still sizeable ice-sheets over north-west Europe and elsewhere in the world. The Antarctic ice-sheet was somewhat enlarged. High pressure over the north-west European ice-cap was a factor in depressing the route of the westerlies down across North Africa, a region for which there is evidence of increased rainfall (van Zinderen Bakker and Maley, 1979). This southward movement of the westerlies in the northern hemisphere was matched by a northern' movement of the westerlies in the southern hemisphere, though to a lesser degree (Faure, 1980). There was a large drop in the temperature of surface water in the northern and southern parts of the Atlantic, but less in the tropical zone where the general fall was only *c.* 3°C, compared with now (Faure, 1980). The upwelling of cold water close to the north-western and south-western (the Benguela Current) coasts of Africa was intensified (Faure, 1980), but whether there were equatorward movements of these currents is disputed (Rognon and Williams, 1977; Talbot, 1980; van Zinderen Bakker, 1976). Latitudinal temperature gradients must have been intensified, with a resultant general increase in wind speeds (cf. Parkin and Shackleton, 1973), including those of the dry winds moving away from terrestrial subtropical anticyclones (van Zinderen Bakker and Maley, 1979) (Fig. 78).

There is some dispute as to whether the increased aridity near the equator was a result of the location of the African subtropical anticyclones nearer to the equator, compressing the intertropical convergence zone (Rognon and Williams, 1977) or whether it was

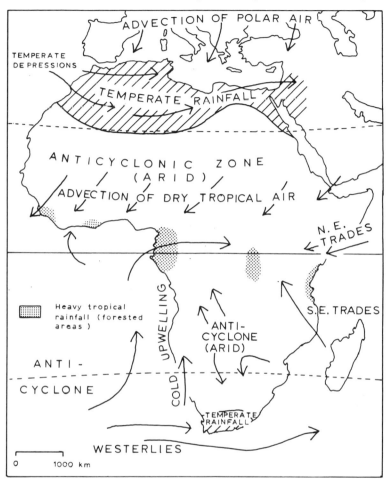

Fig. 78 Diagrammatic reconstruction of mean positions of principal features of general atmospheric circulation over Africa during the last glacial maximum (*c.* 18 000 B.P.). Adapted largely from Rognon and Williams (1977) and van Zinderen Bakker (1976).

achieved by a reduction in the moistness of air masses without any major changes in patterns of atmospheric circulation (Talbot, 1980). The locations of species-rich areas of forest in tropical Africa correspond to places which receive particularly high rainfall today and the alignments of fixed dunes formed during this arid period closely match contemporary wind directions; both pieces of evidence suggest that circulation patterns over tropical Africa were not greatly different from the present at 21 000–12 000 B.P. It is however thought, in agreement with Rognon and Williams (1977), that the anticyclones must have been intensified and somewhat nearer the equator. The main cause of tropical aridity is believed to have been a decreased moisture content of air masses moving in off the oceans. This itself is likely to have been the result of the decreased evaporative potential of the atmosphere at the generally reduced temperatures. A minor factor in the case of tropical Africa was reduction in the area of open water as a result of the spread of sea-ice and the lowering of sea-levels by up to perhaps 120 m.

One interesting contrast with the present during the glacial maximum was the relative increase in moistness of the north-east trades as compared with the south-east trades over East Africa. The explanation may be that, before moving onto East Africa, the north-east trades followed a more southerly route than they do at present, and that the longer sea-passage allowed the winds to become charged with a relatively large quantity of water. It is also likely that the Indian Ocean trade winds in general were relatively moist in comparison with winds originating over the Atlantic. The reason for this is that ocean sediment core analyses have indicated that surface water temperatures to the west of Africa were much more depressed than those to the east at 18 000 B.P. (CLIMAP, unpublished).

On a world scale massive ice melting occurred between 15 000 and 7 000 B.P., being perhaps more rapid before 12 000 B.P. (Faure, 1980). The input of a large volume of cold fresh water is believed to have been responsible for a big delay in the warming of ocean temperatures and it was not until the oceans reached critical temperatures at *c.* 12 000 B.P. that maritime air masses which influenced tropical Africa became really moist (Williams and Adamson, 1980). Pollen diagrams show that a major increase in air temperatures occurred in montane eastern Africa over the 12 000–10 000 B.P. period. At 12 000/10 000 B.P. warmer world-wide temperatures, a great reduction in ice-volume, including that of the north-west European ice-cap, and other factors allowed a relaxation of latitudinal temperature gradients, movement of the westerlies to higher latitudes, a reduced intensity of the subtropical anticyclones and the development of much moister trade winds.

In the period from 10 000 B.P. to the present the characteristics of atmospheric circulation over Africa are to some extent disputed (Rognon and Williams, 1977; van Zinderen Bakker and Maley, 1979). Probably the more arid periods in inter-tropical Africa, for instance the post-*c.* 4000 B.P. period in general compared with the preceeding

6000 years, were marked by intensification and equatorwards movement of the sub-tropical anticyclones. On a smaller time-scale, climatic changes during the last 30 years are also said to be related to movements of the anticyclones towards and away from the equator, with a concomitant reduction and expansion of the equatorial rain belt (Lamb, 1977). Van Zinderen Bakker and Malcy (1979) believe that temperate depressions regularly brought winter rainfall to the central Sahara in the period preceding *c.* 6500 B.P.

The reconstruction of the meteorology of the *c.* 30 000–20 000 B.P. period is also contentious (Maley, 1973; Rognon and Williams, 1977). Temperatures were lower generally during this period than now, though not as low as at 21 000–12 000 B.P., and there is evidence of rather moist conditions, not only in tropical Africa, but also along both margins of the Sahara (Maley, 1973) and in the Arabian Desert (McClure, 1976). It should, however, be noted that there is evidence that the White Nile was hardly flowing at the time (Williams and Adamson, 1980). If this evidence is soundly based, then the climate, at least of much of eastern Africa, could not have been as moist as post-12 000/10 000 B.P. According to Maley (1973) there may have been hemispheric ice imbalance at the time. An exceptionally cool Antarctica may have casued northward displacement of general zonal circulation, causing *inter alia* the extension of the summer monsoon northwards well into the Sahara. At the same time, the westerlies in the northern hemisphere may have been somewhat depressed to the south by anticyclonic conditions over somewhat cool northern Europe. It is, however, noted that the Kalahari region was rather wet at 30 000–20 000 B.P. (Heine, 1979), in possible contradiction to Maley's model, and more data is needed before this or other reconstructions of general circulation can be confidently accepted for the 30 000–20 000 B.P. period.

Even if atmospheric circulation over Africa during the Quaternary is incompletely understood, there nevertheless is considerable evidence that the times of climatic events in tropical Africa during the Upper Quaternary are correlated with those in Europe, not only on a large scale, but in some cases also in detail. A good example is the Little Ice Age, which was marked by cold temperatures and an increase in ice extent generally in the world, and which witnessed a minor glacial maximum also in Africa. Another example is the cold period at *c.* 10 500–10 000 B.P. in north-west Europe (the Upper Dryas Stadial) when re-advance of some glaciers interrupted a general climatic warming. There is evidence from several lakes in tropical Africa (e.g. Chad, Victoria, Kivu, the Ethiopian Rift lakes) of recessions at this time. I would also like to draw attention to the climatic change to some what drier conditions soon after 4000 B.P.: from the ecosystem point of view this seems to have been the most important climatic event of the last 10 000 years. Parallels with north-west Europe are perhaps not so obvious for this climatic change as for the two already mentioned, but it is worth pointing out that there is a tendency to attribute many of the vegetation changes seen in Upper Holocene pollen diagrams from north-west Europe to human disturbance and the role of climatic change may have been under-estimated. In Northern Ireland, for example, there is evidence that blanket bogs started to grow soon after 4000 B.P. and the current trend is to attribute this spread of mountain mires to the influence of agricultural man (but see Smith, 1975). It would be desirable to re-evaluate some of the European evidence for environmental change during the Holocene in the light of the African evidence.

It remains to discuss the dating of the environmental events inferred from distributional evidence. Clearly the last period of forest expansion commenced at 12 000/10 000 B.P. and it is probable that there have been numerous contractions and expansions of forest in tropical Africa corresponding to glacial and interglacial periods. The cool moist climate of > 30 000–20 000 B.P. may have allowed expansion of montane ecosystems, though it is noted that this expansion did not correspond to the time of minimum temperatures. The Afroalpine Belts of the various mountains of East Africa have not been in contact with one another during the Quaternary. The similarity of the fish fauna of lakes and rivers stretching from west to east across northern tropical Africa must be due in part to connections between 10 000 and 4000 B.P. The persistence of Lakes Tanganyika and Malawi for a long time is related partly to their topographic configurations and partly to their positions in relatively moist zones in Africa. The relatively high number of endemics in the Chari-Longone river system may be connected with the persistence of a wet climate in the Cameroon/Gabon area during dry periods, as indicated by the forest distribution studies.

Chapter 10

Some Matters Arising

Evolution in Tropical Forest Organisms

A study of the patterns of distribution shown by a group of related organisms can help us to appreciate some of the factors which determine evolutionary processes. This is why Hall and Moreau's (1970) atlas of passerine bird distributions in Africa is called "An Atlas of Speciation in African Passerine Birds" and why Kingdon's (1971 etc.) work on East African mammals is subtitled "An Atlas of Evolution in Africa". Distributional evidence alone is uninformative about the rates of evolutionary processes; to appreciate these, patterns of distribution must be considered in the light of evidence of environmental history dated by absolute means.

There is little doubt that differentiation of populations within forest species in tropical Africa is principally associated geographically with the long-established forest core areas in West Africa, Cameroon/Gabon, eastern Zaire and near the East African coast. The evidence certainly supports the prevailing orthodoxy that geographical isolation is normally essential for speciation in free-living, sexually-reproducing animals (Bush, 1975; Haffer, 1974; Mayr, 1969, 1976).

Populations of disjunct species which occur outside the core areas are only rarely differentiated from core area populations. Thus, few of the montane forest species which occur in either all or some of the isolated montane forests of Kenya (Elgon, Kulal, Marsabit, etc.) show differentiation within Kenya or between Kenya and either East Zaire or the East Coast montane forests. Again, with the notable exception of some of the butterflies in supposedly man-isolated forest fragments to the south of the main Congo forest block (Carcasson, 1964), there is little differentiation shown by populations of species in patches of forest isolated from one another by man's activities following the introduction of agriculture. Evidence given elsewhere in this book suggests that many of the montane disjunctions within Kenya, and between Kenya and elsewhere, have arisen since 12 000/ 10 000 B.P. and that widespread destruction by man of moister forest types in central and eastern Africa has only occurred during, at most, the last 3000 years. It is thought that many of the Kenyan montane disjunctions actually date to the earlier part of the post 12 000/ 10 000 B.P. period, penetration of species arriving in new areas becoming increasingly restricted by established populations. Two conclusions can be drawn concerning the rates of evolutionary processes. First, the rate of differentiation of isolated populations has generally been slow and, second, the rate of extinction of populations in core areas has also been slow, at least since 12 000/10 000 B.P. The latter claim rests on the fact that gradients of species richness away from former refugia are very well defined, there being very few cases of species whose ranges do not include at least one core area.

With reference particularly to birds, the findings are in line with the opinions of Mayr (1969, 1976), but cannot be reconciled with some of those of Lack (1971, 1976). Mayr holds that species vary in their dispersal capacities, that competitive exclusion often prevents establishment of long-distance wanderers (see also MacArthur and Wilson, 1967; Mayr and Diamond, 1976), that niche expansion can be rapid in the absence of competitors (see also Diamond, 1970; Moreau, 1966) and that speciation is a slow process. Lack believed that, in general, long-distance dispersal is a common phenomenon and that dispersal barriers are unimportant in limiting ranges. He attributed the high proportion of endemic species on oceanic islands to rapid ecological shifts by new immigrants, the length of time of residence being much less important. Such ecological shifts following colonization of new areas may well have occurred also in the case of forest species in tropical Africa, but the evidence suggests that the rates of these shifts, as shown by morphological differentiation, are usually much less rapid than Lack envisaged.

Taxa disjunct between the forest core areas show a wide range of differentiation in their isolated populations. Given the probable multiplicity of forest connections and disruptions between at least some of these core areas during the Quaternary, it is difficult to determine the time at which any particular disjunct distribution originated (Fig. 79). Hence, for any particular taxon, rates of differentiation cannot be determined in the absence of other evidence.

It is thought that two important factors determining the number of species present in any particular area of forest in tropical Africa are

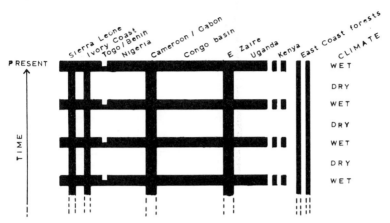

Fig. 79 Very simplified model of forest history in tropical Africa to illustrate persistence of forest in core areas and periodic spead of forest elsewhere in response to moist climatic episodes. In fact, the cycle has certainly not been so regular as here illustrated, and intermediate conditions have probably frequently prevailed. Furthermore, forest, albeit impoverished, is likely to have always persisted locally away from core areas, even during very arid periods. The extension of forest across the Togo/Benin savanna gap during the early part of each moist phase is conjectural.

altitude and distance from core areas. The decline in species diversity with altitude reflects the intolerance of many species to low temperatures. The decline in species diversity away from core areas is related to differential rates of range expansion. The number of species present in core areas today is not related to modern environmental conditions, but rather to those which prevailed during Quaternary arid periods. It would be interesting to determine the area and habitat diversity of each core area refugium in an attempt to isolate which of these factors was the most significant influence on species' numbers. This might well vary between different groups of organisms.

A similar picture of repeated contractions and expansions of forest during the Quaternary is reported for South America and there too speciation is believed to be related to the isolation of populations in core areas during arid periods (Haffer, 1969, 1974, 1977). There is believed to have been a greater number of forest refugia in South America than in Africa and some of the South American refugia were also relatively large. These may be important reasons why the numbers of species in many groups of organisms is much higher in South American than in African forests (Haffer, 1974).

Range Expansion Rates of Forest Trees

The model of forest history outlined in earlier chapters allows exploration of some of the factors which determine the abilities of species to expand their ranges. Here, a single example is taken to illustrate some of the possibilities and difficulties. The problem considered is the influence of the types of seeds or fruits possessed by forest trees on their rates of range expansion. The sample area chosen is Uganda and western Kenya (Kakamega Forest) (Fig. 80), a region for which there is palynological evidence of forest spread at 12 000/ 10 000 B.P. (Hamilton, 1972; Kendall, 1969; Livingstone, 1967) and in which lowland forests show a well-defined pattern of decreasing species-richness from west to east (Hamilton, 1974a). The latter pattern is believed to be due largely to variation in the abilities of species to enlarge their ranges out of an arid-period forest refugium in E. Zaire. This refugium may have extended into extreme western Uganda in the Kayonza region and, less likely, also in the Bwamba region. A minor forest refugium may have existed somewhere close to the present-day mouth of the River Kagera where it flows into Lake Victoria. Incidentally, forest expansion is not envisaged in terms of a wave of forest moving across the country, but rather, must have been by the infiltration of forest species into non-forest vegetation types and by the gradual enlargement and eventual coalescing of outlying forest patches.

Distributions in Uganda are here considered in relation to the four flora-areas recognized for the "Flora of Tropical East Africa" (1952 etc.). Species lists for each of these flora-areas are basically as employed in Hamilton (1974a) and the inventory for Kakemega Forest is after Lucas (1968) but omitting shrubs and trees too small to be included in Hamilton (1974a). Species have been classified into six groups according to their supposed primary means of dispersal. The allocation of species to groups was based on the literature (Keay, 1957; Jones, 1956; Ridley, 1930; van der Pijl, 1972), on my own observations in Uganda and, mainly for species or genera not covered by the literature, on the basis of the morphology of seeds and fruits (e.g. Fig. 81). The six groups are:

(1) Species with wind-dispersed disseminules possessing plumes.

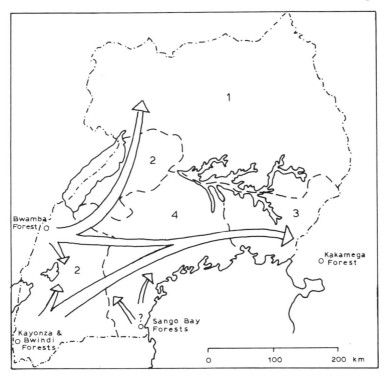

Fig. 80   Map of Uganda showing the four flora-areas (numbered 1 to 4) used for the "Flora of Tropical East Africa" (1952 etc.) and postulated directions of movement of forest species across the country following the onset of moister conditions at 12 000/10 000 B.P. The main forest refugium during the preceding arid period lay in E. Zaire, with an extension into south-western Uganda (Kayonza-Bwindi area) and perhaps also to the north of Ruwenzori (Bwamba Forest area). There may have been a minor forest refugium on the north-west/western side of Lake Victoria (Sango Bay area): this may perhaps have consisted of riparian forest along the Kagera River. Modified from Hamilton (1975b).

This is a small group of four species: *Alstonia boonei, Bombax buonopozense* and two species of *Funtumia*.

(2) Species with wind-dispersed disseminules having wings (17 species).

(3) Species with wind-dispersed disseminules lacking well developed plumes or wings. Only the two species of *Mitragyna* are placed here.

(4) Species with animal-dispersed disseminules which are sufficiently small to be carried by birds or fruit bats. Many of these

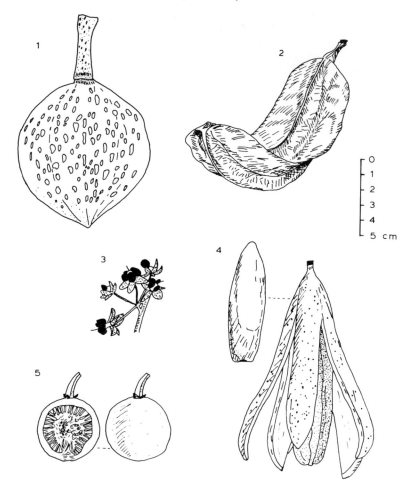

Fig. 81   Fruits and seeds of some Ugandan tree species. 1. *Caloncoba crepiniana*; 2. *Tetrapleura tetraptera*; 3. *Ochna* sp.; 4. *Entandrophragma utile*; 5. *Ficus mucuso*. No. 4 is classified as wind-dispersed, nos 3 and 5 as being capable of dispersal by birds or fruit bats and nos 1 and 2 as being animal-dispersed, but too large to be carried by flying animals.

disseminules are also eaten by terrestrial animals. This is the largest group, with 170 species.

(5) Species with animal-dispersed disseminules too large to be carried by flying animals. The 28 species of the group are listed on Table 10. *Parinari excelsa* and *Raphia farinifera* are marginal members.

(6) Species with disseminules of uncertain dispersal mode (62

Table 10   Lowland forest tree species found in Uganda or west Kenya with disseminules too large to be carried by flying animals

Allanblackia kimbiliensis	*M. myristica*
Antrocaryon micraster	*Myrianthus arboreus*
Balsamocitrus dawei	*Oncoba routledgei*
Caloncoba crepiniana	*O. spinosa*
Carapa grandiflora	*Oxyanthus speciosus*
Chrysophyllum pentagonocarpum	*Parinari excelsa*
C. pruniforme	*Picralima nitida*
Desplatsia dewevrei	*Raphia farinifera*
Euadenia eminens	*Tabernaemontana holstii*
Klainedoxa gabonensis	*T. odoratissima*
Leplea mayombensis	*T. usambarensis*
Mammea africana	*Tetrapleura tetraptera*
Mildbraediodendron excelsum	*Treculia africana*
Monodora angolensis	*Voacanga thouarsii*

species). Most of the disseminules are probably often animal-dispersed and nearly all are small enough to be carried by birds or fruit bats.

Table 11 shows the numbers and percentages of species in the above categories with various types of distribution, ranging from restricted (confined to western Uganda) to widespread (reaching Kakamega Forest). The most obvious results are that few species with wind-dispersed disseminules have very restricted distributions, that species with small animal-dispersed disseminules tend to increase in percentage representation with distance from source and that species with large animal-dispersed disseminules mostly have restricted ranges. The last two of these findings seem to be in agreement with general opinion that bird- or bat-dispersed disseminules are better dispersed than those transported only be terrestrial animals.

This result cannot be accepted uncritically. Among other factors, the possible influence of generation time has not been considered. Suppose, for example, that trees with large animal-dispersed disseminules take longer on average to reach maturity than do those with small animal-dispersed disseminules, then the former might be expected to have less extensive ranges than the latter, solely because of a lower number of generations since 12 000/10 000 B.P. This possibility is explored with reference to Table 12(a), which compares the distributions in Uganda of species found in young and old forest types. It is presumed that species of younger forest types tend to reach maturity more rapidly than do those of older stages in forest

Table 11 Distribution of lowland forest trees in Uganda and western Kenya according to fruit/seed type

	A Species restricted to western Uganda No. (%)	B Species of intermediate distributon in Uganda No. (%)	C Species extending to eastern Uganda No. (%)	D Species reaching western Kenya No. (%)
1. Species with wind-dispersed plumed seeds	0 (0)	2 (2)	2 (2)	1 (1)
2. Species with wind-dispersed winged fruits/seeds	2 (4)	9 (7)	7 (7)	4 (7)
3. Species with wind-dispersed fruits lacking plumes or wings	0 (0)	2 (2)	0 (0)	0 (0)
4. Species with animal dispersed fruits/seeds small enough to be transported by birds or fruit bats	25 (54)	77 (58)	61 (63)	45 (79)
5. Species with animal dispersed fruits/seeds unlikely to be carried by flying animals	8 (17)	15 (11)	7 (7)	2 (4)
6. Other species	11 (24)	28 (21)	20 (21)	5 (9)
Totals	46 (99)	133 (101)	97 (100)	57 (100)

Definition of distributional categories (Flora-areas are as used for "Flora of Tropical East Africa" (1952 etc.) and as shown on Fig. 80). A, species confined to Flora-area 2; B, species found in Flora-area 2 and one other flora-area, but not in Flora-area 3; C, species recorded from Flora-area 3 (all also occur elsewhere); D, species recorded from Kakamega Forest, Kenya (Lucas, 1968).

Table 12　(a) Distributions in Uganda of primary and secondary forest tree species recorded from (i) Budongo Forest and (ii) Kibale/Itwara Forest

	Number of flora-areas from which spp. are recorded				Total no. of spp.
	1	2	3	4	
(i) Budongo Forest					
Tree spp. recorded from woodland or *Maesopsis* plots	0	3 (12%)	7 (27%)	16 (62%)	26
Tree spp. recorded from mixed or *Cynometra* plots	2 (8%)	9 (35%)	11 (42%)	4 (15%)	26
(ii) Kibale/Itwara Forest					
Trees found in woodland or forest gaps	0	2 (12%)	4 (25%)	10 (62%)	16
Trees found in older forest types	6 (9%)	10 (15%)	29 (44%)	21 (32%)	66

(b) Comparison of dispersal methods of primary and secondary forest trees in Budongo and Kibale/Itwara Forests

	Plumed seeds	Winged fruits/ seeds	Bird/ bat dispersed	Other animal dispersed	Unclas- sified	Totals
(i) Budongo Forest						
Tree spp. recorded from woodland or *Maesopsis* plots	1 (4%)	0	22 (85%)	1 (4%)	2 (8%)	26
Tree spp. recorded from mixed or *Cynometra* plots	1 (4%)	3 (12%)	12 (64%)	4 (15%)	6 (23%)	26
(ii) Kibale/Itwara Forest						
Trees found in woodland or forest gaps	2 (12%)	0	12 (75%)	0	2 (12%)	16
Trees found in older forest types	7 (11%)	1 (2%)	46 (70%)	6 (9%)	6 (9%)	66

Data for Budongo Forest from Eggeling (1947) and for Kibale/Itwara Forest from Osmaston (1959). Some species at Budongo were recorded from more than one forest type, but in the Kibale/Itwara lists species appear in only one or the other of the two types.

development. The lists are for two different forests in western Uganda (both in Flora-area 2). One set of data relates to species recorded from four plots in Budongo Forest (Eggeling, 1947) and the other to an inventory for Kibale/Itwara Forest (Osmaston, 1959). The four plots in Budongo are Woodland Forest of age 30 years, *Maesopsis* Forest of age 30–40 years, Mixed Forest of age 200–250 years and *Cynometra* Forest of unknown age, but older than Mixed Forest. The lists for the first two, and those for the last two of these plots have been combined to give the two categories shown in Table 12. The classification of species for Kibale/Itwara Forest follows Osmaston's division into woodland and gap species, taken together as one category, and species of older forest types (marked F on his lists).

It is apparent from Table 12(a) that species of younger forest types tend to have relatively wide distributions. For example, 62% of species recorded from younger forest types, both at Budongo and Kibale/Itwara, are found in all four flora-areas, compared with only 15% and 32% of the species of maturer forest types in the two forests, respectively. It therefore seems that generation time, in addition to disseminule type, helps to determine the distribution of tree species. But what if these two variables are themselves correlated? Table 12(b) shows that this is indeed the case. Most notably, relatively high proportions of species of younger forest types have small animal-dispersed disseminules and large animal-dispersed disseminules are mainly a feature of species of mature forest types.

I do not claim that this matter is fully explored here, but merely give it as an example of the type of analysis which might prove rewarding to pursue in detail in the future.

Peat Formation in Eastern Africa

The rate of peat accumulation in eastern Africa can vary greatly between different mires and at different times at any one site. It would be wrong to suppose that the factors determining peat formation are well understood, but sufficient information now exists to warrant some speculations.

Fig. 82 shows some of the main pathways through which organic matter comes to be deposited on or eroded from a mire surface. It is believed that the rates of gain or loss along some of these pathways can vary greatly. Dealing first with the *in situ* processes of primary production and decomposition, it is thought that, as elsewhere in the

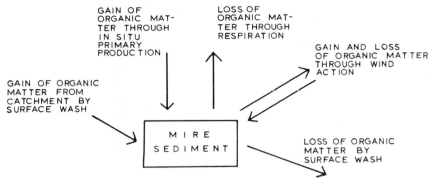

Fig. 82 Simple model showing some pathways through which organic matter is gained or lost from the surface of a mire. For respiration, read decomposition.

world, the balance tends to be tipped in the direction of peat accumulation by constant waterlogging, low temperatures or low pH values (Moore and Bellamy, 1973). The influence of the first two of these is shown in a general way by the tendency for peatlands in eastern Africa to be concentrated in areas of higher rainfall and lower temperature. In the case of a peat deposit in which gains or losses of organic matter through other channels have always been negligible, then the climate at any particular time is thought to be the chief factor determining whether any peat is accumulating and, if so, at what rate.

Mire surfaces which are subject to a substantial flow of surface water have the potential both to receive surface-transported organic matter from elsewhere, and to lose it through erosion. The importance of surface water flow during the history of a mire deposit can be assessed by three characteristics: mineral content of the peat, fossil plant remains, and topographic position of the mire.

Mineral matter can reach a mire surface through the atmosphere or by surface wash from surrounding slopes. The importance of the latter may in part be judged by the sizes of mineral particles in the sediment, larger particles being less likely to have been transported by wind, and in part by the regularity of the distribution of mineral matter in the sediment body, greater irregularity along either the horizontal or vertical axes raising the likelihood that there has been a major wash component. It is argued that the presence of mineral matter wash from surrounding slopes indicates environmental processes potentially also capable of depositing or removing organic matter from the surface of the growing mire.

The vegetation type of a mire is known to be related to the quantity of nutrients entering the mire by surface water flow (Moore and

Bellamy, 1973). The latter depends on factors such as the volume of the flow, the rock type and the degree of vegetation cover in the catchment. Thus, other factors being equal, the presence of a peat body formed by an oligotrophic plant community, such as one rich in *Sphagnum*, suggests that there has been little nutrient input from surrounding slopes. This in turn suggests little surface water flow and hence also little organic matter movement along the surface. On the other hand, the former existence of a mesotrophic or eutrophic community, such as one dominated by a species of *Cyperus*, indicates that there may have been substantial surface transport of organic matter.

The topographic position of a mire deposit is obviously important in determining whether it is liable to be subject to substantial surface water flow. Both the general shape of the mire surface in relation to the surrounding landscape and whether or not a marginal canalizing zone is present must be considered. Marginal wet zones serve to inhibit the penetration of water from surrounding slopes to central mire areas and are mainly a feature of lower altitude mires in climatically wetter areas. They occur at Kamiranzovu Swamp and at some of the south-west Ugandan mires.

The varying importance of changes in precipitation, temperature and surface wash are illustrated by reference to a number of examples. Unfortunately, the number of reasonably well-dated sediment profiles is small. Karimu Swamp is a mire at 3040 m on the plateau area of the Aberdares (Fig. 83). The sediments are currently under detailed investigation by R. A. Perrott. It can be seen from Fig. 84 that there may have been two periods of peat formation, one extending from very roughly 32 600–24 000 B.P. and the other beginning soon before 9000 B.P. The two peat horizons are separated from one another by a substantial band of clay. This pattern is believed to be related to climatic history in a fairly simple way, the central clay band being deposited under a dry climate, when there was little stabilizing vegetation on slopes around the mire, and the peat bands dating to wetter periods. It is thought that there was probably rather little organic matter movement onto or off the mire during the periods of peat accumulation. The reasons for this belief are that the mire is large, both in an absolute sense (several kilometres across) and in relation to the area of its catchment, and that oligotrophic conditions are suggested, at least at the present time, by the mire vegetation, which includes abundant *Sphagnum*.

The history of peat accumulation of Kamiranzovu Swamp, Rwanda (1950 m), is striking and informative. Peat accumulated

Fig. 83 Karimu Swamp, Aberdares Range, Kenya, 3040 m. This is a very large mire with much *Carex monostachya*. Bamboo and *Cliffortia* thickets are present on the slope beyond. An isolated giant groundsel is growing in the foreground.

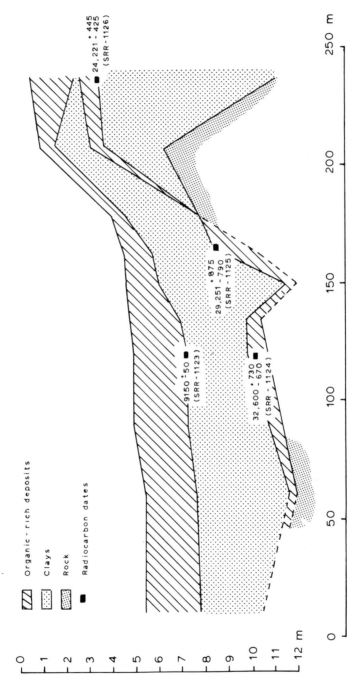

Fig. 84 Upper Quaternary sediments of Karimu Swamp on the plateau area of the Aberdares, Kenya. Clay-rich sediments are sandwiched between two organic deposits, the lower of which is itself locally underlain by clays. Judging by the ^{14}C dates, there was probably some removal of the lower organic-rich stratum prior to deposition of the upper clays. The shape of the underlying rock surface is probably related in part to the disposition of individual lava flows.

steadily between *c.* 37 630 and about 12 600/11 000 B.P., since when the mire surface has stagnated. The mire was dominated for most of this period by a *Sphagnum/Erica/Xyris* community and, considering this and the fact that the mire is today very flat and has a well defined marginal wet zone, it is likely that, as at Karimu, there has been rather little transportation of organic matter by surface water flow during the peat accumulating phase. It is therefore thought that climatic change must have been responsible for causing cessation of peat growth. Now, we know from much evidence that the period *c.* 21 000–12/10 000 B.P. was marked by less rainfall than more recent times and it is considered that the period of peat growth was dependent on the lower temperatures which prevailed before 12 600/ 11 000 B.P. and which permitted organic accumulation during the relatively arid period of the last ice age.

Kaisungor Swamp, Cherangani, and Badda Bog, Ethiopia, are both small valley mires which, I believe, have sometimes been subject to substantial surface water flow. Both accumulated peat up to sometime between 12 000 and 10 000 B.P. and again after very approximately 4000 B.P., but not, or at a very slow rate, during the intervening period. By analogy with Kamiranzovu, it is postulated that lower temperatures may have helped to offset the influence of drier climate in permitting the first phase of peat growth. But neither a fall in temperature nor a fall in rainfall can be invoked to explain why peat started accumulating again after 4000 B.P., since this date marks an important change to a drier climate in eastern Africa with at the most only minor temperature changes. In my view the lack of accumulation of organic matter between *c.* 10 000 and 4000 B.P. is due to substantial erosion of the organic matter from the mires by surface wash. This itself is taken to be due to increased surface water flow under the wetter climate and possibly also to more luxuriant growth of the mire dominants. Both these mires are now, and almost certainly always have been, dominated by tussock-forming species. Water flowing through the mires will have been channelled between the tussocks and it is postulated that under wetter climatic conditions the tussocks would have grown more luxuriantly, possibly reducing the protective cover of vegetation lining the inter-tussock channels as a consequence of greater shading.

There is some evidence of a higher rate of soil erosion during the drier post-4000 B.P. period than during the preceeding wetter period. This is shown, for example, by increased quantities of inorganic matter in sediments beneath Lake Kimilili and Sacred Lake. There is also evidence of a high rate of erosion maintained for a short period at the transition to a more humid climate at *c*. 12 000/10 000 B.P. A high rate of sedimentation at this time is reported for Laboot Swamp, Lake Rutundu and Kawasenkoko Swamp. It is suggested that the high erosion rate was due to the effects of heavy precipitation falling on slopes which had not yet been covered by a dense mantle of vegetation and which may also have been topographically poorly adapted to the new climatic regime. High sedimentation rates during the transition from the arid to the moist phase are also reported from the Sahel Zone (Talbot, 1980).

Chapter 11

Quaternary Man and Environment in East Africa

Interest in Fossil Man

East Africa has become pre-eminent in the study of early man. Reasons include the following (Isaac, 1975):

(1) The region has the longest known record of occupation by hominids and their closest relatives. Fossils date back to 22 million years and are particularly numerous for the last 6 million years.
(2) East Africa lies within the biogeographical zone which supported man's hominid ancestors.
(3) Earth movements associated with the rift valleys have repeatedly created sedimentary basins in which fossils and archaeological sites could be preserved with a minimum of disturbance.
(4) Continual volcanic activity provides a basis for K-A dating and geophysical chronology.

A driving force behind many investigations of early hominids has been interest in the course of human evolution. By this is meant not only changes in the physical characteristics of man, but also his technological and social development and his varying relationship with the environment. In the past, it has often been held that pre-agricultural man made little impact on his environment, but increasingly this view is being questioned. Today, it seems likely that man has been an important modifying influence in savanna ecosystems in tropical Africa over a very long period of time.

Quaternary Hominids

Man is the only surviving species of the Hominidae, the family which includes man and his nearest relatives (von Koenigswald, 1962). The most closely related groups to the Hominidae are the apes (family Pongidae) and the extinct genus *Parapithecus* (family Parapithecidae) which together are included with the Hominidae in the superfamily Hominoidea.

Most important fossil hominid sites in East Africa are associated with the Eastern Rift Valley. The most famous site is Olduvai in northern Tanzania, where a gorge has cut through and exposed a long series of deposits, including four major beds (numbered I to IV) and some overlying more recent strata. Olduvai Gorge contains an exceptionally long record of hominid fossils and artefacts, the range of time represented being from soon after 1·89 million years to *c.* 200 000 B.P. (M. D. Leakey, 1975). Another major locality for fossil hominids is the Omo/Lake Turkana area: there are three principal fossiliferous localities which taken together have sediments extending from *c.* 6 million years to the present (Coppens *et al.*, 1976). There is a scarcity of hominid fossils in East Africa for the period 500 000–50 000 B.P. (Pilbeam, 1975).

By the beginning of the Quaternary (*c.* 2·5 million B.P.) it is known that the ancestors of man were well established as ground-living, bipedal, social and, to some extent, flesh-eating animals (Isaac, 1975), but the patterns of evolution shown by hominids during the Quaternary are debated. There seem to have been periods of relatively rapid change at *c.* 1 250 000 ± 250 000 and 75 000 ± 25 000 B.P. (Pilbeam, 1975). During the late Pliocene and most of the Lower Quaternary (i.e. *c.* 5–1·25 million years), two or perhaps three hominid species were present, probably sympatrically, in East Africa (Clark, 1976; Howell and Isaac, 1976; R. E. F. Leakey, 1976). A species distinct from the others was *Australopithecus robustus*, a small brained (endocranial volume *c.* 500 ml), large toothed, rugged skulled, markedly sexually dimorphic and largely vegetarian species. The classification of the remaining hominids is controversial. Two "species" may have been present, one which has been assigned to the genus *Homo* and the other a gracile species of *Australopithecus* (*A. africanus*). Both species had unspecialized dentition, such as is characteristic of omnivores, and it is possible that *Australopithecus africanus* is ancestral to *Homo*. Fossils referred to *Homo* have been described from rocks dating back to perhaps 3 million years and even at this early date a skull is known with the remarkably large endocranial volume of 775 ml.

Between about 1·25 ± 0·25 million years and 75 000 ± 25 000 B.P., the only hominid known world-wide is *Homo erectus* and this is believed to lie on the genetic lineage between the *Homo* of the Lower Quaternary and *H. sapiens*. Fossils have been found in Africa, Asia and Europe. *Homo erectus* shows much variation, including variation in brain size (775–1225 ml (Clark, 1976)), probably the result of regional differentiation and genetic drift within a single genetic system. Some groups may have evolved in isolation for relatively long periods of time and it is possible that some populations failed to contribute genes to future stocks.

Homo erectus was succeeded in the Upper Quaternary (at *c.* 75 000 B.P.) by *H. sapiens*. Fossils predating *c.* 40 000 B.P. differ from those of modern man and have been designated as either Neanderthal man, *H. sapiens neanderthalensis*, recorded from North Africa and Europe, or Rhodesian man, *H. sapiens rhodesiensis*, known from a few finds in sub-saharan Africa. According to some authorities, the skull of *Homo sapiens* differs from that of *H. erectus* in showing changes believed essential for the development of the voice-box and the use of language.

The Archaeological Record

Stone implements, being resistant to weathering, form the principal record of man's material culture for all but the most recent times. There is, however, no doubt that objects made of perishable materials such as bone and wood contributed substantially to prehistoric technologies (Coles and Higgs, 1969). Stone tools are known from Africa earlier than in any other part of the world. Traditionally, stone tool assemblages from Africa have been placed into three categories according to their supposed times of origin, the Earlier, Middle and Later Stone Ages (and Intervening First and Second Intermediate Periods) (Cole, 1964). This classification has been criticized for its potential in confusing categories based on lithic characteristics, with categories based on time (Phillipson, 1977), and is probably less used today than formerly. The Earlier Stone Age (E.S.A.) includes the Acheulian and Oldowan industries, the M.S.A. is a rather vague category thought to be associated with Rhodesian Man and the L.S.A. includes late-Upper Quaternary industries and is characterized by small (microlithic) impliments.

The oldest known stone industry is the Oldowan, named after Olduvai Gorge, where it is known throughout Bed I and into basal Bed II. The Oldowan is found over a large part of the African continent and in rocks dating back *c.* 2·5 million years (Isaac, 1976). Tool-making hominids have thus been present throughout the East African Quaternary. Although direct evidence is lacking, it is commonly believed that Oldowan implements were manufactured by early *Homo* and/or perhaps *Australopithecus africanus*. The tools are informal and include choppers, polyhedrons, discoids and scrapers (M. D. Leakey, 1975). The most characteristic of these is the chopper, an implement with a length of 5–20 cm and manufactured, in the case of a pebble, by removal of flakes from one end (Fig. 85). The intersections of the flake scars form a sharp and uneven edge and the tools were probably used for cutting, pounding and digging.

The Oldowan is succeeded by the Acheulian (*sensu lato*), dating

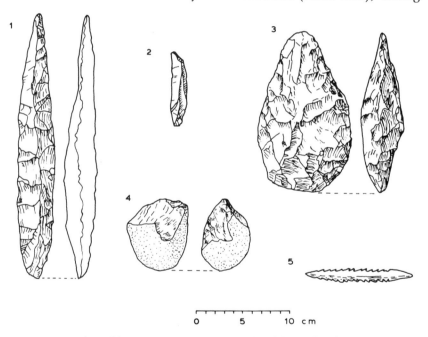

Fig. 85   Stone tools and harpoon. 1. Lupemban bifacial lanceolate from Kinshasha, Zaire; 2. Kenya Capsian blade from Gamble's Cave, Kenya; 3. Acheulean hand axe from Bed IV, Olduvai Gorge, Tanzania; 4. Chopper from Bed I, Olduvai Gorge, Tanzania; 5. Bone harpoon head from Ishango, Lake Edward. 1, 2 and 5 from J. D. Clark (1970) "The Prehistory of Africa" by permission of Thames and Hudson Ltd and 3 and 4 reprinted by permission of Faber and Faber Ltd from "The Archaeology of Early Man" by J. M. Coles and E. S. Higgs (1969).

from perhaps 1·4 million years (Isaac, 1975) to *c.* 50 000 B.P. The Acheulian is widely spread in Africa, though poorly represented in some regions which are either very arid or heavily forested today. Elsewhere, it is known from parts of Europe and Asia. At Olduvai, the Acheulian commences within Bed II, its appearance being co-incident with the demise of the Villifranchian fauna. The industry is regarded as the work of *Homo erectus.*

The most conspicuous feature of the Acheulian is its uniformity and lack of any great change over a very long period of time. This having been said, Acheulian assemblages fall into two rather distinct, but contemporaneous, categories, known respectively as the Developed Oldowan and the "classic" Acheulian (M. D. Leakey, 1975). The classic Acheulian is characterized by abundant large tools such as handaxes (Fig. 85; often thought of as the distinctive Acheulian implement), cleavers, and knives; smaller tools, such as choppers, spheroids, scrappers and anvils, can also be common. The Developed Oldowan differs in being dominated by small-sized implements, large tools being rare. Various theories have been advanced for the co-existence of these two rather different tool assemblages (e.g. M. D. Leakey, 1975). Perhaps the most likely explanation is that the industries were appropriate for different activities, the classic Acheulian being associated more with plant-gathering and the Developed Oldowan with hunting. This is suggested, for instance, by an association between sites of large animal butchery and the Developed Oldowan (Clark, 1975).

Acheulian sites are preferentially found close to water-courses (Clark, 1975; Isaac, 1975). Apart from satisfying the need to drink regularly, the location of occupation sites near rivers and lakes would often have provided *Homo erectus* with ready access to a range of ecosystem types, including riparian forest and savanna. Riparian forest may have provided shade, a refuge and a source of fruits (Isaac, 1975), while hunting may have been mainly a savanna activity. Archaeological sites vary greatly in density of bone refuse, suggesting variation in the contribution of meat to the diet and it is thought that vegetable foods were always important (Isaac, 1975). A full range of mammals, including large mammals, were exploited. Group size is estimated at around 10–50.

According to Isaac (1975), the Acheulian in Europe is probably no older than 700 000 years and may be as young as 500 000–400 000 years. This expansion of man into the temperate zone suggests an increase in the adaptability of *Homo erectus.* In general, however, the marked uniformity of the Acheulian contrasts with the proliferation of industries in the relatively brief post-Acheulian period. In post-Acheulian times, the archaeological record indicates:

(1) a great geographical expansion in the range of man,
(2) an extension in the range of staple foods,
(3) a great elaboration of the maximum level of technology and material culture,
(4) increasingly pronounced geographical differentiation and greater specificity in regional adaptations and
(5) material traces of spiritual and symbolic activity (Isaac, 1975).

These changes are together believed to be related to both increase in brain capacity and the development of increasingly sophisticated language.

The Acheulian is succeeded in Africa by three industries, occurring to a large extent in geographically distinct parts of the continent. The transition is roughly dated at, or slightly before the end of the early Würm glacial maximum at *c.* 60 000 B.P., which was probably marked by aridity over much of tropical Africa. North Africa was part of the Mousterian Industrial Area associated with Neanderthal man (Clark, 1960, 1970). The other two African industries (traditionally assigned to the First Intermediate Period) are the Fauresmith and the Sangoan, believed to be the work of Rhodesian man. The Fauresmith is very similar to the Acheulian and is found principally in southern Africa, with apparently disjunct occurrences also in highland East Africa and Ethiopia. It could be that in the latter areas (e.g. Mt Kenya and the Aberdares) Fauresmith man was restricted to high altitudes by his need to avail himself of permanent streams, water being scarce at lower altitudes (Cole, 1964). The Sangoan industry is confined to areas of tropical Africa which today receive more than 100 cm mean annual rainfall (Cole, 1964) and this culture was apparently the first to occupy extensive parts of the present forest zone of West and Central Africa (Clark, 1965). In contrast to the Acheulian, handaxes and cleavers are absent, being replaced by forms (including heavy-duty "core-axes" and "picks") which were clearly used for wood-working. It is suggested that the movement of man into a zone which today carries forest was assisted by the disruption of the forest cover under the prevailing dry climate. It is possible that much of the occupied region was covered by tree-rich savanna.

The Fauresmith and Sangoan were replaced perhaps shortly before 40 000 B.P. by Middle Stone Age cultures, an event possibly associated with the spread of modern man (Clark, 1970). In drier parts of Africa the M.S.A. cultures (such as the Stillbay) were characterized by light-duty equipment including projectile points, knives of various kinds and carefully rounded stone balls (Clark, 1965). In wetter regions, the Sangoan was developed into the Lupemban, the only major difference in the distributions of the two cultures being the absence of the Lupemban south of the Zambezi (Clark, 1965, 1970; Cole, 1964). According to Clark and Cole, this retraction in range might be due to greater aridity in southern Africa after *c.* 40 000 B.P. The Lupemban tool-kit, which includes a characteristic elongated lanceolate type with bifacial retouch, is clearly associated largely with wood-working.

Later Stone Age industries are characterized by the production of large punch-struck blades (before *c.* 8000 B.P.) and microliths. The latter are small blades or flakes, blunted by retouch on one or more edges and were probably mainly used hafted to other materials to make complicated tools. Although L.S.A. implements are known from East Africa as early as *c.* 18 000 B.P., it is believed that it was only at around 12 000/10 000 B.P. that L.S.A. cultures spread widely throughout the region (Phillipson, 1977). This date is of course of great environmental significance, marking a major change from general aridity to much more humid climates in tropical Africa. At several sites, bone analysis indicates a change in hunting with an increased emphasis on smaller, less gregarious creatures (Phillipson, 1977). The latter would have increased in abundance in response to the greater vegetation cover.

Despite a general uniformity in eastern Africa from Ethiopia to the Cape (Oliver and Fagan, 1975), L.S.A. industries show greater variation, presumably related to environmental specialization, than is evident at earlier times (Phillipson, 1977). The makers of L.S.A. artefacts were almost certainly of Bushman/Hottentot stock and, with minor exceptions, were only replaced or absorbed over much of East Africa with the spread of Bantu-speaking people *c.* 2000 years ago. In southern Africa these hunters and gatherers persisted widely as far north as Zimbabwe up to about 100 years ago, but today they have become restricted by the spread of agriculture and occur mainly in the arid region of the Kalahari. Isolated groups of hunters-gatherers, including the Hadza of Tanzania, still persist very locally in more northern parts of Africa. The Hadza language is believed by some authorities to be related to that of the Kalahari bushmen.

A distinctive African L.S.A. culture is one with an emphasis on fishing which flourished over very large parts of the southern Sahara at the time of the early Holocene high lake stands (Smith, 1980; Sutton, 1974). This culture is also known to have occurred along the

Nile and as far south as Lakes Turkana, Nakuru and Edward in East Africa. Bone harpoons (Fig. 85) were in use back to at least 9000 B.P. and the earliest pottery known from East Africa, dating to the seventh millennium B.C., is associated with this culture. The culture flourished at *c.* 9000–7500 B.P. and, according to Sutton (1974), showed a minor revival during the second high Holocene lake stands at *c.* 6000–5000 B.P.

The introduction of domesticated animals and of cultivation resulted in a revolution in the relationship between man and environment. Cattle were probably introduced into Africa from a centre of domestication in western Asia (Clark, 1970; Payne, 1964). Pastoralists first appeared in the Sahara shortly after 7000 B.P., driving herds of cattle and "shoats" (goats and/or sheep) and the pastoral way of life spread rapidly across much of the Sahara down to 10°N and from the longitude of Timbuctu to that of the Nile. The Saharan Neolithic persisted until shortly after 4500 B.P., when increased aridity resulted in most of the area becoming unsuitable for habitation by pastoral man (Smith, 1980).

The origins of plant domestication in tropical Africa have been discussed by Clark (1976), Harlan *et al.*, (1976), Oliver and Fagan (1975), Shaw (1976) and Stemler (1980). There is a consensus that the concept of centres of origin, that is places where plants were first domesticated and out of which cultures diffused, is not particularly helpful when dealing with the origins of many of the indigenous tropical African crops, such as yams, oil palm, sorghum and some of the millets. It is envisaged that the practice of cultivation was a consequence of aridification in the Sahara after *c.* 4500 B.P. and the movement of pastoral people southwards into areas occupied by hunters and gatherers who previously lacked domesticates. This population movement appears to have been associated with the origins of plant domestication south of the Sahara and it is thus thought that cultivation may have begun in tropical Africa (though not specifically in East Africa) as early as 4000 B.P. Early domesticates are believed to have included sorghum and millets. The oldest fossil evidence of domesticated forms of indigenous African grasses is 1000 B.C. (Mauritania) and 245 A.D. (Sudan).

In East Africa the transformation from hunting and gathering to agriculture is believed to be associated with the arrival of people from elsewhere introducing the local population to livestock and crops (Clark, 1976). The oldest known bones of domestic animals in East Africa have been discovered in sites of the Stone Bowl culture, which is recorded from the Eatern Rift Valley and adjoining plateau areas of

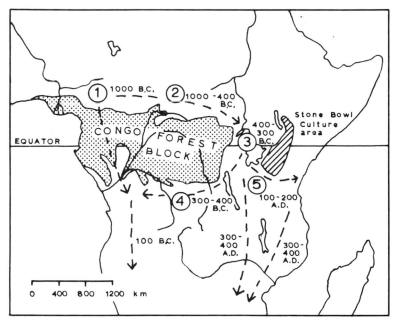

Fig. 86 Part of tropical Africa showing the area yielding finds of the Stone Bowl Culture and stages in the spread of Bantu speakers. The numbers refer to stages mentioned in the text. Adapted from Phillipson (1977).

Kenya and northern Tanzania (Fig. 86) (Bower *et al.*, 1977; Oliver and Fagan, 1975; Onyango-Abuje, 1977; Phillipson, 1977). These cattle-herders were certainly in East Africa in the first millennium B.C. and may have been present by the middle of the second millennium B.C. (Clark, 1976) and thus it is likely that their arrival is part of the general southern movement of pastoralists across Africa induced by aridity after *c.* 4500 B.P. Finds include stone pestles and mortars, pottery, baskets and beads of semi-precious stones; links with the north or north-east are indicated by some artefacts (Oliver and Fagan, 1975). The persistent use of stone tools similar to those of the Late Stone Age people who preceeded them (Onyango-Abuje, 1977) suggests a fusion of old and new cultures (Oliver and Fagan, 1975). There is no direct evidence of cultivation, but it is possible that the stone vessels typical of this culture could have been used for preparing food from a cultivated grain (Clark, 1976).

There is some evidence that pottery (Kansyore ware) and perhaps cereal cultivation and cattle-keeping were present in the Lake Victoria region for a brief period before the introduction of iron-working (Oliver and Fagan, 1975). However, there is little doubt that major expansion, if not perhaps the introduction, of cultivation in East Africa was a consequence of the spread of Bantu-speaking people into and within the region during the period *c.* 400 B.C.–400 A.D. (Phillipson, 1975, 1977). These people also introduced iron-working (Huffman, 1970), as well as the pottery types known as Urewe (Dimple-based), Kwale and Lelusu ware (Phillipson, 1977). Today, Bantu-speaking people are dominant over virtually all of Africa south of the Equator, but linguistic analysis clearly shows that the Bantu language group is new, probably originating from a small nuclear area during comparatively recent years. Following earlier work by Guthrie (1967) and others, Phillipson (1977) has put forward the following reconstruction (here simplified) of the expansion of Bantu-speakers across Africa, taking regard of both the linguistic and archaeological evidence (Fig. 86):

(1) By 1000 B.C., there was early development of Bantu speech in the Cameroon area among a stone tool-using population which at a relatively late date obtained domestic goats and may have had some form of cultivation.

(2) *c.* 1000–400 B.C. these people dispersed eastwards along the northern fringes of the equatorial forest. They came into contact with mixed-farmers, from whom they adopted the herding of cattle and sheep and the cultivation of cereal crops, notably sorghum. Knowledge of iron-working was almost certainly also acquired during this period.

(3) *c.* 400–300 B.C. Bantu-speakers reached the inter-lacustrine region (including western East Africa) where they established an Early Iron Age culture (with Urewe ware).

(4) *c.* 300–100 B.C. movement continued around the flank of the Congo forest and contact was achieved to the south of the forest with another group of Bantu-speakers who had earlier moved directly southwards from Cameroon.

(5) *c.* 100–200 A.D. people descended from the Urewe ware-makers, moved southwards and eastwards to the coasts of Kenya and northern Tanzania, establishing settlements characterized by Kwale ware.

The neolithic history of the area to the south of the main Congo forest, that is Katanga and neighbourhood, appears to be still very little understood. This is an area in which savanna occurs over large areas believed to be climatically suitable for forest (Aubréville, 1949; Oliver and Fagan, 1975). Judging by incipient speciation shown by some butterflies (Carcasson, 1964), some of the remnant forest patches within the derived savanna may have been isolated from one another and from the main forest block for a long period of time. Fragmentation of the forest would appear to have been earlier than in the case of Uganda where there is little differentiation between isolated butterfly populations. Possibly, some of the avifaunal contrasts between the northern and southern parts of the central Congo forest (Diamond and Hamilton, 1980; Hamilton, 1976a) may also be due to a long history of forest disturbance by man in the south.

Around the beginning of the second millennium A.D., early Iron Age pottery was succeeded between Kivu and central Kenya by coarser, roulette-decorated ware (Oliver and Fagan, 1975). Comparable pottery is still produced today in several of the Bantu-speaking interlacustrine kingdoms (Phillipson, 1977). Dimple-based ware and associated iron-working never penetrated into the Kenyan Rift area. Here the Stone Bowl culture persisted until well into the second millennium A.D. when it also was replaced by a culture making roulette-decorated pottery (Oliver and Fagan, 1975). The roulette-decorated pottery was introduced into East Africa by largely pastoral, Nilotic-speaking people from the north. The pottery tradition was readily absorbed by the Bantu agriculturalists, but in other respects the arrival of the Nilotic-speakers was less welcome and it is possible that the centrally-organized Bantu kingdoms of Uganda and its neighbourhood may have arisen at this time, partly as a reaction to Nilotic influence (Phillipson, 1977). A standard theme of early oral tradition in the interlacustrine region is of interaction between incoming pastoralists and established agriculturalists.

Several plants which are today widely grown in tropical Africa have been introduced from other continents. The inadequacy of present knowledge concerning early agricultural development in tropical Africa is well illustrated by the banana/plantain (*Musa*), which is of south-east Asian origin and which has been in Africa for many hundreds of years (McMaster, 1962). The earliest historical record of the banana in Africa is from an Arabic source dating to the early tenth century (Phillipson, 1977) and the plant may have been transported to the East African coast by Malayo-Polynesians (Purseglove, 1976). The route by which *Musa* penetrated into inland Africa is uncertain. Both the Zambezi valley (Purseglove, 1976) and Ethiopia (McMaster, 1962) have been mentioned as possibilities. Maize, common bean (*Phaseolus vulgaris*), groundnut (*Arachis hypogaea*), sweet potato (*Ipomoea batatas*) and cassava (*Manihot esculenta*) were introduced to Africa by the Portugese following the Columban discovery of America (Purseglove, 1976).

Some Interactions of Man and Environment

Man as a hunter and gatherer is essentially a savanna dweller and there is a striking difference between his impact on forest and savanna ecosystems. Until recent times, man's intervention into wetter types of forest ecosystem has probably been negligible. Even since the introduction of cultivation and iron-working, his main interest in forested areas has generally been the destruction of the forest and its replacement, with a greater or lesser degree of permanency, by either crops or savanna communities. In contrast, hominids have inhabited African savannas throughout the Quaternary and at least some features of savanna ecosystems must have been influenced by this long occupancy.

The influence of climatic changes on early hominids is poorly known, but presumably oscillations in human population density paralleled oscillations in the ecosystems which man inhabited. The distribution of Acheulian artefacts indicates that *Homo erectus* avoided heavily forested and arid regions, and presumably, within the savanna zone, certain types of savanna were more favoured than others. Climatic oscillations may thus have been responsible for repeatedly increasing and decreasing the amount of contact between human populations, thereby creating opportunities for divergence and selection in genetic and cultural traits. In some areas, however, such as parts of East Africa, human cultures might have been buffered against climatic oscillations by the continued existence of a range of ecosystem types in topographically diverse landscapes (Isaac, 1975).

Today, the great majority of savanna ecosystems are regularly burnt by man. The earliest archaeological evidence for Africa of the use of fire by man (e.g. as indicated by the presence of hearths) appears to come from Kalambo Falls, with an age of *c.* 60 000 B.P. (Clark, 1970). In France there are indications that man was a fire-user as early as 400 000 B.P. (Lumley, 1975) and, given the geographical distribution of the Acheulian culture, the technology must have been known to *Homo erectus* also in Africa at an early date. Burning is such an ubiquitous feature of modern savanna ecosystems that some of the characteristics which such ecosystems would possess in the absence of man-induced burning are difficult to judge. Fire exclusion plots in savanna ecosystems nearly always show a great increase in the biomass of woody plants. It is probable that many areas which today are grass-dominated or which carry a scattered growth of bushes or trees would have supported more woody types of vegetation before regular burning by man. In this context it has been suggested that the miombo (*Brachystegia* woodland) which covers much of Tanzania, Zambia and neighbouring regions has largely replaced dry forest types (van Zinderen Bakker, 1969a). These could have been similar to the isolated patches of the community known as transition woodland in Malawi (Chapman and White, 1970), the vegetation of which is physiognomically and floristically intermediate between forest and woodland. When this replacement occurred is unknown, but palynological evidence from Kalambo Falls shows the presence of *Brachystegia* woodland well back into the Upper Quaternary.

There was a major extinction of mammals, particularly large mammals, in Africa at very approximately the date of the transition from Acheulian to later cultures (Martin, 1966). Similar major extinctions occurred elsewhere in the world during the Upper Quaternary and cover a wide range of dates, but always apparently coincident either with the arrival of man in an area or with a change in his material culture (Martin, 1966). It thus seems that man was the responsible agent. In the case of Africa, over-hunting and the discovery of the use of poison have been advanced as possible causes (Hamilton, 1974b; Verdcourt, personal communication), and it is likely that, given the scale of the extinctions, a major factor must have been ecosystem modification on a massive scale. We can envisage that replacement of *Homo erectus* by *H. sapiens* led to an intensification of man's exploitation of his environment, with burning on a scale not indulged in before, and the development of new hunting techniques.

Two possible evolutionary consequences of man's increasingly important position in savanna ecosystems are briefly mentioned. First, the decrease in biomass of woody plants would have increased the relative importance of herbaceous plants. Perhaps declining opportunities for one set of organisms might have been paralleled by increasing opportunities for another, but whether the length of time is sufficient for much adaptive radiation to occur is unknown. Second, a consequence of burning and of human activities in ecosystems generally can be to introduce a new type of patchiness. Greater diversity in the environment on a local scale may have been responsible for breaking down the reproductive barriers between some taxa and encouraging the production of new ecotypes.

The introduction of cattle added a new element into some East African ecosystems. An advantage of cattle or of other domestic animals or plants to man is the channelling of ecosystem productivity into forms that can readily be harvested. In the absence of the introduction of energy and usually also of nutrients into an ecosystem from elsewhere, a consequence of this channelling is a general reduction in ecosystem productivity. Also, the domestic organisms may, on a longer or shorter time-scale, cause changes to ecosystems inimical to the interests of the domestic organisms themselves. In the case of dometic animals, the degradation of the habitat which may result as a consequence of over-stocking is well known and is briefly described in the next chapter. In the case of annual crops, such as maize, sorghum or millets, the whole ecosystem is severely disrupted by the stripping of the vegetation cover prior to sowing and the continued major interference in the ecosystem through weeding during the period of crop growth. Cultivation usually involves a seasonal increase in the area of bare soil and thus an enhanced potential for soil erosion. The actual rate of soil removal from cultivated land is influenced by many factors, including the rhythm of cultivation compared with that of the seasons, soil permeability, topography and the existence of erosion-prevention practices.

A small amount of evidence is available on the dating of early agriculture and its effects on East African ecosystems. Livingstone (1975) has suggested that an increase in *Acalypha* pollen sometime before 4000 B.P. in the Lake Mahoma diagram from Ruwenzori may have been a consequence of agriculture in the lowlands around the mountain. If this is so, then agriculture in East Africa is older than is suggested by the archaeological record. Major changes in vegetation in a forested landscape are shown by three pollen diagrams from south-west Uganda (Figs 87 and 88; Morrison and Hamilton, 1974). Deforestation is estimated to have commenced at very roughly 1000 B.P. and three phases of disturbance can be recognized. In stage 1, trees such as *Alchornea hirtella* growing on lower slopes were felled and there is an increase in the pollen of secondary forest trees and shrubs. Stage 2 witnessed a replacement of secondary forest trees, such as *Neoboutonia*, by herbs and shrubs, such as *Dodonaea* and *Justicia* which are characteristic of more intensely managed land. Finally, in stage 3, upper slope forests, which had previously escaped clearance, were felled. Soil erosion, resulting from forest clearance, caused deposition of much silt on one of the mires, leading to a change in mire vegetation to dominance by *Typha*. Over 5 m of sediment were deposited during the agricultural period in Lake Bunyonyi.

Changes in pollen diagrams from high altitude sites in eastern Africa resulting from agricultural disturbance have been described in an earlier chapter. It is noted here that agricultural disturbance does not always result in an increase in grass pollen, as might be expected,

Fig. 87. Moist Lower Montane Forest, Bwindi Forest, S.W. Uganda, altitude about 2300 m. This forest is influenced by selective felling, but is otherwise more or less undisturbed by man. *Podocarpus milanjianus* is silhouetted in the top right foreground. The forest contains a small gorilla population. Compare with Fig. 88.

Fig. 88   Agricultural land, Rukiga Highlands, S.W. Uganda, *c.* 2200 m. Eucalyptus trees (introduced from Australia) grow in the foreground and terraced fields can be seen beyond. This locality is only a few kilometres from that shown on Fig. 87 and the land would once have been covered by a similar forest type.

but that particularly in drier areas there are often falls in grass pollen. These are attributed to a reduction in grass vigour as a consequence of grazing, and the destruction of grass inflorescences and pollen by burning.

Chapter 12

The Future of the East African Environment

During the Quaternary man has progressed from being a relatively minor player in a restricted number of ecosystem types to become the leading actor with influence extending to even the most remote and inhospitable environments. Two stages in man's development in East Africa have already been noted, a long hunting and gathering stage and a relatively short stage marked by food production. Taking these stages together, progress proceeded at an accelerating rate and sometimes with periods of revolutionary change in the adaptation of human populations to particular environments. There were increases both in the number of habitats utilized by man and in the intensity with which these habitats were exploited. Mainly within the last 100 to 150 years East Africa has entered a third stage in development, characterized by huge increases in the exchanges of raw materials, energy, technology and cultural values, both between different parts of East Africa and between East Africa and elsewhere. This transformation has been accompanied by a great increase in the complexity of human organization. Modern East African societies are so complicated, are changing so fast and, in certain respects, are so incompletely understood that major uncertainties surround attempts to predict the future. This account focuses on some of the major trends which are believed to have occurred in the environment during the last few years and indicates some of the possible consequences if these trends are continued into the future.

A major trend which will undoubtedly greatly influence the environmental future of East Africa is population increase. At the time of the 1967/1969 censuses the populations of Kenya, Tanzania and Uganda were estimated at 10·9, 12·2 and 9·5 million, respectively, with annual growth rates of c. 3% and increasing (Morgan, 1973). As an example of changes since 1967/1969, the 1978 population of Kenya has been estimated at 14·7 million (Kenya Development Plan for 1979–1983, as reported in the Daily Nation 23.3.79). The growth rate for Kenya in 1979 is thought to have been as high as 4% (Standard 6.9.79). Projections of population changes into the future are difficult, but if current rates of increase are maintained the population of Kenya will reach 34 million in 2000 A.D. Even if family planning becomes widely practiced, the country is still expected to have 28 million inhabitants by the turn of the century (Kenya Development Plan for 1979–1983, as reported in the Daily Nation 23.3.79).

Within East Africa the distribution of population is very uneven with concentrations in the high rainfall areas around Lake Victoria, in the highlands and along the coast. With prevailing land-use practices, many of the rural pockets of high population have been unable to support their increasing populations or at least have failed to supply full and attractive employment, and there has been a substantial drift of people, particularly of young men, away from these areas in recent years. The emigrants have tended to settle either on land which is relatively unfavourable for small-scale agriculture or else have sought employment in towns or cities. Despite this movement to the towns, East Africa is still relatively little urbanized; in 1967/1969, for instance, over 90% of the Kenyan population still lived in the countryside (Morgan, 1973). However, urban populations are increasing at much faster rates than overall regional values (Standard 6.9.79) and the proportion of the Kenyan population still residing in rural areas is certainly much reduced from the 1967/1969 level. It can be safely predicted that the already serious problems faced by urban areas in the provision of services and employment will become greatly aggravated in the future. The growth of urban centres has been uneven and, in 1967/1969, four cities, Nairobi, Mombasa, Dar-es-Salaam and Kampala, held over half the urban population. For a few people the move to the town is to take up jobs or educational vacancies which have been previously secured, but for many the move is a consequence of unemployment or under-employment in the region as a whole, the urban centres being perceived as places offering greater opportunities for monetary gain or personal fulfillment. At present, many urban dwellers still retain social and economic links with rural small-holdings and this offers a degree of security to the urban poor, but the proportion of such people is likely to decline in the future resulting in a heightening of urban problems.

The rising East African population is bound to make ever greater demands on the environment. Clearly to maintain living standards at current levels, supplies of food and many other products will have to increase in line with the population increase, requiring for example an approximate doubling in food production over the period 1980–2000 A.D. In practice, however, demands on the environment, whether realized or not, are likely to rise out of all proportion to the rate of population increase. Among factors which can be expected to contribute to this are:

(1) a general rise in material expectations,
(2) pressure to set aside more land for the production of export crops, thus removing land from the production of internally consumed products (Standard 1.9.79), and
(3) higher per capita energy and material costs of maintaining an urban, as opposed to a rural, population.

Agricultural products, such as coffee and tea, are at present by far the most important earners of foreign exchange for East Africa as a whole. It is possible that manufactured non-agricultural commodities and tourism will contribute increased proportions of the total, but agricultural exports can be expected to predominate as earners of foreign exchange for the foreseable future. On the other side of the coin, by far the biggest category of imports into East Africa is that which includes transport-related goods, such as petroleum products, vehicles and vehicle parts. Efficient transportation networks are widely regarded as vital to the running of modern societies and it is highly unlikely that the demand for vehicles or petroleum will slacken. The East African economies have been severely affected by recent increases in the price of oil and, as this price continues its apparently inexorable rise, so too is pressure likely to grow to transfer additional land to the growing of export crops.

Increasing urbanization has been accompanied by an ever greater disparity between the amounts of materials and energy utilized by town and country, an imbalance enhanced by the concentration of high-income groups in cities. The only one of the governments of the East African countries to introduce a measure to cut down the rate of urban drift is Tanzania, where permission to move to a city is only given to those who have already secured employment. This is part of a general political philosophy emphasizing rural development and the government intends that eventually the countryside will be perceived by citizens as an environment as rewarding as the city for earning a living.

The demands on natural resources can be met, in theory, either by increasing the area of utilized land or by increasing the efficiency of resource exploitation. In fact, the extent of highly productive or moderately productive land in East Africa is severely limited by the distribution of rainfall. This is a particularly serious factor in Kenya where only 17% of the land is regarded as suitable for intensive agriculture. With the notable exceptions of forest reserves and parts of the southern highlands of Tanzania, there are few areas of high rainfall in East Africa which are not already being extensively managed for food production; in general, demand for more food will have to be met by an increase in the productivity of existing agricultural land. This will involve the spread of new agricultural practices, a slow process in conservative agricultural societies. In terms of resources generally, it is unlikely that much progress will be made in equating supply with demand in the absence of a much lower population growth rate than now. A widespread acceptance of family planning would, however, be itself largely dependent on a radical change in social attitudes. It is likely therefore that the demand for basic products will exceed that which can be supplied from East African resources. The decline of self-sufficiency will increase the need for food imports. In such a scenario the problems arising from both the limited availability and the inefficient distribution of imported foodstuffs may be expected to contribute towards the regular occurrence of famine.

The controls over resource utilization have changed dramatically since the end of the last century. Prior to this time, there were few extensive political organizations in East Africa, there was virtually no monetary economy and most resources were managed on a very local scale. During this subsistence stage, it seems likely that there was in general an equilibrium between the available resources and the level of demand, given the relatively low population and perceived needs of the people. This is not to say that man's relationship with his environment did not change nor that environmental stress did not occur. The stage may well have witnessed an increasing population, an extension of the area of intensively managed land and a declining productivity per unit area as a result of a declining soil fertility. There must also have been some major changes in agricultural practices connected with the adoption of new crops, particularly maize, sweet potatoes and cassava, all of which were introduced to Africa from America during the last few hundred years. Famines are recorded in many oral traditions. In Rwanda, for example, it is said that famine used to occur about every 25 years, a curious periodicity which it has been suggested may be related to fluctuations in human population (Coupez, personal communication).

Colonial governments established the boundaries of the modern East African countries and had much wider perspectives of the economic resources of the region than had prevailed hitherto. Resource supply was now related not only to the projected requirements of the East African territories, but increasingly also to the needs of other parts of the world, particularly the homelands of the European colonials. The imposition of this new economic order produced a movement away from subsistence and a number of measures were implemented to catalyze this transformation. The most important of these measures in Uganda was the imposition of universal taxation; many people raised the required sum by planting cotton for sale on the export market.

An important concept introduced by the colonial governments was that of the reserved area. Tracts of land, often extensive, were set aside either for single or a small number of mutually compatible uses, other activities being discouraged or prohibited. The principal uses of reserved land were water conservation, forestry, game conservation and, eventually, the preservation of relatively unspoilt ecosystems as national parks. Particularly in the case of highland Kenya, land was also withdrawn from the general estate for large-scale farms settled mainly by Europeans. The implementation of the reserved land concept was feasible during the earlier part of the colonial period when the population was relatively low; major additions to reserved land would be impossible today. Within reserved areas resources could be managed more efficiently for particular purposes than would otherwise have been the case and the system has proved so advantageous that reserved areas have persisted with relatively minor changes to their boundaries up to modern times. This generalization is true even of large European-style farms in Kenya, albeit usually with a change of ownership during recent years. These farms were established originally mainly to supply food to the colonial homelands, but increasingly this export role was superseded by that of supplying agricultural products to urban areas in East Africa. The relative efficiency of these farms in terms of the quantity of food produced for sale per unit area of land has been an important factor in preventing their break-up and possibly the same consideration will remain an effective argument against their dismantling in the future.

The role of the government administrator has changed along with the social, economic and political development of East Africa. In the case of reserved land an obvious shift has been away from the business of demarkation of reserves and the evolution and establishment of management techniques to the more complicated and difficult tasks of retaining the reserves and warding off pressures to enlarge the small-holding estate. The boundaries of reserved areas have become increasingly well defined, in fact as well as theory, leading to increased difficulties in policing to prevent illegal activities which can include felling timber, burning and grazing domestic stock. Also, some national parks have suffered severely from the problems of managing populations of large animals in unnaturally defined eco-systems.

The implementation of government land-use policy has always depended on a variable mixture of enforcement and persuasion. In the case of reserved land the balance has tended to lie in the direction of enforcement, but education has not been forgotten and many attempts have been made to persuade people of the value of individual sacrifice for the benefit of the long-term interests of the country as a whole.

The transition from foreign- to self-rule in the early 1960s resulted in certain changes in the relationship between the governors and the governed. Administrators derived from local social groups are often aware in a more personal way of the aspirations of the population and may have a relatively realistic view of the limitations of government power. On the other hand, the detachment of many colonial administrators also had some advantages: policies could be conceived and implemented with less danger of bias towards particular local groups and unpopular measures could be enforced more readily. It is sometimes argued that the transition to independence should have produced a move away from authoritarianism in favour of persuasion in the implementation of land-use decisions. This admirable intention is, however, probably unrealistic given the ever-growing conflicts between alternative land-uses. Difficulties in communication between rulers and ruled seem liable to continue, in many cases reinforced by major differences in social background and formal education.

Scientific research has an important role to play in the management of natural resources. Research carried out by universities and government bodies is today augmented by projects under the auspices of the United Nations and other international organizations. The latter support some excellent research work, but communication is often poor between them and the East African governments and also between the various international bodies themselves.

Political events and philosophies have played important roles in determining development patterns during both colonial and modern times and can be expected to do so in the future. The last 10 years have witnessed particularly striking contrasts in these respects between the East African countries and, partly as a result of these developments, there has been a reduction in their economic and social links. Kenya has shared with Tanzania the advantage of political stability since independence. It has adopted a pragmatic policy combining considerable central planning with measures which encourage diversity and individual initiative. The registration of small-holdings has made it worthwhile for farmers to improve their techniques and, although there are obvious regional differences, the efficiency of farming in some areas has increased greatly over recent years. Kenya still retains many large farms inherited from settler days. It is a serious dilemma as to whether these farms should be retained in view of their important role in supplying food to towns or whether further estates should be subdivided into small-holdings under resettlement schemes to assuage land hunger. Uganda, since about 1970, has witnessed breakdown in central government authority and very high inflation, with the consequences of much illegal encroachment into reserved land and a move back towards a more subsistence-based economy. This recent history has underlined the importance of stable and effective government for the management of resources and for long-term planning. Tanzania has adopted a policy of encouraging village-based development along communal lines. Individual initiative based on the profit motive is discouraged at the expense of collective schemes. Whether this policy is working is a matter of dispute. Although at present Tanzania is the only one of the East African countries to be a major importer of basic foods, it can be argued that the development policy conceived by the government is a long-term one, involving the difficult business of developing new social structures, and that in the long-term collectivist development will lead to a more rewarding existence for a greater proportion of the population than would otherwise be the case.

Considering now the possible fates of particular resources, it is certain that it will be the more productive (wetter) areas which will be subject to the greatest conflicts between different land-users. Such areas are today the chief suppliers of food and wood products and they also have vital roles as water catchments and in providing dry season grazing for the herds of the pastoralists. It was the policy of colonial governments, largely retained, to maintain a forest cover on mountains above an altitude of approximately 2150 m, the principal objectives being the protection of water catchments, the prevention of soil erosion and sometimes the provision of timber. Although the loss of water by evapotranspiration tends to be greater under forest than under more open vegetation types and although total annual stream discharge is reduced by the presence of forest in a catchment, there are overwhelming advantages in maintaining a forest cover on the hills. These advantages include a greater chance that streams and springs will maintain their flows outside rainy seasons and reductions in the frequency of flash floods, in soil erosion and in the sediment load carried in the water (Synnott, 1979).

In terms of total energy consumption, wood and charcoal are much more important than petroleum products. Wood-based products are estimated to meet 80% of total energy usage in Kenya and this proportion must be greater in Uganda and Tanzania. At present most people in the countryside still gather fuel locally, but there is already a large commercial trade supplying cities and towns and there is also export of charcoal to Arabia. Although attempts have been made to control fuel exploitation, in general this important sphere of economic activity is unregulated. There are already many signs of ecosystem degradation as a result of fuel harvesting and, because little attempt is presently being made to ensure the future of the resource, there will presumably soon come a time of serious energy shortfall. The other main use of woody plants, as timber, is also an area in which demand will soon exceed sustainable supply. According to United Nations estimates, Uganda will have to import timber soon after the turn of the century if it is not to begin a run-down of its forest capital. This is, however, rather an academic statistic, since it is unlikely that there will be enough timber on a world scale to supply poor countries like Uganda. Further, it assumes that the forest estate in Uganda will be well managed, which at present is not the case.

Perhaps the most critical question of all is whether farmers will be able to produce enough food to feed the growing population. Standards of farming at present vary widely within East Africa, but there remain very extensive areas where the efficiency of food production is low. According to Raynaut (1977) one of the reasons why traditional systems of cultivation are becoming inadequate is because periods of fallow are too short to restore soil fertility. If food demand is to be met, there will have to be a transformation of many agricultural systems, with, in particular, the systematic growing of fodder crops and the implementation of new methods of regenerating soils, such as crop rotation. There is much anectodal evidence demonstrating a greatly increased rate of soil erosion, largely because of bad cultivation practices in recent years. One effect of this erosion is to threaten the viability of hydroelectric works, such as the Tana River scheme, through the very rapid accumulation of silt behind dams (Daily Nation and Standard 26.7.79).

From the scientific point of view, methods of improving farming techniques and of decreasing rates of soil erosion are fairly well known. According to Makina (1979) the chief problems in implementing the necessary measures are ensuring the profitability of innovations to farmers and establishing communications between scientists, agricultural extension officers and farmers. Inadequate communication can easily ruin the best-intentioned schemes, as the following example for Rwanda demonstrates. Rwanda is a hilly country with a very high population density and a very serious soil erosion problems; when in power, the Belgians compelled villagers to build terraces. The scheme was, however, regarded as an alien imposition and after independence terrace maintenance was neglected and today the terraces have all but completely disappeared. (The persistence of terraces in neighbouring Uganda—see Fig. 88—can be attributed to the existence of a more enlightened educational programme.)

On the whole, the willingness with which a country changes its systems of farming as a response to market forces and the flow of ideas contrasts with the general conservatism of pastoralists in East Africa. Livestock, particularly cattle, occupy a central position in the cultures of pastoral societies and the whole fabric of these societies is threatened by the transformation to a monetary economy (Shorter, 1974). Within the pastoral societies, both the wealth of an individual and also his ability to withstand a period of environmental stress such as drought depends largely on the size of his herds. Within the limits imposed by tribal boundaries there is unregulated competitive grazing of the pastures. Ecological degradation due to overgrazing has accelerated in recent years, not only in East Africa, but generally in the pastoral regions of Africa and this has rendered these areas highly susceptible to drought. There have been recurrent food shortages and in some cases deaths of people and animals in large numbers through starvation. This has led to international recognition of the extent of the problem, sometimes referred to as that of "desertification". According to Lamprey (1978) the immediate causes of this ecological degradation are overgrazing and excessive tree felling, the latter to supply fuel and fencing. Overgrazing first affects herbaceous plants and later trees and shrubs and is accompanied by erosion, compaction and desiccation of the soil (Fig. 89). Many examples are known of areas which were covered by lush grass and scattered trees at the turn of the century and are now converted to unpalatable thorn thicket riddled by bare and hardened cattle tracks.

Fig. 89   Overgrazed land near Voi, Kenya. Thorn scrub riddled by bare and hardened cattle tracks, as shown in the picture, is a common result of overgrazing.

Some of the causes of habitat over-exploitation by pastoralists are increases in the numbers of people and livestock and a growing tendency for people to aggregate around centres of security and services, particularly boreholes. These centres are today surrounded by ever-widening circles of denudation. In Kenya and Uganda, famine was largely averted during the 1968–1976 drought by massive international food aid, but for many reasons food subsidy cannot be regarded as a long-term solution to the problem. Dependence on outside help leads to the demoralization of the pastoral people and, in any case, external aid is an uncertain source of supply, prone to corruption and various types of interruption (e.g. as happened in Uganda during the 1979–1980 drought in Karamoja according to numerous newspaper reports, e.g. Sunday Nation 29.7.79). There is little evidence of effective measures being introduced to solve the problem of overgrazing and an increasing number of people will be forced to abandon the pastoral way of life.

Although land management practices are implicated as the main causes of ecosystem degradation in semi-arid Africa (e.g. Lamprey, 1978), there has been keen interest in the contribution of "natural" climatic fluctuations to desertification. Grove (1977) has summarized the evidence for climatic change during recent years. The 20–30 years preceding 1898 were marked by greater rainfall over much of Africa than during the next 20 or so years, when there were a number of widespread and severe droughts, especially in 1913 (see also Nicholson, 1980). The 1950s and early 1960s were marked by relatively high precipitation in many areas, with a peak in the levels of many East African lakes in *c.* 1964. Grove (1977) thinks that the severity of the recent drought (that of *c.* 1968–1976) was partly due to the build-up of human and cattle populations in semi-arid Africa during the relatively favourable conditions of the preceding two decades. There is some evidence that changes in the albedo of semi-arid Africa associated with overgrazing may have an adverse influence on rainfall, ecosystem degradation due to overgrazing itself resulting in a reduction in precipitation.

The governments of the East African countries accept that they must play an important role in ensuring the survival of both the indigenous species of animals and plants and also of examples of ecosystems which have been relatively little disturbed by man. The conservation of large savanna animals in particular has often been justified on economic grounds, since they contribute considerable quantities of foreign exchange earned through tourism. Their conservation has usually been based on the withdrawal of large though mostly rather arid areas of land from the food-productive estate. The financial argument has little appeal to land-hungry people except where they benefit directly from the revenue. There is therefore a growing effort to explain to the public the wider justification for nature conservation. The success of this educational programme is likely to be an essential element in policies designed to protect many of the plants and animals of East Africa.

The importance of national parks and forest nature reserves as a refuge for wildlife has grown with the increased intensity of agriculture outside the reserves. The reserve areas have also become increasingly isolated as islands which may imprison herds of large animals which are naturally nomadic. For example, many parks are situated in relatively dry areas which would naturally tend to be attractive to elephants only during the rainy seasons and the result of the permanent confinement of the elephants to the parks has been the build up of populations to levels which eventually are not sustainable in the dry season. Vegetation degradation by elephants has been reported from many parks during the last 20 years. A case in point is Tsavo National Park in Kenya. Here, in spite of the existence of an extensive buffer zone of cattle ranges around the park (regarded by the park authorities as part of the "Tsavo ecosystem"), agricultural expansion in neighbouring wetter areas has restricted the movements of Tsavo elephants, causing them to become increasingly confined to the park. Vegetation degradation by the elephants has been marked in particular by the destruction of *Acacia* and *Commiphora* trees and their replacement by grassland or low thorn scrub (Wright and Wainaina, 1972); this began in the late 1950s and reached alarming proportions and in the 1960s and early 1970s there were calls for some of the elephants to be culled. This policy was never put into effect and there were widespread elephant deaths during the drought of 1968–1974. A culling policy would certainly be inappropriate today, with the massive decline in the Tsavo elephant population due to poaching since 1976.

The illegal slaughter of animals, both within and outside national parks or other protected areas, has reached alarming proportions in recent years. While this is true of all three East African countries, the situation at present is most critical in Uganda, with large-scale poaching during the 1970s followed by uncontrolled mass-killings after the 1979 revolution (Anon, 1979; Edroma, 1979). As an example, the number of elephants in Kabalega (Murchison) Falls National Park is estimated to have decreased from 15 000 in 1972 to 2448 in 1976 to less than 1000 in September 1979. Very little wildlife remains in Ruwenzori (Queen Elizabeth) National Park (Fig. 90): the elephant population was estimated at 2850 in 1973, 704 in 1976 and about 50 in July 1979 and the hippopotamus population declined from roughly 14 000 in 1971–1976 to perhaps about 100 by September 1979. It is unlikely that there are any rhinoceros alive anywhere in Uganda today.

For East Africa as a whole the two herbivorous species which have been most affected by poaching have been the elephant and the black rhinoceros, the former valued for its ivory and the latter for its horn. The chief market for rhinoceros horn is not as an aphrodisiac, as is commonly supposed, but rather is for dagger handles in North Yemen. According to aerial surveys of large mammals in the "rangelands" of Kenya, the elephant population declined from 59 800–87 600 in 1977 by no less than 26·5% in 1978, while in the same year

Fig. 90   Fig tree with lions, Ruwenzori National Park, Uganda. The large mammal population in this park has been decimated since this photograph was taken in 1967.

the rhinoceros population dropped from 3636 by an incredible 68·6% (Stelfox *et al.*, 1979). Widespread poaching of rhinos, elephants and other animals is also recorded from Tanzania (Cheffings and Binks, 1979; Anon, 1979). If these trends continue, rhinos and savanna elephants will soon have disappeared from each of the East African countries and it can be predicted that, as this happens, the poachers will turn their attention increasingly to other species.

It is important that examples of wetter types of ecosystems survive (Fig. 91). Here we have an interesting example of interaction between an international perspective and the realities on the ground. If forest

Fig. 91   Bwindi Forest, Uganda. This species-rich forest, together with neighbouring Kayonza Forest, should be a prime objective for conservation in Uganda.

conservation could be effected by international bodies, then undoubtedly the most important forests to conserve would be those situated in the core areas described in a previous chapter. Areas such as East Zaire, the Usambaras and the Ulugurus are relatively rich in species and probably also, for any given species occurring both within and without core areas, are also genetically diverse. But conservation can actually only be enforced at a national level and it cannot be assumed by the government of any one country that the governments of others will necessarily act in the interests of the international community as a whole. Partly for this reason, it is desirable that each country should view nature conservation in terms of those ecosystems contained within its boundaries, taken in isolation. Thus, although on a broad scale, Kakamega Forest is one of the most impoverished lowland forests of the Guineo-Congolian type in East Africa, it is the only example of this forest type in Kenya and large parts of it should undoubtedly be conserved.

Appendix

Indicator Values of Selected Pollen Types

The concept that pollen types have certain values as indicators of past vegetation or environment is one widely used by palynologists (e.g. by Flenley, 1979) and the environmental significance of a few of the pollen types encountered in East African pollen diagrams are described below. One point needs to be emphasized: the presence or degree of abundance of a pollen type in a pollen diagram is not a consequence of a single factor, but rather of a combination of circumstances and it may be misleading to equate the presence or degree of abundance of a pollen type with one particular set of conditions. Thus, high values of Gramineae in a diagram could indicate a (relatively) undisturbed semi-arid environment, or cultivation under a moist climate, or indeed they could have resulted in a number of other ways. Again, a pollen type may increase in abundance as an environmental factor changes up to a certain value, but decline thereafter. Taking the example of a tree like *Juniperus*, relatively low levels of human disturbance might result in an increase in this species, which is fire-tolerant and can act as a colonizer, but at high levels of human activity the population of the tree might well decline as a consequence of felling for timber and fuel.

Afrocrania

This is a distinct pollen type produced by only one East African species, *A. volkensii*, a widely distributed tree which can reach a height of 25 m. *Afrocrania* is found up to an altitude of just over 3000 m. It is a moisture-loving species which in Kenya is distributed over a relatively wide range of topographic types at high altitudes, but becomes restricted to valleys below the altitude of the Bamboo Zone (Wimbush, 1957). *Afrocrania* is often particularly abundant on volcanic soils; it forms a woodland with *Agauria* at 2300–2800 m on two of the Virunga Volcanoes (Lebrun, 1942, quoted in Lind and Morrison, 1974) and is found under *Juniperus* forest on the east side of Mt Meru (Lind and Morrison, 1974).

Surface pollen samples indicate that *Afrocrania* pollen has a low relative export ability and where it is abundant in pollen diagrams, the tree is very likely to have been growing close to the site. *Afrocrania* is more abundant in the Katenga and Butongo diagrams than the Muchoya diagram, even though the latter is situated at a higher and, for *Afrocrania*, apparently more suitable altitude. Katenga and Butongo, but not Muchoya, have recent volcanic deposits in their catchments and perhaps *Afrocrania* was responding to their presence. This explanation accords with the presence of an *Afrocrania* peak just above an ash band in the Lake Mahoma pollen diagram.

Alchemilla

Alchemilla pollen is usually easily recognizable though occasionally it may be confused with other small tricolpate types. Shrubby species of *Alchemilla* are often common in the Afroalpine Belt and, at least in the case of Mt Elgon, are also found in the understory of *Philippia* thicket down to *c.* 3200 m. Herbaceous species of *Alchemilla* are widely distributed in montane vegetation. On Mt Elgon, for example, herbaceous Alchemillas are more or less constant members of the more open types of forest undergrowth at altitudes above *c.* 2200 m and are present in many areas of grassland and on mires. In western Uganda, species of herbaceous *Alchemilla* grow on mires down to at least 1900 m.

Surface soil samples from under *Alchemilla* scrub on Mt Elgon contain very much higher quantities of *Alchemilla* pollen (generally over 50% of total pollen; Hamilton, 1972) than do bryophyte polster samples collected at 2 m on *Dendrosenecio* trees above the *Alchemilla* scrub (less than 4% of total pollen; Hamilton and Perrott, in press, a), suggesting that relatively little *Alchemilla* pollen is dispersed in the atmosphere. Surface samples from sites with herbaceous species of *Alchemilla* in the vicinity yield low values of *Alchemilla* pollen (Hamilton and Perrott, in press, a). All this evidence together suggests that abundant *Alchemilla* pollen in a diagram indicates the presence of shrubby species of *Alchemilla* close to the sample site. *Alchemilla* has higher values in the upper, as compared with the lower part of the Koitoboss Bog diagram from Mt Elgon and this may be due to an increase in *Alchemilla* growing on *Carex* tussocks under drier climatic conditions.

Celtis-type

Celtis-type pollen is produced by *Celtis, Chaetacme aristata* and *Hymenocardia acida*. The latter can be distinguished from the others under good conditions of preservation and with care (Hamilton, 1976b). All East African species of *Celtis* except one, *C. integrifolia*, are forest trees and the genus is abundant in many lowland forests in Uganda. Two species, *Celtis africana* and *C. durandii*, occur at relatively high as well as low altitudes, *C. africana* being found up to *c.* 2300 m, often in rather dry forest types, and *C. durandii* growing up to *c.* 1850 m generally in rather moister forest types than *C. africana*. Both species are either absent from or very rare in the montane forests of western Uganda, as well as in those of Burundi (Lewalle, 1972). *Celtis integrifolia* is a tree of dry woodlands and is very locally distributed in East Africa, being confined to north-east Uganda. *Chaetacme aristata* is a small spreading tree or shrub which is often very common in forest understory and on forest edges; it is present up to *c.* 2150 m. *Hymenocardia acida* is a small woodland tree found below *c.* 1500 m.

Celtis-type pollen is found in many surface samples from montane East Africa but is relatively abundant only in those from Ruwenzori, which is situated in a climatically moist area. Unlike other long-distance pollen types in surface samples from the Ericaceous and Afroalpine Belts of Ruwenzori, *Celtis*-type is significantly more abundant in surface samples from west-facing, as opposed to east-facing, slopes (Table 13) and this is believed to be due to the presence of much more extensive lowland forest at the foot of the range on the west as compared with the east. Apart from other factors, it is thought that forest destruction has been more extensive on the eastern side. Many of the other long-distance pollen types are produced by taxa abundant in montane forest, which is roughly equally distributed on both sides of the mountain. Comparison of a pollen diagram from a west-facing valley (that from Lake Kitandara) with one from an east-facing valley (Lake Bujuku) shows a relatively large decrease in *Celtis* and a relatively large increase in Gramineae pollen at the supposed time of forest clearance, providing convincing evidence that *Celtis*-type pollen is here produced largely by species growing in lowland forest. *Celtis*-type pollen appears and becomes

Table 13　Comparison of long-distance pollen spectra of surface samples from east- (Bujuku) and west- (Kitandara) facing valleys on Ruwenzori[c]

Valley		Number of grains									
		Po[d]	Ur	Ac	Ma	Ra	Ol	Ce	My	Do	Fi
Bujuku	Observed	208	184	135	112	64	46	32[b]	10	12	8
	Expected[a]	204	167	135	109	64	50	50[b]	12	11	9
Kitandara	Observed	178	131	120	95	58	48	63[b]	13	8	9
	Expected[a]	182	148	120	98	58	44	45[b]	11	9	8

[a] Expected if randomly distributed.
[b] Observed and expected values significantly different ($p > 99\%$). (All other values are not significantly different.)
[c] All samples are from the Ericaceous and Afroalpine Belts.
[d] Key to pollen types. Po, *Podocarpus*; Ur, Urticaceae; Ac, *Acalypha*; Ma, *Macaranga kilimandscharica*; Ra, *Rapanea rhododendroides*; Ol, *Olea*; Ce, *Celtis*-type; My, *Myrica*; Do, *Dodonaea viscosa*; Fi, *Ficus*-type.

common in the Lake Victoria pollen diagram after *c.* 12 000 B.P. (Kendall, 1969) and is regarded as having originated from lowland forest, as in the case of the Ruwenzori diagrams. All of this suggests that rarity of *Celtis*-type pollen in the basal part of the Lake Mahoma pollen diagram was due to rarity or absence of lowland forest around the foot of the mountain at the time.

In some pollen diagrams from relatively dry montane areas, for instance Mt Badda, Ethiopia, *Celtis*-type pollen, while still remaining uncommon, actually shows an increase following the onset of agricultural disturbance. This could be due to the spread of *Celtis africana* or *Chaetacme* in secondary lower montane forest or thicket.

Dendrosenecio-type

This pollen type is produced by giant groundsels (*Senecio*, subgenus, *Dendrosenecio*) and by *Crassocephalum mannii* (Hamilton, 1972; Livingstone, 1967). It is distinguished from most other Tubiflorae by being large and by having relatively short spines. Giant groundsels are a characteristic component of Afroalpine vegetation, but vary greatly in size and density from mountain to mountain, only forming dense woodland on the wettest mountains, Ruwenzori and the Bufumbira Volcanoes. *Crassocephalum mannii* is a small tree or shrub in wetter areas, with an altitudinal range 1220–2440 m (4000–8000 ft) in Kenya according to Dale and Greenway (1961).

High values of *Dendrosenecio*-type pollen have been encountered in many surface samples from the Afroalpine Belt of Ruwenzori and in three pollen diagrams, also from Ruwenzori, from Lakes Bujuku and Kitandara in the Afroalpine Belt and Lake Mahoma at 2960 m in the Montane Forest Belt. In the case of Lake Mahoma, high values are found only in the basal sediments. Considering the association shown in surface samples from Ruwenzori between high values of *Dendrosenecio*-type pollen and the more or less close presence of giant groundsel forest, the most reasonable explanation for the high values of *Dendrosenecio*-type pollen in the lower part of the Lake Mahoma diagram is that giant groundsels were abundant close to the lake and this in turn suggests temperature depression compared with now. Livingstone (1967), however, has argued that the vegetation represented in the lower part of the Lake Mahoma diagram may have been determined partly by the immaturity of the soils on the moraines which surround the lake; indeed, he contends that there may have been no lowering of temperature. I regard the first part of Livingstone's statement as probable, but the second as unlikely. There is no evidence that giant groundsels are ever species of early seral stages in vegetation development today and measurements on Mt Kenya have shown giant groundsels to have a very slow growth rate (Hedberg, 1969b). Furthermore, if temperatures had been similar to today, pollen types belonging to fast-growing Montane Forest Belt species would be expected to be more abundant than is the case.

Surface samples, even those from *Senecio* woodland, and pollen diagrams from high altitudes on Mt Elgon contain much lower values of *Dendrosenecio*-type than is the case on Ruwenzori.

Ericaceae

Pollen termed Ericaceae in surface samples and pollen diagrams is of a tetrad type, and is produced by the shrubs and trees of the genera *Agauria, Blacria, Erica, Philippia* and *Vaccinium. Ficalhoa laurifolia*, which is sometimes included in the Ericaceae, has different pollen. Microphyllous Ericaceae (especially *Philippia*) are abundant in the Ericaceous Belt (*c.* 3300–3650 m), being most luxuriant on Ruwenzori and being much lower in stature and more widely spaced on dry mountains where there is often an extensive development of grassland in the Ericaceous Belt. Microphyllous Ericaceae can be common at altitudes below the Ericaceous Belt: tree Ericaceae are abundant in the upper part of the Montane Forest Belt on Ruwenzori, *Philippia benguelensis* is found on stony sites in western eastern Africa down to *c.* 1000 m (Lewalle, 1972) and species of *Erica* and occasionally *Vaccinium* occur on mires in western Uganda and Rwanda down to *c.* 1950 m. *Agauria salicifolia* which is a broad-leafed woodland tree is found over a wide altitudinal range, being recorded down to 1800 m in Burundi (Lewalle, 1972) and up to 3200 m on Mt Elgon.

Pollen of Ericaceae is sometimes abundant in surface samples. In the case of Mt Elgon, high values of Ericaceae pollen have been found only in surface samples from Ericaceae thickets, the pollen being very rare elsewhere; in the case of most non-thicket samples containing Ericaceae pollen on Elgon, the pollen could have been derived from nearby thickets by surface wash. There is a parallel here with *Calluna* pollen, which in Britain has been found to be very poorly dispersed in the atmosphere (Peck, 1973). In general, Ericaceae pollen is much more abundant in surface samples from the Ericaceous and Afro-alpine Belts of Ruwenzori than Mt Elgon and it is thought that, as with *Dendrosenecio*-type pollen, this is due in part to the greater abundance and vigour of the parent plants.

Pollen of Ericaceae is often common in pollen diagrams. In some cases, for instance in the Kamiranzovu diagram and in the upper part of the Muchoya diagram, this is clearly due to the past presence of Ericaceae plants on the mires close to the sample sites. In other cases, the Ericaceae pollen is believed to have been derived from dry land species. The presence of Ericaceae pollen in pollen diagrams from sites in the Montane Forest Belt is sometimes believed to be due to depression of the vegetation belts. Ericaceae pollen is probably a better indicator of such depression in drier areas in which Ericaceous species are more or less absent from montane forest vegetation. It is, however, noted that the pollen diagram from Kilimanjaro appears to be exceptional in that Ericaceae pollen is present in substantial quantities even though the site is believed to have always been situated in the Montane Forest Belt. *Erica arborea* grows near the site today (Coetzee, 1967) and it is assumed that special local factors allowed this species or perhaps other Ericaceae species to grow locally in the past. This illustrates the problem of recognizing depression of vegetation zones in pollen diagrams from montane eastern Africa.

Gramineae

Grass pollen is readily identifiable, but difficult to subdivide usefully.

Several authors (Coetzee, 1967; Hamilton, 1972; Morrison, 1968; Osmaston, 1958) have attempted to use size statistics to distinguish between different grass species or groups of grasses characteristic of various vegetation types, but this approach has yielded little success. Measurements of grass pollen in surface samples have, however, shown that mountain bamboo, *Arundinaria alpina*, produces little pollen (Hamilton, 1972; Osmaston, 1958).

Grasses are present and, indeed, often abundant in almost all vegetation types in East Africa, leading to doubts as to the interpretability of changes in the Gramineae curves in pollen diagrams (Livingstone, 1967). However, in the investigation of pollen deposition on Mt Elgon, it was found that Gramineae values of over 30% total pollen were found in all surface samples from grassland and rocky ground communities and values of less than 30%, and usually less than 10%, in samples from all other vegetation types. A sample from bamboo forest yielded 24% Gramineae pollen, a high value for forest vegetation. Size measurements show that the grass pollen in this sample was not derived from bamboo. It is suggested that the low pollen production of the upper vegetation stratum in bamboo forest is responsible for raising the representation of Gramineae pollen, much of which is probably derived from grasses in the undergrowth.

Surface samples and, in the case of Mt Elgon, pollen trap samples show that the quantity of grass pollen carried up from low altitudes and deposited at high altitudes is markedly greater on Ruwenzori than on Mt Elgon (Hamilton, 1972; Hamilton and Perrott, in press, a). The explanation is believed to be a combination of vegetation and land-use differences. In general, Ruwenzori lies in a climatically moister part of East Africa than Mt Elgon, and there are extensive areas of tall grassland, including large expanses of elephant grass (*Pennisetum purpureum*) below the forest boundary, often covering land believed to be climatically suitable for forest. In the case of Mt Elgon, grass pollen production is believed to be relatively depressed in the agricultural/savanna zone found below the lower forest boundary by a combination of factors, including decreased grass vigour under the generally drier climate, decreased grass vigour due to heavier grazing by domestic animals and increased destruction of grass inflorescenses and pollen by more frequent burning. These factors are believed to be responsible for the apparently paradoxical situation of decreased Gramineae representation following the supposed date of agricultural introduction, in pollen diagrams, from Mt Elgon and other relatively dry areas.

Hagenia

Hagenia pollen is a readily identified type produced only by *Hagenia abyssinica*. The latter forms a spreading tree of up to 25 m height and is a light-requiring species, not regenerating under a dense canopy. *Hagenia* is usually common in the Upper Montane Forest Zone; in the case of Mt Elgon, *Hagenia* is more abundant in this zone (*c.* 3000–3300 m) on the moister western slopes, where it forms a more or less continuous canopy over *Rapanea*, than on the drier eastern slopes, where although still common it is more closely restricted to the forest margins and clearings. At lower altitudes, *Hagenia* is the commonest dicotyledonous tree in bamboo forest on west Mt Elgon (2450–3000 m). It is also common in the Bamboo Zone on the Bufumbira Volcanoes, but is infrequent with bamboo on Ruwenzori. *Hagenia* seems to be the dominant tree throughout the Montane Forest Belt (2550–3050 m) on west Mt Meru, where it is found with an understory of *Stoebe* (Hedberg, 1951). As with many other species, *Hagenia* descends to lower altitudes in climatically wetter areas, reaching *c.* 1800 m on the western slopes of Mt Elgon (Dale, 1940), about the same altitude on the Rukiga Highlands, and 1700 m in Burundi (Lewalle, 1972). At lower altitudes (Lower Montane Forest Zone), *Hagenia* becomes increasingly confined to a forest-edge and colonizing role, being absent or uncommon in dense forest, where the "gap niche" is filled by such species as *Macaranga kilimandscharica* and *Neoboutonia macrocalyx*. *Hagenia* is abundant in derived woodland with *Dodonaea* and *Myrica* in the Rukiga Highlands and is abundant on well drained lava fields in the Albert National Park (Robyns, 1948) and on the lava slopes of the Virunga Volcanoes.

Surface samples show that *Hagenia* pollen is moderately well dispersed in the atmosphere. It is sometimes common in pollen diagrams and high values are believed usually to indicate the presence of Upper Montane Forest or bamboo forest close to the site. In some cases, increases in *Hagenia* in pollen diagrams can be attributed to human disturbance.

Myrica

Myrica pollen is readily recognizable. Of the four species known from East Africa, only two, *Myrica kandtiana* and *M. salicifolia*, are widely distributed and it is likely that one or both of these constitute the source of *Myrica* pollen found in published surfaces samples and pollen diagrams. The pollen of the two species is very similar. *Myrica kandtiana* is a swamp plant found at relatively low altitudes, usually below 2000 m and with a highest known occurrence at 2260 m on Muchoya Swamp in south-west Uganda. *Myrica salicifolia* is a dryland species. In the vegetation survey of Mt Elgon (Hamilton and Perrott, 1980), *Myrica kandtiana* was not encountered and only two individuals of *M. salicifolia*, both juvenile, were found, one in a *Juniperus* forest and the other in a *Philippia* thicket, the altitude of both sites being *c.* 3000 m. *Myrica salicifolia* is common in derived woodland, on upper slope sites and ridges on Ruwenzori, and in the Rukiga Highlands, occurs in scrub thicket at *c.* 2500–3000 m on dry Mt Kadam (Wilson, 1962) and is common on well-drained lava fields in the Albert National Park (Robyns, 1948). *Myrica usambarensis*, which may be conspecific with *M. salicifolia*, is listed by Lewalle (1972) as growing on rocky ground with *Philippia benguelensis* at 1600 m in Burundi. The upper altitudinal limit of *M. salicifolia* appears to be normally *c.* 3000 m, but var. *alpina* is said to reach 3300 m on the Virunga Volcanoes (Robyns, 1948). These records, together with my observations in the field, indicate that *Myrica salicifolia* is a light-demanding and drought-tolerant species. I have never seen mature trees in dense montane forest.

Myrica pollen is abundant in parts of the *Muchoya* diagram. In the upper part of the diagram, the source of this pollen is likely to have been *Myrica kandtiana*, since the existence of swamp forest is demonstrated by the abundance of wood in the peat and the *Myrica* curve is very jagged, indicating a very local source. In the lower part of the diagram, however, corresponding to a time when Muchoya was a lake, *Myrica salicifolia* may well have been the parent species, since the presence of *M. salicifolia*, but not *M. kandtiana*, is consistent with the rest of the pollen record. *Myrica* is abundant in the lower part of the Mahoma diagram and the altitude of this site, together with the type of terrain in the area, makes it highly likely that *M. salicifolia* was the species present. In this case, *Myrica* was probably growing at lower altitudes, its pollen being transported up to the lake in the atmosphere.

Relatively abundant *Myrica* before *c.* 12 000/10 000 B.P., as seen at Muchoya and Mahoma, is a feature of many other pollen diagrams of sufficient age from eastern Africa and is attributed to the widespread occurrence of open dry forest or dry montane woodland on the mountains under a generally rather arid climate. *Myrica* is exceptionally abundant at Mahoma and it is suggested that this may reflect the absence then, as now, of *Juniperus procera* and *Podocarpus gracilior* from Ruwenzori. These species are potential competitors which are believed to have been present on many of the other eastern African mountains at the time.

Olea

The pollen of *Olea* is usually readily identifiable. Three species are likely to have contributed to pollen diagrams and surface samples from eastern Africa, *Olea africana, O. hochstetteri* and *O. welwitschii. Olea africana* is often abundant in drier montane forests, being found abundantly betweeen 2000 and 3000 m on east Mt Elgon and is usually absent from western Rift forests, though present on lava and ash fields in the Albert National Park (Robyns, 1948). *Olea hochstetteri* is also a common species of dry montane forests, being often found with *O. africana*, but it is also found in moister montane forests. It is present on upper hillslopes in Bwindi Forest and on

---

Figs 92–94   Pollen grains from Quaternary peat deposits (all × 1000 mag.).
Fig. 92   1. Fern bean (naked monolete fern spore), Kamiranzovu Swamp, Rwanda, depth 750–5 cm, Zone B; 2. *Polypodium*-type, Kamiranzovu Swamp, Rwanda, depth 250–5 cm, Zone B; 3–6. *Pteris*-type, Laboot Swamp, Mt Elgon, depth 55–6 cm, Zone B (3 and 4 and 5 and 6 are different foci on the same grains); 7. *Sphagnum*, Kamiranzovu Swamp, Rwanda, depth 750–5 cm, Zone B; 8. *Juniperus*-type, Laboot Swamp, Mt Elgon, depth 1–2 cm, Zone A; 9. *Podocarpus*, Kamiranzo-vu Swamp, Rwanda, depth 250–5 cm, Zone B; 10. Gramineae, Kuwasenkoko Swamp, Rwanda, 160–5 cm; 11. Cyperaceae, Kamiranzovu Swamp, Rwanda, depth 750–5 cm, Zone B; 12. *Myrica*, Kamiranzovu Swamp, Rwanda, depth 750–5 cm, Zone B; 13. *Acalypha*, Koitoboss Bog, Mt Elgon, depth 180–5 cm, Zone B; 14. *Faurea*-type, Koitoboss Bog, Mt Elgon, depth 0–5 cm, Zone A; 15. Myrtaceae, Koitoboss Bog, Mt Elgon, depth 0–5 cm, Zone A.
Fig. 93   1–4. *Sparganium*-type, Kamiranzovu Swamp, Rwanda, depth 750–5 cm, Zone B (1 and 2 and 3 and 4 are different foci on the same grains); 5. *Dombeya*, Kamiranzovu Swamp, Rwanda, depth 750–5 cm, Zone B; 6. *Impatiens*, Kamiranzo-vu Swamp, Rwanda, depth 1300–5 cm, Zone D; 7–12. Chenopodiaceae-type, Badda Bog, Ethiopia, 237–8 cm, Zone C (similar types are found in Badda Zone D; 7 and 8, 9 and 10 and 11 and 12 are different foci on the same grains).
Fig. 94   1–2. *Dendrosenecio*-type, Koitoboss Bog, Mt Elgon, depth 180–5 cm, Zone B (2 foci on the same grain); 3–4. *Dendrosenecio*-type, Kuwasenkoko Swamp, Rwanda, depth 160–5 cm (two foci on the same grains; note accompanying *Helichrysum*-type which shows size difference); 5–6. *Stoebe*, Koitoboss Bog, Mt Elgon, depth 180–5 cm, Zone B (two foci on the same grain); 7–8 *Ilex*, Kamiranzovu Swamp, Rwanda, depth 1300–5 cm, Zone D (two foci on the same grain); 9. *Alchemilla*, Koitoboss Bog, Mt Elgon, 0–5 cm, Zone A; 10. Umbelliferae, Kamiran-zovu Swamp, Rwanda, depth 250–5 cm, Zone D; 11. *Hagenia*, Kamiranzovu Swamp, Rwanda, depth 750–5 cm, Zone B; 12. *Cliffortia*, Kamiranzovu Swamp, Rwanda, depth 1300–5 cm, Zone D; 13. Ericaceae, Kamiranzovu Swamp, Rwanda, depth 250–5 cm, Zone B.

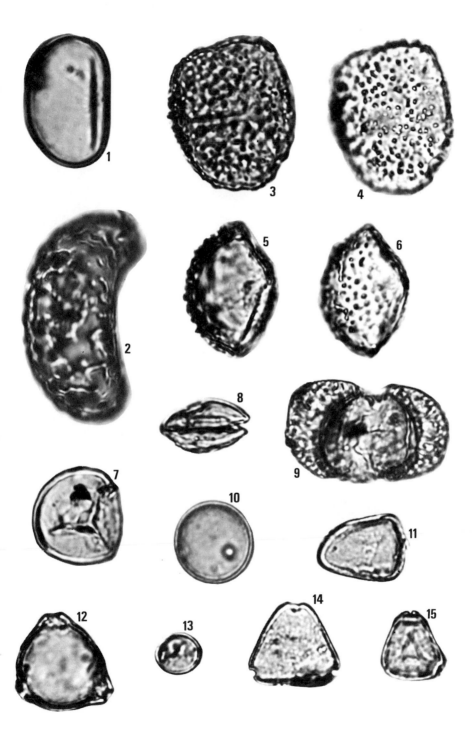

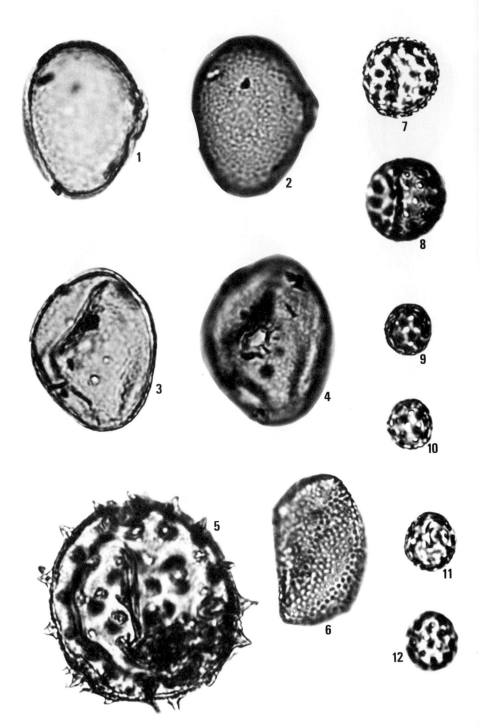

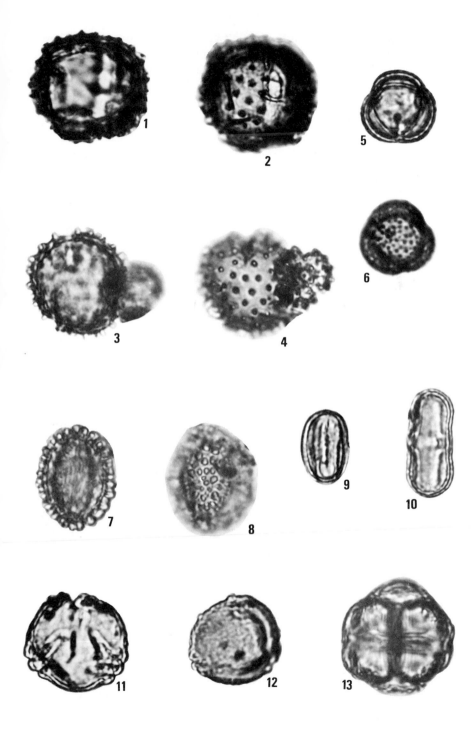

Ruwenzori, western Uganda. *Olea welwitschii* occurs up to 2150 m in wetter montane forests on Mt Elgon and is common in many lowland forests in Uganda. In Budongo Forest, the species is regarded as an early colonizer (Eggeling, 1947).

Olea pollen is common in many surface samples and has moderate relative export ability. In pollen diagrams it sometimes shows rather little change in abundance as other pollen types are changing massively, but this does not necessarily mean that climatic changes have not caused large-scale shifts in forest composition, since the various species of *Olea* together grow in a wide spectrum of forest types. Bonnefille (1971a) has distinguished *Olea africana* pollen from that of the other species by means of the larger cells of its reticulum and this distinction has been employed in the counting of the Koitoboss Bog diagram from Mt Elgon with rewarding results. *Olea africana* is seen to increase together with *Podocarpus* in the upper part of the diagram, providing confirmatory evidence that the *Podocarpus* rise present here is a result of a shift to drier climate.

Podocarpus

Podocarpus is a wind-pollinated genus of gymnosperms producing winged pollen which is often abundant in pollen diagrams and which is unlikely to be confused with that of any other indigenous East African plant. The recently introduced *Pinus* produces similar pollen which is, however, usually larger. Of the four species of *Podocarpus* found in East Africa (Melville, 1958), only two are widely distributed, *Podocarpus gracilior* being typical of drier montane forests than *P. milanjianus*. Only *Podocarpus gracilior* is known from Ethiopia and only *P. milanjianus* from western Rift montane areas (where *P. usambarensis* also occurs, but very rarely; Melville, 1958). Both species occur on many of the Kenyan mountains and the distribution of the two on Mt Elgon illustrates their differences in moisture relationships. *Podocarpus gracilior* is the only species present on the drier north and east slopes and *P. milanjianus* the only species present on the wetter western slopes; both species grow together on the Kimilili transect on the south, where the climate is moist, though not as moist as on the west.

Podocarpus pollen rises are marked features of many East African Upper Quaternary pollen diagrams and may well have been contemporaneous with one another. The most probable explanation is that the rises are due to a general shift to a drier climate over a wide area, but a fully satisfactory explanation awaits greater understanding of the ecology of *Podocarpus*, particularly *P. milanjianus*. In the case of Ethiopia, the *Podocarpus* pollen increase was presumably due to an increase in the population of *P. gracilior* and, in the case of West Rift montane areas, the increase presumably related to *P. milanjianus*, which may have been able to expand its numbers on ridge sites under a drier climate. Concerning Mt Elgon, the rise is greater in the Lake Kimilili than the Koitoboss Bog pollen diagram and, since a greater proportion of pollen in the former is believed to have been derived from drier slopes, *P. gracilior* is probably the main species contributing to the rises.

Urticaceae

Urticaceae pollen is porate, small and typically rather featureless (Hamilton, 1976b). Most Urticaceae species are herbs or small shrubs found in the understory of forests. They are probably particularly common between 2000 and 3000 m, especially in moister areas, though it should be noted that in the vegetation survey of Mt Elgon no differences in abundance of Urticaceae plants on the moister and drier transects were noted. Urticaceae herbs can be abundant beneath dense bamboo stands. Species of the genus *Urera* are unusual in being climbers and one species, *U. hypselodendron*, is montane. This was by far the commonest climber encountered in the vegetation survey of Mt Elgon and was recorded between 2100 and 3000 m. Some members of the family are found on nitrophyllous sites, in which role they can be associated with human disturbance.

Surface samples suggest that Urticaceae pollen is more abundant in moist forest types than dry. Urticaceae constituted over 10% of total pollen in all montane forest surface samples on the wetter Kimilili transect on Mt Elgon, but was always less than 7% in samples from the drier Koitoboss transect (Hamilton and Perrott, in press, a). Again, surface samples from above the forest limit on Mt Elgon show increased percentages of Urticaceae towards the west, the wetter aspect (Hamilton, 1972).

Urticaceae pollen has a high relative export ability. It is interesting that little of the pollen in either surface samples or pollen diagrams originates from *Urera hypselodendron*, which has distinguishable pollen, despite the apparently favourable position for pollen dispersal of the plant in the forest canopy and its general abundance. Most Urticaceae pollen must originate from the forest undergrowth and presumably the lightness of the pollen grains is a factor in aiding their dispersal out into the general atmosphere.

References

Adamson, D. and Williams, F. (1980). Structural geology, tectonics and the control of drainage in the Nile basin. *In* "The Sahara and the Nile" (M. A. J. Williams and H. Faure, eds), pp. 225–252. A. A. Balkema, Rotterdam.

Agnew, A. D. Q. (1974). "Upland Kenya Wild Flowers." Oxford University Press. 827 pp.

Andersen, S. T. (1967). Tree-pollen rain in a mixed deciduous forest in South Jutland (Denmark). *Rev. Palaobotan. Palynol.* **3,** 267–275.

Andersen, S. T. (1974). Wind conditions and pollen dispersal in a mixed deciduous forest II. Seasonal and annual pollen deposition 1967–1972. *Grana* **14,** 64–77.

Anon (1979). Shocking news from Uganda. *Swara* **2,** 23.

Aubréville, A. (1949). Climats, forêts et désertification de l'Afrique tropicale. Société d'Éditions Géographiques, Maritimes et Coloniales, Paris. 351 pp.

Ayodele Cole, N. H. (1974). Climate, life forms and species distribution on the Loma Montane grassland, Sierra Leone. *Bot. J. Linn. Soc.* **69,** 197–210.

Baker, B. H. (1967). Geology of the Mount Kenya area. *Geol. Surv. Kenya Rep.* no. **79,** 78 pp.

Baker, B. H. and Wohlenberg, J. (1971). Structure and evolution of the Kenya Rift Valley. *Nature, Lond.* **229,** 538–542.

Balinsky, B. I. (1962). Patterns of animal distribution on the African Continent. *Ann. Cape Prov. Mus.* **2,** 299–310.

Battarbee, R. W. and McCallan, M. E. (1974). An evaporation tray technique for estimating absolute pollen numbers. *Pollen Spores* **16,** 143–150.

Battiscombe, E. (1936). "Trees and Shrubs of Kenya Colony." Govt. Printer, Nairobi. 201 pp.

Beadle, L. C. (1974). "The Inland Waters of Tropical Africa." Longman, London. 365 pp.

Beals, E. W. (1969). Vegetational change along altitudinal gradients. *Science, N.Y.* **165,** 981–985.

Bergstrom, E. (1955). British Ruwenzori Expedition, 1952: glaciological observations—preliminary report. *J. Glaciol.* **2,** 468–476.

Bigalke, R. C. (1968). Evolution of mammals on Southern continents, 3. The contemporary mammal fauna of Africa. *Q. Rev. Biol.* **43,** 265–300.

Birks, H. J. B. (1973). "Past and Present Vegetation of the Isle of Skye." Cambridge University Press. 415 pp.

Bishop, W. W. (1963). The later Tertiary and Pleistocene in Eastern Equatorial Africa. *In* "African Ecology and Human Evolution" (F. C. Howell and F. Bourlière, eds), pp. 246–275. Aldine Publishing Co., Chicago.

Bishop, W. W. (1967). "Annotated Lexicon of Quaternary Stratigraphical Nomenclature in East Africa" (W. W. Bishop and J. D. Clark, eds). University of Chicago Press, Chicago and London.

Bishop, W. W. (1969). Pleistocene stratigraphy in Uganda. *Geol. Surv. Uganda. Memoir* **no. X.** Govt. Printer, Uganda. 128 pp.

Bishop, W. W. and Posnansky, M. (1960). Pleistocene environments and early man in Uganda. *Uganda J.* **24,** 44–61.

Bonnefille, R. (1970). Premiers résultats concernant l'analyse pollinique d'échantillons du Pléistocène inférieur de l'Omo (Ethiopie). *C. r. Acad. Sci., Paris* **270,** 2430–2433.

Bonnefille, R. (1971a). Atlas des pollen d'Ethiopie. Principales espèces des forêts de montagne. *Pollen Spores* **13,** 15–72.

Bonnefille, R. (1971b). Atlas des pollen d'Ethiopie. Pollen actuels de la basse vallée d l'Omo, récoltes botaniques 1968. *Adansonia* **11,** 463–518.

Bonnefille, R. (1972). Associations pollinique actuelles et Quarternaire en Ethopie. Thèse, Univ. Parix VI. 513 pp.

Bonnefille, R. (1976). Implications of pollen assemblage from the Koobi Fora Formation, East Rudolf, Kenya. *Nature, Lond.* **264,** 403–407.

Bonnefille, R. (1979). Méthode palynologique et reconstitutions paléoclimatiques au Cénzoique dans le Rift Est Africain. *Bull. Soc. géol. Fr.* **21,** 331–342.

Bonnefille, R. and Letouzey, R. (1976). Fruits fossiles d'*Antrocaryon* dans la vallée de l'Omo (Ethiopie). *Adansonia* **16,** 65–82.

Bonnefille, R. and Riollet, G. (1980). "Pollen des Savanes d'Afrique Orientale." Éditions du Centre National de la Recherche Scientifique, Paris.

Bonnefille, R. and Vincens, A. (1977). Représentation pollinique d'environnements arides à l'est du Lac Turkana (Kenya). Supplément au Bulletin AFEQ, 1977–1, no 50.

Bonny, A. P. (1976). Recruitment of pollen to the seston and sediment of some Lake District lakes. *J. Ecol.* **64,** 859–887.

Booth, A. H. (1954). The Dahomey Gap and the mammalian fauna of the West African forests. *Revue Zool. Bot. afr.* **1,** 305–314.

Booth, A. H. (1957). The Niger, the Volta and the Dahomey Gap as geographic barriers. *Evolution, Lancaster, Pa.* **12,** 48–62.

Booth, A. H. (1958). The zoogeography of West African Primates: a review. *Bull. Inst. fr. Afr. noire Sér. A* **20**, 587–622.

Boucher, K. (1975). "Global Climate". The English Universities Press Ltd. 326 pp.

Boughey, A. S. (1954–1955). The vegetation of the mountains of Biafra. *Proc. Linn. Soc. Lond.* **165**, 144–150.

Boutique, R. and Verdcourt, B. (1973). "Flora of Tropical East Africa: Haloragaceae." Crown Agents, London. 9 pp.

Bouxin, G. (1974). Etude phytogéographique des plantes vasculaires du marais Kamiranzovu (forêt de Rugege, Rwanda). *Bull. Jard. bot. Nat. Belg.* **44**, 41–159.

Bouxin, G. (1976). Ordination and classification in the upland Rugege Forest (Rwanda, Central Africa). *Vegetatio* **32**, 97–115.

Bouxin, G. (1977). Structure de la strate arborescente dans un site de la forêt de montagne du Rwanda (Afrique Centrale). *Vegetatio* **33**, 65–78.

Bowen, D. Q. (1978). "Quaternary Geology." Pergamon Press, Oxford.

Bower, J. R. F., Nelson, C. M., Waibel, A. F. and Wandibba, S. (1977). The University of Massachusetts' Later Stone Age/Pastural "Neolithic" comparative study in Central Kenya: an overview. *Azania* **12**, 119–146.

Brock, P. W. G. and MacDonald, R. (1969). Geological environment of the Bukwa mammalian fossil locality, Eastern Uganda. *Nature, Lond.* **223**, 593–596.

Burke, K. and Wilson, J. T. (1972). Is the African plate stationary? *Nature, Lond.* **239**, 387–390.

Bush, G. L. (1975). Modes of animal speciation. *Ann Rev. Ecol. Syst.* **6**, 339–364.

Butzer, K. W. (1976). The Mursi, Nkalabong, and Kibish Formations, lower Omo basin, Ethiopia. *In* "Earliest Man and Environments in the Lake Rudolf Basin" (Y. Coppens *et al.*, eds), pp. 12–23. University of Chicago Press, Chicago and London.

Butzer, K. W. (1980). Pleistocene history of the Nile Valley in Egypt and Lower Nubia. *In* "The Sahara and the Nile" (M. A. J. Williams and H. Faure, eds), pp. 253–280. A. A. Balkema, Rotterdam.

Butzer, K. W., Isaac, G. L., Richardson, J. L. and Washbourn-Kamau, C. K. (1972). Radiocarbon dating of East African lake levels. *Science, N.Y.* **175**, 1069–1076.

Capart, A. (1949). Sondages et carte bathymétrique. Exploration hydro-biologique du Lac Tanganyika (1946–1947). *Inst. Roy. Sci. Nat. Belg.* **1**, 3–27.

Carcasson, R. H. (1964). A preliminary survey of the zoogeogaphy of African butterflies. *E. Africa Wild Life J.* **2**, 122–157.

Carte Lithologique du Rwanda (s.a.). Ministère de l'agriculture et des affaires économiques service géologique, Rwanda.

Chaney, R. W. (1933). A Tertiary flora from Uganda. *J. Geol.* **41**, 702–709.

Chapin, J. P. (1932). The birds of the Belgian Congo. *Bull. Am. Mus. nat. Hist.* **65**, 1–756.

Chapman, J. D. and White, F. (1970). "The Evergreen Forests of Malawi." Commonwealth Forestry Institute, University of Oxford. 190 pp.

Charnley, F. E. (1959). Some observations on the glaciers of Mt Kenya. *J. Glaciol.* **3**, 483–492.

Cheffings, J. and Binks, A. (1979). Tanzania—recent impressions. *Swara* **2**, 8–13.

Chesters, K. I. M. (1957). The Miocene flora of Rusinga Island, Lake Victoria, Kenya. *Palaeontographica* **101**, 30–71.

Clark, J. D. (1960). Human ecology during Pleistocene and later times in Africa south of the Sahara. *Curr. Anthrop.* **1**, 307–324.

Clark, J. D. (1965). The Later Pleistocene cultures of Africa. *Science, N.Y.* **150**, 833–847.

Clark, J. D. (ed.) (1969). "Kalambo Falls Prehistoric Site", Vol. 1. Cambridge University Press.

Clark, J. D. (1970). "The Prehistory of Africa." Thames and Hudson. 302 pp.

Clark, J. D. (1975). A comparison of the Late Acheulian industries of Africa and the Middle East. *In* "After the Australopithecines" (K. W. Butzer and G. L. Isaac, eds), pp. 605–659. Mouton Publishers, The Hague and Paris.

Clark, J. D. (1976). African orgins of man the toolmaker. *In* "Human Origins" (G. L. Isaac and E. R. McCown, eds), pp. 1–53. W. A. Benjamin, California.

Clark, J. D. and Cole, S. (ed.) (1957). Proceedings of the third Pan-African Congress on Prehistory, Livingstone, Northern Rhodesia, 1955. Chatto and Windus, London.

Coe, M. J. (1967). The ecology of the Alpine Zone of Mt Kenya. *Monographiae Biologicae* **17**. W. Junk, The Hague. 136 pp.

Coetzee, J. A. (1967). Pollen analytical studies in East and Southern Africa. *Palaeoecol. Afr.* **3**, 1–146.

Cole, S. (1964). "The Prehistory of East Africa." Weidenfeld and Nicolson, London. 382 pp.

Coles, J. M. and Higgs, E. S. (1969). "The Archaeology of Early Man." Penguin, England. 454 pp.

Combe, A. D. and Simmons, W. C. (1933). The volcanic area of Bufumbira, Part 1. *Geol. Survey Uganda Memoir* **no. 3**. Govt. Printer, Uganda.

Coppens, Y., Howell, F. C., Isaac, G. L. and Leakey, R. E. F. (ed.) (1976). "Earliest Man and Environments in the Lake Rudolf Basin." University of Chicago Press, Chicago and London. 615 pp.

Curry-Lindahl, K. (1968). Zoological aspects on the conservation of vegetation in Tropical Africa. *In* "Conservation of Vegetation in Africa South of the Sahara" (I. and O. Hedberg, eds), pp. 25–32. *Acta phytogeogr. suec.* **54**.

Daily Nation. (A Kenyan newspaper.)

Dale, I. R. (1940). The forest types of Mount Elgon. *J. E. Africa Uganda nat. Hist. Soc.* **45**, 74–82.

Dale, I. R. and Greenway, P. J. (1961). "Kenya Trees and Shrubs." Buchanan's Kenya Estates Ltd, Kenya. 654 pp.

Dandelot, P. (1965). Distribution de quelques espèces de Cercopithedidae en relation avec les zônes de végétation de l'Afrique. *Zoologica africana* **1**, 167–176.

Deuse, P. (1966). Contribution à l'étude des tourbières du Rwanda et du Burundi. Inst. Nat. Recherche Scient. Butare, Rwanda. Publication no. **4**. 115 pp.

Diamond, A. W. and Hamilton, A. C. (1980). The distribution of forest passerine birds and Quaternary climatic change in tropical Africa. *J. Zool., Lond.* **191**, 379–402.

Diamond, J. M. (1970). Ecological consequences of island colonization by southwest Pacific birds. 1. Types of niche shifts. *Proc. natn. Acad. Sci. U.S.A.* **67**, 529–536.

Downie, C. (1964). Glaciations of Mount Kilimanjaro, Northeast Tanganyika. *Bull. geol. Soc. Am.* **75**, 1–16.

Downie, C., Humphries, D. W., Wilcockson, W. H. and Wildinson, P. (1956). Geology of Kilimanjaro. *Nature, Lond.* **178**, 828–830.

East African Meteorological Dept. (1968a). Summary of rainfall in Uganda for the year 1967. Met. Dept., E. Afr. Community, Nairobi.

East African Meteorological Dept. (1968b). Summary of rainfall in Kenya for the year 1967. Met. Dept., E. Afr. Community, Nairobi.

Edroma, E. (1979). "Game Parks Almost Empty." The Nairobi Times Sept. 2nd.

Eggeling, W. J. (1947). Observations on the ecology of Budongo rain forest, Uganda. *J. Ecol.* **34**, 20–87.

Embleton, C. and King, C. A. M. (1968). "Glacial and Periglacial Geomorphology." Edward Arnold, London. 608 pp.

Exell, A. W. (1953). The vegetation of the islands of the Gulf of Guinea. *Lejeunia* **16**, 57–66.

Faden, R. B. (1974). East African coastal-West African rain forest disjunctions. *In* "East African Vegetation" (E. M. Lind and M. E. S. Morrison, eds), pp. 202–203. Longman, London.

Faegri, K. and Iversen, J. (1964). "Textbook of Pollen Analysis". Blackwell, Oxford, 237 pp.

Faure, H. (1980). Le cadre chronologique des phases pluviales et glaciaires de l'Afrique. *In* "Histoire Generale de l'Afrique", vol. 1 (J. Ki-Zerbo, ed.), pp. 409–434. U.N.E.S.C.O., Paris.

Flenley, J. R. (1972). The use of modern pollen rain samples in the study of the vegetational history of tropical regions. *In* "Quaternary Plant Ecology" (H. J. B. Birks and R. G. West, eds), pp. 131–141. Blackwell, Oxford.

Flenley, J. R. (1979). "The Equatorial Rain Forest: a Geological History." Butterworths, London and Boston. 162 pp.

Flint, R. F. (1959). On the basis of Pleistocene correlation in East Africa. *Geol. Mag.* **96**, 265–284.

Flora of Tropical East Africa (1952 etc.). Crown Agents, London.

Gasse, F. (1975). L'évolution des lacs de l'Afar Central (Ethiopie et T.F.A.I.) du Plio-Pléistocène à l'Actuel. Thèse, Univ. Paris VI. 390 pp.

Gasse, F. (1978). Les diatomées holocènes d'une tourbière (4040 m) d'une montagne Ethiopienne: le mont Badda. *Revue algol.* **13**, 105–149.

Gasse, F. and Street, F. A. (1978). Late Quaternary lake-level fluctuations and environments of the Northern Rift Valley and Afar Region (Ethiopia and Djibouti). *Palaeogeog. Palaeoclimatol. Palaeoecol.* **24**, 279–325.

Gasse, F., Rognon, R. and Street, F. A. (1980). Quaternary history of the Afar and Ethiopian Rift lakes. *In* "The Sahara and the Nile" (M. A. J. Williams and H. Faure, eds), pp. 361–400. A. A. Balkema, Rotterdam.

Gautier, A. (1967). New observations on the later Tertiary and early Quaternary in the Western Rift: the stratigraphy and palaeontological evidence. *In* "Background to Evolution in Africa" (W. W. Bishop and J. D. Clark, eds), pp. 73–87. University of Chicago Press, Chicago and London.

George, T. N. (1976). Charles Lyell: the present is the key to the past. *Philosophical J.* **13**, 3–24.

Gill, R. L. O. (1974). African swells, magmatism and plate tectonics. *Nature, Lond.* **247**, 25–26.

Greenwood, P. H. (1974). The cichlid fishes of Lake Victoria, East Africa: the biology and evolution of a species flock. *Bull. Br. Mus. Nat. Hist. Zool. Suppl.* **6**.

Griffiths, J. F. (1962). The climate of East Africa. *In* "The Natural Resources of East Africa" (E. W. Russell, ed.), pp. 77–87. Hawkins, Nairobi.

Grove, A. T. (1967). "Africa South of the Sahara." Oxford University Press. 275 pp.

Grove, A. T. (1977). Desertification in the African environment. *In* "Drought in Africa" (D. Dalby, R. J. H. Church and F. Bezzaz, eds), pp. 54–64. International African Institute. 200 pp.

Grove, A. T. and Pullan, R. A. (1963). Some aspects of the Pleistocene paleogeography of the Chad Basin. *In* "African Ecology and Human Evolution" (F. C. Howell and F. Bourlière, eds), pp. 230–245. Aldine Publishing Co., Chicago.

Grove, A. T., Street, F. A. and Goudie, A. S. (1975). Former lake levels and climatic change in the rift valley of southern Ethiopia. *Geogrl J.* **141**, 177–202.

Groves, C. P. (1971). Distribution and place of origin of the gorilla. *Man* **6**, 44–51.

Grubb, P. J. (1977). Control of forest growth and distribution on wet tropical mountains: with special reference to mineral nutrition. *Ann Rev. Ecol. Syst.* **8**, 83–107.

Guthrie, M. (1967). "Comparative Bantu", Vol. 1. Gregg Press Ltd, Farnborough, England.

Haffer, J. (1969). Speciation in Amazonian forest birds. *Science, N.Y.* **165**, 131–137.

Haffer, J. (1974). Avian speciation in tropical South America. *Publs Nuttall orn. Club* **no. 14**. Cambridge, Massachusetts.

Haffer, J. (1977). Pleistocene speciation in Amazonian birds. *Amazonia* **6**, 161–191.

Hall, B. P. and Moreau, R. E. (1970). "An Atlas of Speciation in African Passerine Birds." British Museum (Natural History), London, 423 pp.

Hall, J. B. (1973). Vegetational zones on the southern slopes of Mount Cameroon. *Vegetatio* **27**, 49–69.

Hall, J. B. and Medler, J. A. (1975). Highland vegetation in south-eastern Nigeria and its affinities. *Vegetatio* **29**, 191–198.

Hall, J. B., Swaine, M. D. and Talbot, M. R. (1978). An early Holocene leaf flora from Lake Bosumtwi, Ghana. *Palaeogeog. Palaeoclimatol. Palaeoecol.* **24**, 247–261.

Hamilton, A. C. (1968). Some plant fossils from Bukwa. *Uganda J.* **32**, 157–164.

Hamilton, A. C. (1969). The vegetation of southwest Kigezi. *Uganda J.* **33**, 175–199.

Hamilton, A. C. (1972). The interpretation of pollen diagrams from highland Uganda. *Palaeoecol. Afr.* **7**, 45–149.

Hamilton, A. C. (1974a). Distribution patterns of forest trees in Uganda and their historical significance. *Vegetatio* **29**, 21–35.

Hamilton, A. C. (1974b). The history of the vegetation. *In* "East African Vegetation" (E. M. Lind and M. E. S. Morrison, eds), pp. 188–209. Longman, London.

Hamilton, A. C. (1975a). A quantitative analysis of altitudinal zonation in Uganda forests. *Vegetatio* **30**, 99–106.

Hamilton, A. C. (1975b). The dispersal of forest tree species in Uganda during the Upper Pleistocene. *Boissiera* **24**, 29–32.

Hamilton, A. C. (1976a). The significance of patterns of distribution shown by forest plants and animals in tropical Africa for the reconstruction of upper Pleistocene palaeo-environments: a review. *Palaeoecol. Afr.* **9**, 63–97.

Hamilton, A. C. (1976b). Identification of East African Urticales pollen. *Pollen Spores* **18**, 27–66.

Hamilton, A. C. and Perrott, R. A. (1978). Date of deglacierisation of Mount Elgon. *Nature, Lond.* **273**, 49.

Hamilton, A. C. and Perrott, R. A. (1979). Aspects of the glaciation of Mt Elgon, East Africa. *Palaeoecol. Afr.* **11**, 153–161.

Hamilton, A. C. and Perrott, R. A. (1980). "The Vegetation of Mt Elgon, East Africa." Research Report for Kenya Govt. 34 pp.

Hamilton, A. C. and Perrott, R. A. (in press, a). Modern pollen deposition on a tropical mountain. *Pollen Spores.*

Hamilton, A. C. and Perrott, R. A. (in press, b). A study of altitudinal zonation in the Montane Forest Belt of Mt Elgon, East Africa. *Vegetatio.*

Harlan, J. R., Wet, J. M. J. de and Stemler, A. B. L. (1976). Plant domestication and indigenous African agriculture. *In* "Origins of African plant domestication" (J. R. Harlan *et al.*, eds), pp. 3–19. Mouton Publishers, The Hague and Paris. 498 pp.

Harvey, T. J. (1976). The paleolimnology of Lake Mobutu Sese Seko, Uganda-Zaire: the last 28 000 years. Ph.D. thesis, Duke University, N. Carolina. 113 pp.

Hastenrath, S. (1977). Pleistocene mountain glaciation in Ethiopia. *J. Glaciol.* **18**, 309–313.

Heath, G. R. (1979). Simulations of a glacial paleoclimate by three different atmospheric general circulation models. *Palaeogeog. Palaeoclimatol. Palaeoecol.* **26**, 291–303.

Hecky, R. E. and Degens, E. T. (1973). Late Pleistocene-Holocene chemical stratigraphy and paleolimnology of the Rift Valley lakes of Central Africa. Tech. Rept. Woods Hole Oceanogr. Inst., Massachusetts. 93 pp.

Hedberg, O. (1951). Vegetation belts of the East African mountains. *Svensk. bot. Tidskr.* **45**, 140–202.

Hedberg, O. (1954). A pollen-analytical reconnaissance in Tropical East Africa. *Oikos* **5**, 137–166.

Hedberg, O. (1957). Afroalpine vascular plants. *Symb. bot. upsal.* **15**, 1–411.

Hedberg, O. (1959). An "open-air hothouse" on Mt Elgon, Tropical East Africa. *Svensk. bot. Tidskr.* **53**, 160–166.

Hedberg, O. (1961). The phytogeographical position of the Afroalpine flora. *Recent Advances in Botany, Sect.* **9**, 914–919.

Hedberg, O. (1963). Afroalpine flora elements. *Webbia* **19**, 519–529.

Hedberg, O. (1964). Features of Afroalpine plant ecology. *Acta phytogeogr. suec.* **49**, 1–144.

Hedberg, O. (1968). Taxonomic and ecological studies on the Afroalpine flora of Mt Kenya. *Hochgebirgsforschung* **1**, 171–194.

Hedberg, O. (1969a). Evolution and speciation in a tropical high mountain flora. *Biol. J. Linn. Soc.* **1**, 135–148.

Hedberg, O. (1969b). Growth rate of the East African Giant Senecios. *Nature, Lond.* **222**, 163–164.

Hedberg, O. (1971). The high mountain flora of the Galama Mountain in Arussi Province, Ethiopia. *Webbia* **26**, 101–128.

Hedberg, O. (1975). Studies of adaptation and speciation in the Afroalpine flora of Ethiopia. *Boissiera* **24**, 71–74.

Heine, K. (1979). Reply to Cooke's discussion of: K. Heine: Radiocarbon chronology of Late Quaternary lakes in the Kalahari, Southern Africa. *Catena* **6**, 259–266.

Heinzelin, J. de (1951). Glacier recession and periglacial phenomena in the Ruwenzori range (Belgian Congo). *J. Glaciol.* **2**, 137–140.

Heinzelin, J. de (1953). Les stades du Récession du Glacier Stanley occidental (Ruwenzori, Congo Belge). *Explor. Parc natn. Albert sér.* **2**, 1.

Hicks, S. (1977). Modern pollen rain in Finnish Lapland investigated by analysis of surface moss samples. *New Phytol.* **78**, 715–734.

Howell, F. C. and Bourlière, F. (ed.) (1963). "African Ecology and Human Evolution." Aldine Publishing Co., Chicago, 666 pp.

Howell, F. C. and Isaac, G. L. (1976). Introduction (to paleoanthropology). *In* "Earliest Man and Environments in the Lake Rudolf Basin" (Y. Coppens *et al.*, eds), pp. 471–475. University of Chicago Press, Chicago and London.

Huffman, T. N. (1970). The Early Iron Age and the spread of the Bantu. *S. Afr. Archaeological Bull.* **25**, 3–21.

Humphries, D. W. (1959). Preliminary notes on the glaciology of Kilimanjaro. *J. Glaciol.* **3**, 475–478.

Humphries, D. W. (1972). Glaciology and glacial history. *In* "The Geology of Kilimanjaro" (C. Downie and P. Wilkinson, eds), pp. 31–71. Geology Dept., University of Sheffield.

Isaac, G. L. (1966). The geological history of the Olorgesailie area. Actes du 5th Congres Panafricain de prehistoire et de l'étude du Quaternaire. Museo Arqueologico de Teneriffe, Islas Canarias.

Isaac, G. L. (1975). Stratigraphy and cultural patterns in East Africa during the middle ranges of Pleistocene time. *In* "After the Australopithecines" (K. W. Butzer and G. L. Isaac, eds), pp. 495–542. Mouton Publishers, The Hague and London.

Isaac, G. L. (1976). East Africa as a source of fossil evidence for human evolution. *In* "Human Origins" (G. L. Isaac and E. R. McCown, eds), pp. 121–137. W. A. Benjamin, California.

Janssen, C. R. (1973). Local and regional pollen deposition. *In* "Quaternary Plant Ecology" (H. J. B. Birks and R. G. West, eds), pp. 31–42. Blackwell, Oxford.

Jessen, K. (1949). Studies in the late Quaternary deposits and flora-history of Ireland. *Proc. R. Ir. Acad. Ser. B* **52**, 85–290.

Johannesen, I., Krosshaug, L. and Kingston, B. (1967). Site type classification in Rwoho Central Forest Reserve with reference also to Bugamba Central Forest Reserve. Uganda Forest Dept.

Johnston, H. (1902). "The Uganda Protectorate." Hutchinson and Co., London. 1018 pp.

Jones, E. W. (1956). Ecological studies on the rain forest of Southern Nigeria, IX (contd). The plateau forest of the Okumu Forest Reserve. *J. Ecol.* **44**, 83–117.

Keay, R. W. J. (1954–1955). Montane vegetation and flora in the British Cameroons. *Proc. Linn. Soc. Lond.* **165**, 140–143.

Keay, R. W. J. (1957). Wind-dispersed species in a Nigerian forest. *J. Ecol.* **45**, 471–478.

Keith, S., Twomey, A., Friedman, H. and Williams, J. (1969). The avifauna of the Impenetrable Forest, Uganda. *Am. Mus. Novit.* **No. 2389**, 1–41.

Kendall, R. L. (1969). An ecological history of the Lake Victoria basin. *Ecol. Monogr.* **39**, 121–176.

Kenworthy, J. M. (1964). Rainfall and the water resources of East Africa. *In* "Geographers and the Tropics: Liverpool Essays" (R. W. Steel and R. M. Prothero, eds), pp. 111–137. Longman, London.

Kenworthy, J. M. (1966). Temperature conditions in the tropical highland climates of East Africa. *E. Afr. Geogr. Rev.* **4**, 1–11.

Kingdon, J. (1971 etc.). "East African mammals: an Atlas of Evolution in Africa." Academic Press, London and New York.

Lack, D. (1971). "Ecological Isolation in Birds." Blackwell, Oxford. 404 pp.

Lack, D. (1976). "Island Biology: Illustrated by the Land Birds of Jamaica." Blackwell, Oxford. 445 pp.

Lamb, H. H. (1977). Some comments on the drought in recent years in the Sahel-Ethiopian Zone of North Africa. *In* "Drought in Africa" (D. Dalby, R. J. H. Church and F. Bezzaz, eds), pp. 33–37. International African Institute.

Lamprey, H. (1978). The integrated project on arid lands. *Nature and Resources* **14**, 2–11.

Lancaster, I. N. (1979a). Quaternary environments in the arid zone of southern Africa. Dept. Geography and Environmental Studies, University of Witwatersrand, S. Africa. Occasional Paper no. 22. 77 pp.

Lancaster, I. N. (1979b). Evidence for a widespread late Pleistocene humid period in the Kalahari. *Nature, Lond.* **279**, 145–146.

Lancaster, I. N. (1980). Relationships between altitude and temperature in Malawi. *S. Afr. geogr. J.* **62**, 89–97.

Laurent, R. F. (1973). A parallel survey of equatorial amphibians and reptiles in Africa and South America. *In* "Tropical Forest Ecosystems in Africa and South America: a Comparative Review" (B. J. Meggers et al., eds), pp. 259–266. Smithsonian Inst. Press, Washington.

Leakey, L. S. B. (1931). "The Stone Age Cultures of Kenya Colony." Cambridge University Press.

Leakey, L. S. B. (1965). "Olduvai Gorge," Vol. 1. Cambridge University Press.

Leakey, M. D. (1975). Cultural patterns in the Olduvai sequence. *In* "After the Australopithecines" (K. W. Butzer and G. L. Isaac, eds), pp. 477–493. Mouton Publishers, The Hague and Paris.

Leakey, R. E. F. (1976). An overview of the Homidae from East Rudolf, Kenya. *In* "Earliest Man and Environments in the Lake Rudolf Basin" (Y. Coppens et al., eds), pp. 476–483. University of Chicago Press, Chicago and London.

Leburn, J. (1942). La végétation du Nyiragongo. Aspects de végétation des parcs nationaux du Congo. Sér. 1. Institut des parcs nationaux du Congo-Belge. 121 pp.

Leith, H. (1975). Primary production in ecosystems: comparative analysis of global patterns. *In* "Unifying Concepts in Ecology" (W. H. van Dobben and R. H. Lowe-McConnell, eds), pp. 67–88. Junk, The Hague.

Léonard, J. (1965). Contribution à la subdivision phytogéographique de la

Région guinéo-congolaise d'après la répartition géographique d'Euphor-biacées d'Afrique tropicale. *Webbia* **19**, 627–649.

Lewalle, J. (1972). Les étages de végétation du Burundi occidental. *Bull. Jard. bot. Nat. Belg.* **42**, 1–247.

Lind, E. M. (1956). Studies in Uganda swamps. *Uganda J.* **20**, 166–176.

Lind, E. M. and Morrison, M. E. S. (1974). "East African Vegetation." Longman, London. 257 pp.

Livingstone, D. A. (1962). Age of deglaciation in the Ruwenzori Range, Uganda. *Nature, Lond.* **194**, 859–860.

Livingstone, D. A. (1965). Sedimentation and the history of water level change in Lake Tanganyika. *Limnol. Oceanogr.* **10**, 607–610.

Livingstone, D. A. (1967). Postglacial vegetation of the Ruwenzori Mountains in Equatorial Africa. *Ecol. Monogr.* **37**, 25–52.

Livingstone, D. A. (1971). A 22 000-year pollen record from the plateau of Zambia. *Limnol. Oceanogr.* **16**, 349–356.

Livingstone, D. A. (1975). Late Quaternary climatic change in Africa. *Ann Rev. Ecol. Syst.* **6**, 249–280.

Livingstone, D. A. (1980). Environmental changes in the Nile headwaters. *In* "The Sahara and the Nile" (M. A. J. Williams and H. Faure, eds), pp. 339–359. Blakema, Rotterdam.

Livingstone, D. A., Tomlinson, M., Friedman, G. and Broome, R. (1973). Stellate pore ornamentation in pollen grains of the Amaranthaceae. *Pollen Spores* **15**, 345–351.

Logan, W. E. M. (1946). An introduction to the forests of Central and Southern Ethiopia. *Imp. For. Inst. Oxford, paper* no. 24. 66 pp.

Lucas, G. L. (1968). Kenya. *In* "Conservation of Vegetation in Africa South of the Sahara" (I. and O. Hedberg, eds), pp. 152–166. *Acta phytogeogr. suec.* **54**.

Lumley, H. de (1975). Cultural evolution in France and its paleoecological setting during the Middle Pleistocene. *In* "After the Australopithecines" (K. W. Butzer and G. L. Isaac, eds), pp. 745–808. Mouton Publishers, The Hague and Paris.

Lundgren, B. (1971). Soil studies in a montane forest in Ethiopia. Dept. Forest Ecology and Forest Soils, Stockholm. 35 pp.

MacArthur, R. H. and Wilson, E. A. (1967). "The Theory of Island Biogeography". Princeton University Press. 203 pp.

Mainguet, M. and Canon, L. (1976). Vents et paléovents du Sahara. Tentative d'approche paléoclimatique. *Revue Géogr. phys. Géol. dyn.* **18**, 241–250.

Mainguet, M., Canon, L. and Chemin, M. C. (1980). Le Sahara: géomorphologie et paléogéomorphologie éoliennes. *In* "The Sahara and the Nile" (M. A. J. Williams and H. Faure, eds), pp. 17–35. Balkema, Rotterdam.

Makina, S. (1979). "Improved farm technology can change Kenyan farmer's life." Daily Nation, Aug. 2nd. Kisumu Show Suppl.

Maley, J. (1970). Contributions à l'étude du Bassin tchadien. Atlas de pollens du Tchad. *Bull. Jard. bot. Nat. Belg.* **40**, 29–48.

Maley, J. (1973). Mécanismes des changements climatiques aux basses latitudes. *Palaeogeog. Palaeoclimatol. Palaeoecol.* **14**, 193–22.

Marchant, S. (1954). The relationship of the southern Nigerian avifauna to those of Upper and Lower Guinea. *Ibis* **96**, 371–379.

Martin, P. S. (1966). Africa and Pleistocene overkill. *Nature, Lond.* **212**, 339–342.

Mayr, E. (1969). Bird speciation in the tropics. *Biol. J. Linn. Soc.* **1**, 1–17.

Mayr, E. (1976). "Evolution and the Diversity of Life." Harvard University Press, Cambridge, Massachusetts. 721 pp.

Mayr, E. and Diamond, J. M. (1976). Birds on islands in the sky: origin of the montane avifauna of Northern Melanesia. *Proc. natn. Acad. Sci. U.S.A.* **73**, 1765–1769.

McCall, G. J. H., Baker, B. H. and Walsh, J. (1967). Late Tertiary and Quaternary sediments of the Kenya Rift Valley. *In* "Background to evolution in Africa" (W. W. Bishop and J. D. Clark, eds), pp. 191–220. University of Chicago Press, Chicago and London.

McClure, H. A. (1976). Radiocarbon chronology of late Quaternary lakes in the Arabian Desert. *Nature, Lond.* **263**, 755–756.

McMaster, D. N. (1962). Speculations on the coming of the banana to Uganda. *J. trop. Geogr.* **16**, 57–69.

Melville, R. (1958). "Flora of Tropical East Africa: Gymnospermae." Crown Agents, London. 16 pp.

Messerli, B., Winiger, M. and Rognon, P. (1980). The Saharan and East African uplands during the Quaternary. *In* "The Sahara and the Nile" (M. A. J. Williams and H. Faure, eds), pp. 87–118. Balkema, Rotterdam.

Milne-Redhead, E. (1954–1955). Distributional ranges of flowering plants in Tropical Africa. *Proc. Linn. Soc. Lond.* **165**, 25–35.

Misonne, X. (1963). Les Rongeurs du Ruwenzori et des régions voisines. Inst. des Parcs Nat. du Congo et du Rwanda, Brussels.

Moore, P. D. and Bellamy, D. J. (1973). "Peatland." Elek Science. 221 pp.

Moreau, R. E. (1966). "The Bird Faunas of Africa and its Islands. Academic Press, New York and London. 424 pp.

Morgan, W. T. W. (1973). "East Africa." Longman, London. 410 pp.

Morrison, M. E. S. (1961). Pollen analysis in Uganda. *Nature, Lond.* **190**, 483–486.

Morrison, M. E S. (1968). Vegetation and climate in the uplands of south-western Uganda during the Later Pleistocene Period, 1. Muchoya Swamp, Kigezi District. *J. Ecol.* **56**, 363–384.

Morrison, M. E. S. and Hamilton, A. C. (1974). Vegetation and climate in the uplands of south-western Uganda during the Later Pleistocene Period, 2. Forest clearance and other vegetational changes in the Rukiga Highlands during the past 8000 years *J. Ecol.* **62**, 1–31.

Morton, J. K. (1961). The upland floras of West Africa—their composition, distribution and significance in relation to climate changes. Comptes Rendus de la IVᵉ Réunion Plénière de l'A.E.T.F.A.T. Lisbon 1961, 391–409.

Morton, J. K. (1972). Phytogeography of the West African mountains. *In* "Taxonomy, Phytogeography and Evolution" (D. H. Valentine, ed.), pp. 221–236. Academic Press, London and New York.

Morton, W. H. (1968). Expedition to the Ruwenzori Mountains, June–July, 1968. Part 1. General account of the expedition, glaciology and geology and recommendations for further work. Water Development Dept., Uganda 17 pp.

Nicholson, S. E. (1980). Saharan climates in historic times. *In* "The Sahara and the Nile" (M. A. J. Williams and H. Faure, ed.), pp. 173–200. Balkema, Rotterdam.

Nilsson, E. (1931). Quaternary glaciations and pluvial lakes in British East Africa. *Geogr. Annlr* 13, 249–349.

Nilsson, E. (1940). Ancient changes of climate in British East Africa and Abyssinia. *Geogr. Annlr* 1–2, 1–79.

Oliver, R. and Fagan, B. M. (1975). "Africa in the Iron Age." Cambridge University Press. 228 pp.

Onyango-Abuje, J. C. (1977). Crescent Island: a preliminary report on excavations at an East African Neolithic site. *Azania* 12, 147–159.

Osmaston, H. A. (1958). Pollen analysis in the study of the past vegetation and climate of the Ruwenzori and its neighbourhood. Uganda Forest Dept. 32 pp.

Osmaston, H. A. (1959). Working plan for Kibale and Itwara Forests. Uganda Forest Dept. 60 pp.

Osmaston, H. A. (1965). The past and present climate and vegetation of Ruwenzori and its neighbourhood. D. Phil. thesis, Oxford University.

Osmaston, H. A. (1967). Plant fossils in volcanic tuffs near the Ruwenzori. *Palaeoecol. Afr.* 2, 25–26.

Osmaston, H. A. (1975). Models for the estimation of firnlines of present and Pleistocene glaciers. *In* "Processes in Physical and Human Geography, Bristol Essays" (R. F. Peel *et al.*, eds), pp. 218–245. Heinemann, London.

Parkin, D. W. and Shackleton, N. J. (1973). Trade winds and temperature changes down a deep-sea core off the Saharan coast. *Nature, Lond.* 245, 455–457.

Parmenter, C. and Folger, D. W. (1974). Eolian biogenic detritus in deep sea sediments: a possible index of Equatorial ice age aridity. *Science, N.Y.* 185, 695–698.

Payne, W. J. A. (1964). The origin of domestic cattle in Africa. *Emp. J. exp. Agric.* 32, 97–113.

Peck, R. M (1973). Pollen budget studies in a small Yorkshire catchment. *In* "Quaternary Plant Ecology" (H. J. B. Birks and R. G. West, eds), pp. 43–60. Blackwell, Oxford.

Perring, F. H. (1959). Topographical gradients of chalk grassland. *J. Ecol.* 47, 447–482.

Phillipson, D. W. (1975). The chronology of the Iron Age in Bantu Africa. *J. African History* 16, 321–342.

Phillipson, D. W. (1977). "The Later Prehistory of Eastern and Southern Africa." Heinemann, London. 323 pp.

Pilbeam, D. R. (1975). Middle Pleistocene hominids. *In* "After the Australopithecines" (K. W. Butzer and G. L. Isaac, eds), pp. 809–856. Mouton Publishers, The Hague and Paris.

Platt, C. M. (1966). Some observations on the climate of Lewis Glacier, Mount Kenya, during the rainy season. *J. Glaciol.* **6**, 267–287.

Polhill, R. M. (1968). Tanzania. *In* "Conservation of Vegetation in Africa South of the Sahara" (I. and O. Hedberg, eds), pp. 166–178. *Acta phytogeog. suec.* **54**.

Potter, E. C. (1976). Pleistocene glaciation in Ethiopia: new evidence. *J. Glaciol.* **17**, 148–150.

Purseglove, J. W. (1976). The origins and migrations of crops in Tropical Africa. *In* "Origins of Africa Plant Domestication" (J. R. Harlan *et al.*, eds), pp. 291–309. Mouton Publishers, The Hague and Paris.

Radwinski, S. A. and Ollier, C. D. (1959). A study of an East African catena. *J. Soil Sci.* **10**, 149–168.

Rahm, U. (1966). Les mammifères de la forêt équatoriale de l'est du Congo. *Ann. Mus. Roy. Afr. Centrale Tervuren Zool.* **149**, 37–121.

Raynaut, C. (1977). Lessons of a crisis. *In* "Drought in Africa" (D. Dalby *et al.*, eds), pp. 17–29. International African Institute.

Richards, P. W. (1963). Ecological notes on West African vegetation, II. Lowland forest of the Southern Bakundu Forest Reserve. *J. Ecol.* **51**, 123–149.

Richardson, J. L. (1964). Plankton and fossil plankton studies in certain East African lakes. *Int. Ver. Theor. Angew. Limnol. Verh.* **15**, 993–999.

Richardson, J. L. (1966). Changes in level of Lake Naivasha, Kenya, during Postglacial times. *Nature, Lond.* **209**, 290–291.

Richardson, J. L. and Richardson, A. E. (1972). History of an African Rift lake and its climatic implications. *Ecol. Monogr.* **42**, 499–534.

Ridley, H. N. (1930). "The Dispersal of Plants Throughout the World." Reeve, Ashford. 744 pp.

Robyns, W. (1947, 1948, 1955). "Flore des Spermatophytes du Parc National Albert," 3 vols. Inst. Parcs Nationaux du Congo Belge, Brussels.

Rognon, P. (1976). Essai d'interprétation des variations climatiques au Sahara depuis 40 000 ans. *Rev. Géogr. phys. Géol. dyn.* **18**, 251–282.

Rognon, P. (1980). Fluviatile piedmont deposits. *In* "The Sahara and the Nile" (M. A. J. Williams and H. Faure, eds), pp. 118–132. Balkema, Rotterdam.

Rognon, P. and Williams, M. A. J. (1977). Late Quaternary climatic changes in Australia and North Africa: a preliminary interpretation. *Palaeogeog. Palaeoclimatol. Palaeoecol.* **21**, 285–327.

Ross, R. (1955). Some aspects of the vegetation of the sub-alpine zone on Ruwenzori. *Proc. Linn. Soc. Lond. Session* **165**, 1952–1953, Pt. 2, 136–140.

Sarnthein, M. (1978). Sand deserts during glacial maximum and climatic optimum. *Nature, Lond.* **272**, 43–46.

Schultz, E. (1979). Preliminary report on the actual pollen rain along the margin of the Murzuk Basin, Central Sahara. *Palaeoecol. Afr.* **11**, 59–63.

Servant, M. and Servant-Valdary, S. (1980). L'environnement quaternaire du bassin du Tchad. *In* "The Sahara and the Nile" (M. A. J. Williams and H. Faure, eds), pp. 133–162. Balkema, Rotterdam.

Shackleton, N. J. (1975). The stratigraphic record of deep-sea cores and its implications for the assessment of glacials, interglacials, stadials and interstadials in the mid-Pleistocene. *In* "After the Australopithecines" (K. W. Butzer and G. L. Isaac, eds), pp. 1–24. Mouton Publishers, The Hague and Paris.

Shackleton, N. J. and Opdyke, N. D. (1973). Oxygen isotope and palaeomagnetic stratigraphy of Equatorial Pacific Core V28–238: oxygen isotope temperatures and ice volumes on a 10^5 and 10^6 year scale. *Quaternary Res.* **3**, 39–55.

Shaw, T. (1976). Early crops in Africa: a review of the evidence. *In* "Origins of African Plant Domestication" (J. R. Harlan *et al.*, eds), pp. 107–153. Mouton Publishers, The Hague and Paris.

Shorter, A. (1974). "East African Societies." Routledge and Kegan Paul, London and Boston. 155 pp.

Smith, A. B (1980). The Neolithic tradition in the Sahara. *In* "The Sahara and the Nile" (M. A. J. Williams, and H. Faure, eds), pp. 451–465. Balkema, Rotterdam.

Smith, A. G. (1975). Neolithic and Bronze Age landscape change in northern Ireland. *In* "The Effect of Man on the Landscape: the Highland Zone" (J. G. Evans *et al.*, eds), pp. 64–74. Council for Br. Archaeol. Res. Rep. no. **11**.

Smith, J. N. B. (1977). Vegetation and microclimate of east- and west-facing slopes in the grassland of Mt Wilhelm, Papua New Guinea. *J. Ecol.* **65**, 39–53.

Snowden, J. D. (1953). The grass communities and mountain vegetation of Uganda. Crown Agents, London.

Spink, P. C. (1949). The equatorial glaciers of East Africa. *J. Glaciol.* **1**, 277–281.

Standard. (A Kenyan newspaper.)

Stelfox, J. G., Kufwafwa, J. W. and Mbugua, S. W. (1979). "Distributions, Densities and Trends of Elephants and Rhinoceros in Kenya, 1977–1978." Kenya Rangeland Ecological Monitoring Unit, Ministry of Tourism and Wildlife, Kenya. 19 pp.

Stemler, A. B. (1980). Origins of plant domestication in the Sahara and the Nile Valley. *In* "The Sahara and the Nile" (M. A. J. Williams and H. Faure, eds), pp. 503–526. Balkema, Rotterdam.

Straka, H. (1966). Palynologia Madagassica et Mascarenica. Fam. 50–59. *Pollen Spores* **8**, 241–264.

Sutton, J. E. G. (1974). The aquatic civilization of middle Africa. *J. African History* **15**, 527–546.

Synnott, T. J. (1979). A report on the status, importance and protection of the montane forests. Integrated project in arid lands, Marsabit District, Kenya. UNESCO/UNEP. 30 pp.

Talbot, M. R. (1980). Environmental responses to climatic change in the West African Sahel over the past 20 000 years. *In* "The Sahara and the Nile" (M. A. J. Williams and H. Faure, eds), pp. 37–62. Balkema, Rotterdam.

Talbot, M. R. and Delibrias, G. (1977). Holocene variations in the level of Lake Bosumtwi, Ghana. *Nature, Lond.* **268**, 722–724.

Talbot, M. R. and Delibrias, G. (1980). A new late Pleistocene-Holocene water-level curve for Lake Bosumtwi, Ghana. *Earth and Planetary Science Letters* **47**, 336–344.

Tappen, N. C. (1960). Problems of distribution and adaptation of the African monkeys. *Curr. Anthrop.* **1**, 91–120.

Temple, P. H. (1964). Evidence of lake-level changes from the northern shoreline of Lake Victoria, Uganda. *In* "Geographers and the Tropics: Liverpool Essays" (R. W. Steel and R. M. Prothero, eds), pp. 31–56. Longman, London.

Temple, P. H. (1966). Lake Victoria levels. *Proc. E. Afr. Acad.* **2**, 50–58.

Temple, P. H. (1967). Causes of intermittent decline of the level of Lake Victoria during the late Pleistocene and Holocene. *In* "Liverpool Essays in Geography", pp. 43–63. Longman, London.

Terborgh, J. W. and Weske, J. S. (1975). The role of competition in the distribution of Andean birds. *Ecology* **56**, 562–576.

Thompson, K. (1973). The ecology of swamps and peatland in East and Central Africa and their classification for agriculture. Proc. Symp. "Classification of peat and peatland", Internat. Peat Soc., Glasgow, Sept. 1973.

Tomlinson, R. W. (1974). Preliminary biogeographical studies on the Inyanga Mountains, Rhodesia. *S. Afr. geogr. J.* **56**, 15–26.

Troughton, J. H. (1972). Carbon isotope fractionation by plants. *In* "Proc. 8th Int. Conf. on Radiocarbon Dating" (T. A. Rafter and T. Grant-Taylor, eds), pp. 40–57. New Zealand Roy. Soc., Wellington.

Tweedie, E. M. (1965). Periodic flowering of some Acanthaceae on Mt Elgon. *J. E. Africa nat. Hist. Soc.* **25**, 92–94.

van der Pijl, L. (1972). Principles of dispersal in higher plants. 2nd edn. Springer-Verlag, Heidelberg and New York. 162 pp.

van Steenis, C. G. G. J (1935). On the origin of the Malaysian mountain flora, 2. Altitudinal zones, general considerations and renewed statement of the problem. *Bull. Jard. bot. Buitenz. Sér. 3* **13**, 289–417.

van Zinderen Bakker, E. M. (1962). A late-glacial and post-glacial climatic correlation between East Africa and Europe. *Nature, Lond.* **194**, 201–203.

van Zinderen Bakker, E. M. (1964). A pollen diagram from equatorial Africa, Cherangani, Kenya. *Geologie Mijnb.* **43**, 123–128.

van Zinderen Bakker, E. M. (1969a). The Pleistocene vegetation and climate of the basin. *In* "Kalambo Falls Prehistoric Site", vol. 1 (J. D. Clark, ed.), pp. 57–84. Cambridge University Press.

van Zinderen Bakker, E. M. (1969b). Biogeography. *Palaeoecol. Afr.* **4**, 139–162.

van Zinderen Bakker, E. M. (1976). The evolution of late-Quaternary palaeoclimates of southern Africa. *Palaeoecol. Afr.* **9**, 160–202.

van Zinderen Bakker, E. M. and Maley, J. (1979). Late Quaternary palaeoenvironments of the Sahara region. *Palaeoecol. Afr.* **11**, 83–104.

Verdcourt, B. (1969). The arid corridor between the north-east and south-west areas of Africa. *Palaeoecol. Afr.* **4**, 140–144.

Verdcourt, B. (1972). The zoogeography of the non-marine Mollusca of East Africa. *J. Conch., Lond.* **27**, 291–348.

Vincens, A. (1979). Analyse palynologique du site archeologique FxJj50, Formation de Koobi Fora, Est Turkana, (Kenya). *Bull. Soc. géol. Fr.* **21**, 343–347.

von Koenigswald, G. H. R. (1962). "The Evolution of Man." University of Michigan Press, 148 pp.

Washbourn, C. K. (1967). Lake levels and Quaternary climates in the Eastern Rift Valley of Kenya. *Nature, Lond.* **216**, 672–673.

Washbourn-Kamau, C. K. (1970). Late Quaternary chronology of the Nakuru-Elmenteita basin. *Nature, Lond.* **226**, 253–254.

Washbourn-Kamau, C. K. (1975). Late Quaternary shorelines of Lake Naivasha, Kenya. *Azania* **10**, 77–92.

Wayland, E. J. (1934). Rifts, rivers, rains and early man in Uganda. *Jl Roy. anthrop. Inst.* **64**, 333–352.

Wayland, E. J. (1952). The study of past climates in tropical Africa. Pan African Congress on pre-history 1947 (L. S. B. Leakey, ed.). Blackwell, Oxford.

Weimarck, H. (1941). Phytogeographical groups, centres and intervals within the Cape Flora. Lunds Univ. årsskrift N.R.Ard. 2 Bd 37, nr. **5**, 143 pp.

Werger, M. J. A. (1973). American and African arid disjunctions. *In* "Pollination and Dispersal" (N. B. M. Brantjes and H. F. Linskens, eds), pp. 117–124. Dept Botany, University of Nijmegen, Holland.

Werger, M. J. A. (1977). Environmental destruction in southern Africa: the role of overgrazing and trampling. *In* "Vegetation Science and Environmental Protection" (A. Miyawaki and R. Ruzen, eds), pp. 301–305. Maruzen, Tokyo.

West, R. G. (1977). "Pleistocene Biology and Geology." 2nd edn. Longman, London.

White, F. (1962). Geographic variation and sepeciation in Africa with particular reference to *Diospyros*. *In* "Taxonomy and Geography", pp. 71–103. Systematics Association Publ. no. **4**.

Whittow, J. B. (1960). Some observations on the snowfall of Ruwenzori. *J. Glaciol.* **3**, 765–772.

Whittow, J. B., Shepherd, A., Goldthorpe, J. E. and Temple, P. H. (1963). Observations on the glaciers of the Ruwenzori. *J. Glaciol.* **4**, 581–616.

Wickens, G. E. (1975). Quaternary plant fossils from the Jebel Marra volcanic complex and their palaeoclimatic interpretation. *Palaeogeog. Palaeoclimatol. Palaeoecol.* **17**, 109–122.

Wickens, G. E. (1976). Speculations on long distance dispersal and the flora of Jebel Marra, Sudan Republic. *Kew Bull.* **31**, 105–150.

Wild, H. (1968). Phytogeography of South Central Africa. *Kirkia* **6**, 197–222.

Williams, M. A. J. and Adamson, D. A. (1980). Late Quaternary depositional history of the Blue and White Nile rivers in central Sudan. *In* "The Sahara and the Nile" (M. A. J. Williams and H. Faure, eds), pp. 281–304. Balkema, Rotterdam.

Williams, M. A. J., Adamson, D. A., Williams, F. M., Morton, W. H. and Parry, D. E. (1980). Jebel Marra volcano: a link between the Nile Valley, the Sahara and Central Africa. *In* "The Sahara and the Nile" (M. A. J. Williams and H. Faure, eds), pp. 305–337. Balkema, Rotterdam.

Wilson, J. G. (1962). The vegetation of Karamoja District, Northern Province of Uganda. Memoirs Research Div., Dept. Agriculture. Series 2, no. **5**, Dept. Agriculture, Uganda.

Wimbush, S. H. (1947). The African alpine bamboo. *E. Afr. agric. For. J.* **13**, 56–60.

Wimbush, S. H. (1957). "A Catalogue of Kenya Timbers." Govt. Printer, Nairobi. 74 pp.

Winter, B. de (1971). Floristic relationship between the northern and southern arid areas in Africa. *Mitt. bot. StSamml., Münch.* **10**, 424–437.

Winterbottom, J. M. (1967). Climatological implications of avifaunal resemblances between south western Africa and Somaliland. *Palaeoecol. Afr.* **2**, 77–79.

Wright, R. G. and Wainaina, F. N. (1972). An initial quantitative survey of woody and herbaceous plants in elephant exclosures, Tsavo West National Park. 27 pp.

Index of Plant and Animal Names

Higher Plants

General Index